WEALTH PLANNING FOR THE MODERN PHYSICIAN

Residency to Retirement

David B. Mandell, JD, MBA
Jason M. O'Dell, MS, CWM
Carole C. Foos, CPA
Sanjeev Bhatia, MD

with contributions from
Michael Lewellen, CFP®
Robert Peelman, CFP®
Andrew Taylor, CFP®
Adam Braunscheidel, CFP®

2020

Wealth Planning for the Modern Physician: Residency to Retirement
David B. Mandell, JD, MBA; Jason M. O'Dell, MS, CWM; Carole Foos, CPA; Sanjeev Bhatia, MD

ISBN: 978-1-7340643-3-9

Manufactured in the United States of America.

Acknowledgements

The principal authors David Mandell, Jason O'Dell and Carole Foos would first like to thank Dr. Sanjeev Bhatia for his work on the book. A busy orthopedic surgeon and father, Sanjeev spent time writing and editing portions of the book and we greatly appreciate it.

In addition, the authors want to thank their colleagues at OJM Group credited as contributing authors –Michael Lewellen, CFP®, Bob Peelman, CFP®, Andrew Taylor, CFP® and Adam Braunscheidel, CFP®. Each provided valuable writing in their areas of expertise – from retirement plans and investing to financial planning and life, disability and long-term care insurance.

This book simply would not have been possible without the work of Kathy Allard, also an OJM Group teammate. Kathy not only oversaw the book project from a high level, keeping all of us on deadlines, but she was also "in the weeds," editing and even proofreading drafts.

Finally, we would like to thank outside editor and proofreader Liz Seif and graphic designer John Miller. They are responsible for improving our grammar, giving the book a consistent written tone and making our graphics look great.

This book was designed to provide information the authors believe to be accurate on the subject matter covered—but the book is sold and/or provided with the understanding that neither the authors, nor the publishers, are offering individualized advice tailored to your (or anyone else's) specific needs. A competent professional should be sought to assist and advise prior to implementing or attempting to implement any of the strategies or plans discussed in this book.

Further, this book references performance data collected over many periods of time. Past performance and results do not guarantee future performance and/or results. Additionally, performance data, as well as laws and regulations, change over time, and these changes could affect the status of information in this book.

The information herein solely provides historical data to discuss and illustrates the underlying principles. This book is not intended to serve as the basis for any financial decision; as a recommendation of any specific investment advisor; or as an offer to purchase or sell any security. Only a prospectus may be used to offer to sell or purchase securities, and a prospectus must be read and considered carefully before investing or sending money.

No warranty is made with respect to the accuracy or completeness of the information contained in this book. Both the authors and publishers specifically disclaim any responsibility for any loss, liability, risk, personal or otherwise, which is or could be incurred as a consequence, directly or indirectly, of the use and application of any of the contents of this book.

The authors of this book are members of OJM Group, LLC; an SEC-registered investment advisor (RIA) with its principal place of business in the State of Ohio. SEC registration does not constitute an endorsement of OJM by the SEC nor does it indicate that OJM has attained a particular level of skill or ability. OJM and its representatives are in compliance with the current notice filing and registration requirements imposed upon registered investment advisers by those states in which OJM maintains clients. OJM may only transact business in those states in which it is registered or qualifies for an exemption or exclusion from registration requirements. For information pertaining to the registration status of OJM, please contact OJM or refer to the Investment Adviser Public Disclosure web site (www.adviserinfo.sec.gov). For additional information about OJM, including fees and services, send for our disclosure brochure as set forth on Form ADV using the contact information herein. Please read the disclosure statement carefully before you invest or send money.

In addition, certain contributors hold the Certified Financial Planner ("CFP") professional designation. The CFP® certification is a financial planning credential awarded by the Certified Financial Planner Board of Standards Inc. (the "CFP Board") to individuals who meet its education, examination, experience and ethics requirements. Eligible candidates are required to have either five years of work experience in the financial planning industry or, in the alternative, three years of related experience and a bachelor's degree from an accredited U.S. college or university. Certificants are further required to complete a CFP Board-Registered Education Program (or possess a qualifying professional credential), clear a personal and professional background check, and pass the CFP® Certification Examination, a 10-hour multiple choice exam divided into three separate sessions. In order to maintain the certification, CFP® designees must also complete at least 30 hours of continuing education every two years on an ongoing basis.

About the Authors

David B. Mandell, JD, MBA, is a partner in OJM Group, attorney, author, and renowned authority in the fields of risk management, asset protection and wealth planning.

He is a co-author of more than a dozen financial resources for physicians, including *For Doctors Only: A Guide to Working Less and Building More* and *Risk Management for the Practicing Physician*, a CME-certified monograph. His previous titles include *Wealth Protection: Build and Preserve Your Financial Fortress* and *Wealth Secrets of the Affluent*, published by John Wiley & Sons.

David's articles have appeared in over 40 national publications, and he has been interviewed as an expert in national media outlets, including Bloomberg and FOX-TV. He has presented lectures, webcasts, and podcasts on asset protection, tax planning, and wealth management for numerous medical societies, associations and educational platforms.

Mr. Mandell graduated with honors from Harvard University. His law degree is from the UCLA School of Law, where he was awarded the American Jurisprudence Award for achievement in legal ethics. While at UCLA, he also earned an MBA from the Anderson School of Management.

Jason M. O'Dell, MS, CWM, is the managing partner of OJM Group, as well as a financial consultant and investment advisor. He has more than 25 years of experience working with high-net worth clients, including physicians and their medical practices.

Jason is a co-author of 12 financial resources for physicians, including *For Doctors Only: A Guide to Working Less and Building More* and *Wealth Protection Planning for Orthopaedic Surgeons*. He has also authored numerous articles and presented lectures, webcasts and podcasts on investment management, retirement planning and a broad scope of financial topics.

Jason graduated with a Bachelor of Arts in Economics from The Ohio State University and has earned a Master of Science degree with an emphasis in financial planning. He is the President of the Board of Directors for the Alzheimer's Association of Greater Cincinnati and serves on the AALU Board of Directors.

Carole Foos is a partner in OJM Group and a Certified Public Accountant (CPA) offering tax analysis and tax planning services to the firm's clients. Carole has over 25 years of experience in accounting, tax planning and financial consulting. She was formerly a manager in the tax department of a Big 4 firm and spent several years in public accounting.

Carole is a co-author of more than a dozen books for physicians, including *Wealth Management Made Simple*, *For Doctors Only* and *Wealth Protection Planning for Dermatologists*. She has also authored numerous articles and presented lectures, webcasts, and podcasts on tax planning, wealth management, and other financial topics.

Carole earned a Bachelor of Science in Business Administration from Xavier University where she majored in accounting. She serves on the University of Cincinnati Economics Center Development Committee and is a member of the AICPA and OSCPA.

Dr. Sanjeev Bhatia is a Board Certified Orthopaedic Sports Medicine Surgeon who has a tremendous passion for helping physicians achieve financial freedom and independence through investing. After graduating from the University of Wisconsin-Madison, he completed his medical studies at Northwestern University Feinberg School of Medicine. Dr. Bhatia then went on to complete orthopaedic surgery residency at Rush University Medical Center (Chicago, IL) and an orthopaedic sports medicine fellowship at the Steadman-Philippon Research Institute (Vail, CO). Dr. Bhatia is presently the Co-Director of the Hip and Knee Joint Preservation Center at Northwestern Medicine Central DuPage Hospital and Faculty at Northwestern University Feinberg School of Medicine.

Contributing Authors

Michael Lewellen, CFP®, is a partner and Director of Financial Planning at OJM Group. He is an experienced financial planner and insurance specialist, who has worked with OJM clients for more than 17 years.

Michael is a co-author of the financial resource *For Ohio Doctors* and more than a dozen articles on retirement planning, insurance and wealth accumulation. He has also presented numerous lectures, webcasts and podcasts on a broad scope of financial topics. Michael graduated from the University of Kentucky with a Bachelor of Science in Business Administration and has earned the Certified Financial Planner™ designation.

Bob Peelman is the Director of Wealth Advisors and a partner at OJM Group. He is an experienced wealth advisor and financial consultant who has worked with physicians, medical practices and individuals for over 17 years. Prior to joining OJM in 2010, Bob was a financial advisor with Morgan Stanley Wealth Management.

Bob is a contributing author of the financial resource *Wealth Management Made Simple* and co-author of more than a dozen articles on investing, retirement planning, and other financial topics. He has also presented numerous lectures, webcasts, and podcasts for regional and national groups. Bob received his Bachelor of Science in Business Administration from the University of Kentucky and has earned the designation of Certified Financial Planner™.

Andrew Taylor, CFP® is a Wealth Advisor and partner at OJM Group. Andrew provides portfolio management and comprehensive financial planning services for physicians and their families. He joined OJM in 2012, following more than 15 years in the financial services industry with Charles Schwab & Co. and Fidelity Investments.

Andrew is a contributing author of *Wealth Management Made Simple*. He has co-authored numerous articles and presented lectures, webcasts, and podcasts on investing, retirement planning, and market analysis. Andrew graduated from the University of Kentucky with a Bachelor of Science in Business Administration from the University of Kentucky and has earned the designation of Certified Financial Planner™.

Adam Braunscheidel, CFP®, is a Wealth Advisor at OJM Group, providing portfolio management and comprehensive financial planning services for OJM clients. He also handles investment research and market analysis for the firm.

Adam joined OJM in 2009 and is a contributing author of *Wealth Management Made Simple*. He is also a co-author of numerous articles and has presented webcasts and podcasts on investing, retirement planning, and other financial topics. Adam graduated from Xavier University with a Bachelor of Science in Business Administration and has earned the designation of Certified Financial Planner™.

Table of Contents

Foreword XV
Introduction XIX

LESSON 1: Financial Planning Basics During Training and Early Practice Years 1

CHAPTER 1.1 Student Loan Debt and Budgeting: An Overview 2
CHAPTER 1.2 First, Protect What You Have Already Built: How to Preserve Your Most Valuable Asset.......... 7
CHAPTER 1.3 Six Tools to Build Retirement Wealth and the Importance of Flexibility and Tax Diversification.......... 15
CHAPTER 1.4 How to Evaluate Career Opportunities Financially and Choose the Right Job.......... 26
CHAPTER 1.5 Estate Planning Essentials for Physicians of All Ages... 33

LESSON 2: Protecting Assets from Potential Liability 46

CHAPTER 2.1 The Importance of Asset Protection.......... 48
CHAPTER 2.2 The Sliding Scale of Asset Protection.......... 51
CHAPTER 2.3 Asset Protection Myths.......... 56
CHAPTER 2.4 The Best Asset Protection is NOT Asset Protection..... 60
CHAPTER 2.5 The Mixed Blessing of Property and Casualty Insurance.......... 64
CHAPTER 2.6 Maximizing Exempt Assets 69
CHAPTER 2.7 Family Limited Partnerships and Limited Liability Companies.......... 76
CHAPTER 2.8 Using Trusts to Shield Wealth.......... 87
CHAPTER 2.9 Protecting Your Home.......... 93
CHAPTER 2.10 Divorce Protection.......... 97

LESSON 3: Tax Planning When in Practice 103

CHAPTER 3.1 Tax Planning: An Overview and Background 104

CHAPTER 3.2 Tax Planning for Employed Physicians 114

CHAPTER 3.3 The Best Tax Treatment for a Medical Practice: S Corp or C Corp in the Post-TCJA World? 125

CHAPTER 3.4 Tax-Advantaged Benefit Plans for Practice Owners ... 130

CHAPTER 3.5 Getting Larger Deductions in Private Practices with Cash Balance Plans 136

CHAPTER 3.6 Why Many Physicians Should Consider Using Non-Qualified Plans to Reach Retirement Goals.................... 143

CHAPTER 3.7 Avoiding High Fees, Conflicts and Potential Liability In Your Practice's Qualified Retirement Plan 153

CHAPTER 3.8 Small Insurance Companies: What to Do Now 163

LESSON 4: Using Insurance Effectively to Protect the Family and Build Wealth 169

CHAPTER 4.1 Paying Bills Even If You Can't Work: Disability Insurance 170

CHAPTER 4.2 Permanent Life Insurance: What it Is......................... 178

CHAPTER 4.3 Permanent Life Insurance: Why It May Make Sense for You 186

CHAPTER 4.4 Five Key Success Factors When Using Permanent Life Insurance and Case Studies 195

CHAPTER 4.5 Long-Term Care Planning: What You Need to Know About the Risk and the Role of Insurance...................................... 209

LESSON 5: Out in Practice — Investing to Reach Your Goals 216

CHAPTER 5.1 How Physicians Are Unlike, and Like, Most Retail Investors, and Why It Matters..................................... 218

CHAPTER 5.2 Why Our Brains Often Fail Us When We Are Investing: What the Science Shows........................... 230

CHAPTER 5.3 Investing With and Without an Advisor 241

CHAPTER 5.4 What to Look For In and Expect From an Investment Advisor 251

LESSON 6: Success Factors for Physicians Approaching and In Retirement 266

CHAPTER 6.1 Retirement Planning: Three Keys to Success 267

CHAPTER 6.2 Four Tactics to Use as You Approach Retirement...... 273

CHAPTER 6.3 Planning for Estate Taxes 279

Conclusion 287

Free Consultation 288

Schedule a Seminar; Request Authors' Articles 289

Additional Resources for Physicians 290

FOREWORD

Thoughts From a Millennial Physician

It is with tremendous honor and humility that I thank you for committing time from your busy schedule to read this book. Medicine, regardless of your specialty, is the best job in the world when done right. Although there are many great professions in this world, there is no other career that consistently serves humanity as personally and positively as that of being a physician or surgeon. In fact, in many cases, the personal joy that we feel by helping a child, adult or elderly person is so great that a few of us would actually consider doing it for free if our financial goals were taken care of and we achieved the optimal balance of work, family and other professional interests. Wouldn't it be great if we could help our patients, in all the ways that we do, on our terms, while being truly financially independent?

Unfortunately, as a millennial physician, I know firsthand that the field of medicine in today's world is much different than what it was years ago when we committed our lives towards this selfless career. Gone are the days where a high paying career that perfectly blended your professional interests and family needs was guaranteed in the location of your dreams upon graduating residency or fellowship. As a physician today, we are constantly fighting the tide of increased work demands and decreased autonomy while declining reimbursements or health system consolidation frequently devalue our contributions to society.

The results of these trends can jeopardize our ability to reach our financial goals, especially for those of us with six figure student debt. In short, medicine today, with its transformative shift in the last decade, has unfortunately resulted in some physicians practicing uninspired medicine due to their continuous struggle against an uphill financial future. Physicians as a whole have a code of ethics, intelligence and character unmatched by any other profession. It is a shame that, despite this, we are often duped or poorly informed financially, often leading to personal and professional stress from an inability to understand non-clinical income and wealth protection. Physician burnout frequently ensues, often for financial reasons, and is a tremendous loss to the hardworking physician, their families and society.

Millennial physicians today have different goals than our predecessors did. Born between 1981 and 1996, we lived through the booming 1990s and then saw economic prosperity take a dramatic turn for the worst with stagnant wage increases and the Great Recession of 2008. In some cases, we saw Baby Boomers who poorly prepared their retirement nest egg be forced to toil for years beyond their retirement age doing uninspired work. Such dramatic life experiences likely explain why most millennials prefer an optimal work-life balance with prudent savings habits prized over excessive spending patterns.

As investors, millennial physicians also have a slightly different mindset than our predecessors. Having seen many physicians in our parents' generation lose their retirement security from improperly managed asset allocations or risky ventures that they knew nothing about, many millennial physicians have chosen to follow their own instincts or go along with their peers when deciding where to invest. They want to know that their financial advisors are not merely salesmen, but true professionals who genuinely have the physicians' best interests at heart and follow the same Hippocratic decree that they do, "First, do no harm."

I know that many of you reading this book will be physicians of the Gen X and Baby Boomer generations. In fact, many of its Lessons are dedicated to helping you with financial issues you face right now, whereas Millennials will grow into some of the planning strategies described here as they age.

Whatever your path, the goals of this book are to inspire you and show you a route to achieving your financial dreams. It is ironic that despite having some of the highest incomes in America, many physicians fail to build a comfortable nest egg and struggle to achieve financial freedom, even well into their retirement years. Unlike those in other fields, most physicians are poorly trained in business matters, especially when it comes to comprehending the impressive might of a compounding asset class and the benefits of protecting their financial livelihood with adequate disability and life insurance and asset protection.

I would like to sincerely thank my co-authors David Mandell, JD, MBA, Carole Foos, CPA, and Jason O'Dell, MS, CWM for their tremendous knowledge in financial matters and steadfast dedication to helping physicians of all stripes, especially millennials, achieve financial freedom early on and forever. Financial freedom is the greatest weapon against the rising physician burnout epidemic and will be critical to ensure that the next generation of doctors can continue to serve humanity in an inspired way.

Sanjeev Bhatia, MD

INTRODUCTION

Helping Physicians With Their Financial Concerns

What should I be doing as a young physician to secure my financial future?

Now that I am out in practice and building assets, how do I protect them from potential liability?

What are the best ways for me to reduce taxes, whether I am in private practice or employed?

I know I need insurances, but how do I understand the products and make smart choices of what fits best for me and my family?

When it comes to investments, who should I trust to manage them and how do I keep myself from making costly mistakes?

I know I would like to retire someday, but how do I make sure I am "on track"?

I am about to retire, what should I be doing differently at this stage of my financial life?

These seven questions are among the hundreds we have heard from our 1,500+ physician clients during the last 30 years – as partners at OJM Group, and in our former financial, accounting/tax and law practices. We wanted this book to educate readers on exactly these issues – and do it in the chronological order in which they arise for physicians as they progress from "residency to retirement." In this way, this book is different than any of our previous books for doctors.

On the other hand, our newest title adds to the lineage of books for physicians that began with David's *The Doctor's Asset Protection Guide* in the mid 1990's, *The Doctor's Wealth Protection Guide* in the late 1990s, *Wealth Protection MD* in the early 2000s, and five editions of OJM Group's *For Doctors Only: A Guide to Working Less and Building More* since the mid-2000s. We also have books written specifically for and with orthopedic surgeons and dermatologists, as well as a Category I CME monograph, now in its eighth edition since 1998.

Fitting with the chronological theme, we have organized the book into six Lessons:

Lesson One: Financial Planning Basics During Training and Early Practice Years
In this Lesson, we explain the key financial strategies that young physicians should focus on while in training and as they enter practice.

Lesson Two: Protecting Assets from Potential Liability
The unfortunate reality for physicians is that the practice of medicine brings potential liability, especially in certain specialties and for those in private practice. In Lesson Two, we explain the myriad of tactics available to shield assets from potential liability.

Lesson Three: Tax Planning When in Practice
Nearly every practicing physician we have spoken with in our combined careers wants to reduce their taxes in legally permissible ways. This Lesson covers this topic from an overview of our tax system to tax reduction strategies used by employed doctors and physicians in private practice.

Lesson Four: Using Insurance Effectively to Protect the Family and Build Wealth
In their prime practice years, most doctors will make many important decisions regarding insurances – especially regarding disability, life and long-term care coverage. Nonetheless, many physicians do not understand the product choices and make poor decisions or are guided by less-than-ideal salespeople. Lesson Four focuses on these products and decisions.

Lesson Five: Out in Practice — Investing to Reach Your Goals

We have recently written a comprehensive book on wealth management and investing for any investor (*Wealth Management Made Simple*), and we would encourage you to get this book if you have not already done so. Go to **www.ojmbookstore.com** and order a free copy using the code **WPR2R**.

As such, our Lesson on investing is relatively physician specific. We cover topics such as why physicians are like the typical U.S. investor, why they are not, and why that matters. We also dig into what medical science tells us about our brains and how they can hinder us when it comes to investing.

Lesson Six: Success Factors for Physicians Approaching and In Retirement

Achieving retirement that meets their timeline and lifestyle goals is the number one financial goal for most doctors. As one approaches and enters this phase, however, there are some crucial "dos" and "don'ts" from a financial perspective.

We hope you find this book's chronological approach helpful. We are confident that, regardless of your age, you could read the book cover to cover and glean a tremendous amount of knowledge. For many of you, this may make sense. For others, you may treat the book as a resource to revisit as one or more financial questions arise over the years.

Regardless of how you utilize the book, we are glad that you have it. We sincerely encourage you to contact us with questions or comments ... or to schedule a time to discuss your unique situation. Feel free to contact us at any time.

David B. Mandell, JD, MBA
mandell@ojmgroup.com

Jason M. O'Dell, MS, CWM
odell@ojmgroup.com

Carole C. Foos, CPA
carole@ojmgroup.com

LESSON 1

Financial Planning Basics During Training and Early Practice Years

In this Lesson, we explain the key financial strategies that young physicians should focus on while in training and as they enter practice.

We discuss the basics of cash flow management, budgeting, and student loan repayment; how to financially evaluate job opportunities and protect the valuable asset of future earning streams; retirement planning vehicles to consider; and the basics of estate planning that young physicians need to know.

CHAPTER 1.1

Student Loan Debt and Budgeting: An Overview

Ask any young physician about their leading financial concerns and invariably student loan repayment will be mentioned at the top of the list, or close to it. Few young doctors are able to make it through college and medical education without significant debt and many have outstanding loans in the low six-figures. This is an unfortunate reality of medical education in the U.S. in the 21st century.

While the stress of loan repayment may hover over young physicians as they train, the practical realities of how to pay back such debt take hold once the first well-paying job begins. Should one focus on debt repayment over retirement savings or college education funding for young children? Does it make more sense to pay down student loans or save for a house down payment? These are practical choices that young physicians and their families face every day. In this chapter, we will briefly address some of these issues and tie them to the importance of disciplined budgeting.

The Challenge of Student Loan Debt

According to the American Association of Medical Colleges, 76% of medical students who graduated in the class of 2016 carried student loan debt.[1] It is not difficult to imagine that, with compounding interest, such debt loads can quickly get out of control.

[1] https://www.aamc.org/system/files/reports/1/september2018anexplorationoftherecentdeclineinthepercentageofu..pdf

Residency and Fellowship – Try to Avoid Capitalization

Student loan costs typically balloon to their highest levels during residency because of a process called *capitalization*. Capitalization is the addition of unpaid interest to the principal balance of the loan. The principal balance of a loan increases when payments are postponed during periods of deferment or forbearance and unpaid interest is capitalized.

Sometimes, it is difficult to avoid capitalization during residency due to high living costs. However, paying some or all of the interest during residency will allow you to significantly slow runaway capitalization, so it is wise to do so if possible.

Income-driven repayment plans have recently become a solution to the capitalization issue because they allow repayment of student loan interest during residency with much more tolerable monthly payments. One example is the Revised Pay As You Earn (REPAYE) program offered through the Department of Education. With REPAYE, the federal government covers 50% of all interest above the monthly payment amount during repayment.

To illustrate, if a resident making $55,000 a year has a student loan of $164,000 at 6% interest, the monthly payment just to cover interest would be $824. Under REPAYE, the resident would have to pay only $300 per month, while the federal government would cover $262 of the monthly interest. Although some interest will still capitalize, the amount—$262 in this example—is more bearable.

First Job – Refinance Your Student Loans

One of the simplest methods of reducing the burden of student loan debt is refinancing your student loans through a private lender when you begin practicing. Refinancing is a relatively easy way to not only consolidate your student loans into one lump sum but also lower your interest rate considerably. Although you may give up certain loan protections inherent in federal student loans and income-based repayment models, the upside of refinancing is typically a dramatic reduction in your interest rate. It is not uncommon to see interest rates lowered by 2%–3%, which will dramatically reduce the cost of debt over a ten-year span. Returning to the example above, a $268,000 loan paid back over 10 years at 6% interest would require a monthly payment of $2,975.35 with $89,042 in total interest. The same loan at a 4% rate would cost $2,713.37 per month with $57,604 in total interest.

Don't Forget Disability Insurance – Protect Your Greatest Asset

In the next chapter, we will discuss the need to protect your greatest asset—your ability to earn income—which could be jeopardized by an accident or health condition. Securing adequate disability income insurance early in your career will protect your student loan debt payment plan along with your ability to generate future income.

First Job – Good Income and the Importance of Budgeting

After patiently accepting a relatively low income during residency and fellowship, it is not surprising that new millennial physicians want financial independence to occur quickly after a few years of practice. Unfortunately, true financial independence often takes longer than most physicians think due to the impact of taxes on a higher salary, debt burdens, and the increased cost of living typically seen with the jump to life as an attending.

Without adequately preparing and adjusting for these costs, a lucrative new salary can easily be inadvertently squandered. In fact, some physicians, despite being among the top 1% of all earners, never achieve financial independence because they misunderstand their cash flow. A budget is a helpful tool that allows you to increase your awareness of where your money is going and how much you are saving. By adhering to a realistic budget you can avoid overshooting your spending and shorten the length of time it will take to achieve your financial goals.

Step 1: Force Yourself to Think about Budgeting

Although time may be in short supply, force yourself to spend a few minutes thinking about your cash flow in your new job. You can efficiently prepare to develop a realistic budget by gathering your utility bills, bank statements, insurance premiums documentation, and credit card statements. Tax returns may give you a good sense of how much money you earn after accounting for taxes. Finally, a spreadsheet program like Microsoft Excel is a useful tool for comparing numbers and adjusting the budget in real time.

Step 2: Keep Your Goals in Front

Write down your short-term, intermediate, and long-term financial goals. Are you trying to buy a house? Are there partnership buy-in costs to save for? Do you want to contribute to your child's 529 college savings plan? What are your retirement goals? By committing these to writing at the beginning of the process, you will keep your desired long-term picture in mind as you allocate expenditures throughout your career.

Step 3: Estimate Your Cash Flow

If you know your anticipated salary, you can start to estimate your monthly after-tax cash flow. Your last tax return may help you estimate how much you will pay in taxes and other costs. Be sure to assess your pay only after you have contributed to your 401(k), IRA, HSA, and other available tax-advantaged vehicles. As we discuss in Chapter 3.2, maximizing contributions to tax-advantaged accounts lowers your adjustable gross income while the larger pretax dollar amounts give your investments more leverage than after-tax dollars would provide in the same fund.

Step 4: Estimate Fixed and Variable Expenses

Using your previously gathered statements, receipts, and bills, separate the costs that will be the same each month (fixed expenses) from those that will change monthly (variable expenses). As an example, mortgage payments, utility bills, and student loan payments are typically construed as fixed while vacation costs and personal spending are often thought of as variable. Don't worry if you can't ascribe a set value to some fixed expenses—remember the budget is meant to be a rough guide of your spending to see what you can afford.

Step 5: Develop Your Budget

Although it is tempting to look at your after-tax salary and want to spend all of it, it is essential to develop the habit of saving early to safeguard your financial future. As a general rule, fixed expenses should not make up more than 50% of your monthly cash flow and variable expenses should not exceed 25%. The goal each month should be to save 25% or more of your take-home pay so you can comfortably achieve your financial goals and prepare for unexpected events. Now that you know your expenses and cash flow, you can adjust these numbers to see how much you can spend in various areas of your life. Be realistic—it will help you adhere to the budget you have developed.

Step 6: Look at Your Budget Regularly and Have Fun

Congratulations! You are pursuing an incredible career and are blessed with tremendous earning potential. Look at your budget from time to time to make sure you respect your finances, but don't be afraid to enjoy the fruits of your hard work.

TAKEAWAY: Student loan debt affects most young physicians. Without careful planning, a six-figure student loan after training can rapidly get out of control. While the goals of debt repayment and saving/investing often necessitate a balancing act, having a sound plan will help you make great strides toward safeguarding your financial future.

CHAPTER 1.2

First, Protect What You Have Already Built: How to Preserve Your Most Valuable Asset

Throughout a physician's career, protecting assets should be one of the goals of holistic wealth management. In later chapters, we focus on how to shield assets from potential liability claims. Here, the focus is on protection against disability and premature death. We address these protections here in Lesson 1 because they need to be implemented at the outset of a doctor's career, even in training. To understand why, let's examine the concept of present value.

Young Physicians' Greatest Asset: Present Value of Future Income

The most important factor for young physicians in building a solid financial foundation for the long term is to protect what they have already built. Many young doctors with little savings and often large student loan debts may ask, "What have I built? I am in severe debt!" (See Chapter 1.1). The answer is that they have built a significant asset that needs protecting: the present value of their future income.

Given the significant investment made to become a practicing physician, it should not be surprising that the value of a doctor's future income is also significant. For example, let's assume that a surgeon is offered a starting salary of $300,000, including benefits. If this surgeon plans on practicing for 30 years (and assuming 3.5% inflation), the present value of this income is $5,517,613, even if the surgeon never makes more than $300,000 per year, including inflation. Most people would think an asset this valuable is worth protecting.

What is needed to protect this asset? That depends on whether they are protecting it just for themselves or for others who are dependent on them. Either way, doctors need to protect their ability to earn this income in the future. Disability income insurance is tool #1 for young physicians to implement.

The Need for Disability Insurance

The disability of the family breadwinner can be more financially devastating to a family than premature death. In both cases, the breadwinner will be unable to provide any income for the family; however, in the case of death, the deceased earner is no longer an expense to the family. On the other hand, if the breadwinner suddenly becomes disabled, he or she still needs to be fed, clothed, and cared for by medical professionals or family members. The medical care alone can cost hundreds of dollars per day. Thus, with a disability, income decreases or disappears and expenses increase. This can be a devastating turn of events; it can lead to creditor problems and even bankruptcy.

Employer-Provided Coverage Often Inadequate

If you are an employee of a university or other large corporation, your employer may provide long-term disability coverage. Group disability policies often limit either the term of the coverage or the amount of benefits paid. For instance, benefits may last only a few years or benefit payments may represent only a small part of your annual compensation. Since this is most commonly an employer-paid benefit, the money received during your disability will be income taxable to you. Additionally, employer or group disability coverage can be terminated at any time for any reason, leaving you without coverage.

Take a good look at what the employer-offered policy covers and buy a private policy if you and the insurance professional on your advisory team decide you need it.

Getting the Best Insurance Coverage for the Money: Personal Disability Coverage

When it comes to getting your own disability policy, consider the following questions:

1. What is the benefit amount? Most policies are capped at a benefit amount that equals 60% of income. You must ask yourself how much money your family would need if you were to become disabled.

   Generally, you want to find companies that offer at least 60% of pre-disability after-tax income with maximums of $17,000 monthly. You can also purchase a policy that supplements your individual and/or group coverage. Carriers will participate up to $25,000 or $30,000.

2. What is the waiting period (elimination period)? This is the period of time that you must be disabled before the insurance company will pay you disability benefits. The longer the waiting period before benefits kick in, the less your premiums will be. Essentially, the waiting period serves as a deductible relative to time—you cover your expenses for the waiting period and then the insurance company steps in from that point forward.

   If you have adequate sick leave and short-term disability and an emergency fund, and you can support a longer waiting period, choose a policy with a longer waiting period to save money. Though waiting periods can last as long as 730 days, a 90-day waiting period may give you the best coverage for your money.

3. How long will coverage last? It's a good idea to get a benefit period that will last until age 66/67, at which point Social Security payments will begin. Be aware that many policies cover you for only two to five years. Unless you are 62 to 67 years old, that would be inadequate because most people want coverage that will pay them until age 67. Unless you are so young that you haven't yet had time to qualify for Social Security, a policy that provides lifetime benefits, at costly premiums, is generally not worth the added expense.

4. What is the definition of *disability*? Definitions vary from insurance company to insurance company and even from policy to policy within the same company.

The definition of *disability* used for a particular policy is of the utmost importance. The main categories are own occupation, any occupation, and loss of income. The own occupation policies, which pay a benefit if you can't continue working in your occupation (even if you can and do work in another occupation after the disability), are the most comprehensive. Two important elements to look for in an own-occupation policy are the following:

1. Are you forced to go back to work in another occupation?
2. Will you receive a partial benefit if you go back to work gradually after the disability and still make less than you did before the disability?

5. Does the policy offer partial benefits? If you are able to work only part-time instead of your previous full-time hours, will you receive benefits? Unless your policy states that you are entitled to partial benefits, you won't receive anything unless you are totally unable to work. Also, are extended partial benefits paid if you go back to work and suffer a reduction in income because you cannot keep up the same rigorous schedule as before you became disabled? Important note: partial benefits may be added to some policies in a rider and should be seriously considered, as only 3% of all disabilities are total disabilities. Some policies even have a recovery benefit payable if a business has lost clients during the disability due to the insured not being able to serve them and the insured has lost income as a result. The insured does not have to be disabled at all—there can just be loss of income due to disability-related attrition.

6. Is business overhead expense covered? If you are a practice owner, whether you have a $10,000 or $20,000 monthly disability benefit, you likely don't have enough to cover your lost income PLUS the costs of running the practice. Though most companies have limited how much an individual can get in a monthly benefit (often

60% of after-tax monthly income, capped at $30,000 per month), many carriers still offer up to $50,000 or more per month to cover business overhead expense.

7. Is it noncancelable or guaranteed renewable? The difference between these two terms—*noncancelable* and *guaranteed renewable*—is very important. If a policy is noncancelable, you will pay a fixed premium throughout the contract term. Your premium will not go up for the term of the contract. If it is guaranteed renewable, the policy cannot be canceled but your premiums could go up. Ideally you want a policy that is both noncancelable and guaranteed renewable.

8. How financially stable is the insurance company? Before buying a policy, check the financial soundness of the insurer. If your insurer goes bankrupt, you may have to shop for a policy later in life, when premiums are more expensive. Standard & Poor's, A.M. Best Co., Duff and Phelps, and Moody's all rate insurers.

Protecting Future Income for Dependents: Life Insurance

Young physicians with financial dependents—typically children and/or spouses, but sometimes other family members—need to focus on protecting their future income not only against disability, but also against death. For this reason, life insurance is tool #2 recommended to protect your foundation.

As with disability income insurance, you first need to determine the amount of coverage you need. What expenses would need to be covered in the event of your death? A mortgage, education funding for children, income support for your spouse, car loans, and other debts are just a few examples to consider. Here are few of the most common types of life insurance:

Term Life Insurance

Given its affordability, term life insurance is the most common type of life insurance policy. The premium on a term policy is low compared to other types of life insurance policies because it carries no cash value and provides protection for a limited period of time (referred to as a *term*). This limited time frame is usually 10 to 20 years, though some companies offer a 30-year term product. A term life insurance policy pays a specific lump sum to your designated beneficiary upon your death. Thus, it plays an important role in providing temporary death protection for your family (or practice/partners as part of a buy–sell arrangement).

Permanent Life Insurance

Beyond term insurance, the rest of the products below are all considered "permanent" life insurance. The category of permanent insurance products are the those that, unlike term, do carry cash values along with death benefits and can last for the entirety of the insureds life – out to age 100, 115 and beyond (i.e., they are "permanent" so long as the required premiums are paid on time).

Within the general category of "permanent insurance", there are a host of different products. Unfortunately, many physicians refer to all permanent products as "whole life", but, as you will see below, whole life is only one category of permanent policies. Let's examine a few of the leading permanent products here:

Whole Life Insurance

Whole life insurance pays a death benefit to the beneficiary you name and offers you a cash value account with tax-deferred cash accumulation. It has a fixed premium that can't increase during your lifetime (as long as you pay the planned amount), and your premium is invested for you long term. Because it has the cash accumulation component, whole life insurance can offer benefits such as tax reduction, wealth accumulation, asset protection, and estate planning. However, whole life insurance does not allow you to invest in separate accounts (i.e. money market, stock, and bond funds). Thus, your policy's returns will be tied to the insurance company's ability to invest its capital, which is often tied to interest rates.

Universal Life Insurance

Universal life (UL) insurance is similar to whole life insurance but has more flexible premiums. It may be attractive to younger buyers whose ability to pay premiums fluctuates. Because it is so flexible, universal life insurance can offer benefits like tax reduction, wealth accumulation, asset protection, and estate planning. If the insurance company does poorly with its investments, the interest return on the cash portion of the policy could decrease. In this case, less money would be available to pay the cost of the death benefit portion of the policy and future premiums might be necessary in addition to the premiums originally illustrated.

A Hybrid: Equity-Indexed Universal Life Insurance

Equity-indexed universal life insurance (EIUL) is a universal policy that allows you to select from a list of stock market indices to grow your cash value. If the investments fail, a guaranteed minimum death benefit is paid to your beneficiary upon your death.

EIUL gives you more upside than a traditional UL policy because the insurance company contractually agrees to credit the policy's cash value with the same return as that of the stock market index the policy holder chooses (typically the S&P 500 Index, but it can be the Dow Jones, NASDAQ, EAFA, Euro Stoxx, or others) realized over the same period of time, subject to a cap and a floor. Thus, the policy owner has the upside of the indices to the cap but the risk of the same indices to the floor. Typically, floors for an annual return begin at around 0% (no loss of principal) and caps are around 10%.

EIUL policies vary from carrier to carrier. Some allow only for 50% or 75% participation (others offer 100%) of the rate of return from the S&P. This means that if the S&P 500 returns 10%, you may get only 5% or 7.5%. The policyholder must pay particular attention to the carrier's contractual obligations.

Variable Universal Life Insurance

Variable universal life insurance (VUL) pays your beneficiary a death benefit. The amount of the benefit is dependent on the success of your investments. If the investments fail, there is a guaranteed minimum death benefit paid to your beneficiary upon your death. Variable universal life insurance gives you more control of the cash value account portion of your policy than any other insurance type. A form of universal life insurance, it has elements of both life insurance and a securities contract. Because the policy owner assumes investment risks, variable universal products are regulated as securities under the Federal Securities Laws and must be sold with a prospectus.

Private Placement Variable Universal Life Insurance

Private Placement Variable Universal Life insurance (PPVUL) shares most of the characteristics of VUL. However, PPVUL differs from VUL in a few ways that make this type of insurance more attractive to the ultra-wealthy. Essentially, these policies are treated as private placement securities and have great flexibility in their design and management, while still enjoying the tax and asset protection benefits of life insurance. Relatively few physicians own PPVUL.

As you can see, there are many types of permanent life insurance and some are complex. In Lesson 4, we dive deeply into each option, pros and cons, why many physicians utilize permanent life insurance and who should avoid it. We also describe a few key success factors when using permanent life and how they play out in a few case studies.

> **TAKEAWAY:** A young physician's most valuable asset is the present value of his or her future income. This asset should be protected against the risks of disability and premature death through proper insurance coverages.

CHAPTER 1.3

Six Tools to Build Retirement Wealth and the Importance of Flexibility and Tax Diversification

If getting to a financially secure retirement is one of your most important wealth planning goals, you would not be alone. According to a number of physician studies, as well as our own experience in working with well over 1,500 doctors, retirement planning is the leading financial objective in the profession.

While we will get into more depth on the various tools one can use to build wealth for retirement in Lessons 4 and 5, and address pre-retirement and intra-retirement strategies in Lesson 6, we provide an overview of retirement options here in Lesson 1. Our reason for this is simple – the earlier you focus on this long-term goal, the better – as the case study demonstrates powerfully. Thus, in this chapter, we will briefly describe six retirement-focused wealth tools and discuss the importance of both flexibility and tax diversification in every doctor's long-term retirement planning.

Why It's Important to Save Now

> *"Compound interest is the eighth wonder of the world. He who understands it, earns it ... he who doesn't ... pays it."*
> ~ Albert Einstein

Whether Einstein said these exact words is debated, but the truth behind them is not. It is one of the most important lessons of wealth management: the value of getting time on your side. The simple fact is that *when* you start saving outweighs how *much* you save. Let's see this concept in action with an example.

Case Study: Three Investors Save for Retirement

Amy, Bernie, and Chad enjoy the same 7% annual investment return on their retirement funds. The only difference is when and how often they save.

Amy invests $5,000 per year beginning at age 18. At age 28, she stops. She has invested $50,000 over 10 years.

Bernie invests the same $5,000 per year but begins where Amy left off. He begins investing at age 28 and continues until he retires at age 58. Bernie has invested $150,000 over 30 years.

Chad is our most diligent saver. He invests $5,000 per year beginning at age 18 and continues investing until retirement at age 58. He has invested $200,000 over 40 years.

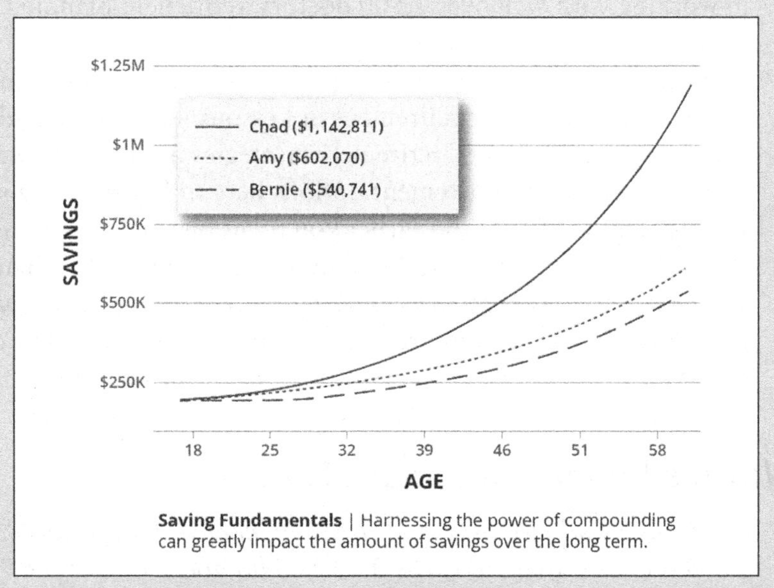

Saving Fundamentals | Harnessing the power of compounding can greatly impact the amount of savings over the long term.

Figure 1.3.1

Bernie has invested three times as much as Amy, yet Amy's account has a higher value. She saved for just 10 years while Bernie saved for 30 years. This is the power of compound interest: the investment return that Amy earned in her 10 early years of saving is the key—its impact is so significant that Bernie couldn't catch up, even though he saved for an additional 20 years.

The best retirement saver is obviously Chad, who began saving early and never stopped. Note that he saved much more than either Amy or Bernie. This shows the value of even "singles and doubles" (to use a baseball analogy): you do not need to hit home runs to reach retirement goals if you save steadily and (ideally) begin early.

It is clear from the case study that compound interest favors those who start saving early, which is why we discuss this in this opening Lesson aimed at physicians in the early phase of their career. However, even if you are an established physician who is late getting started because of military training, a late entrance into medicine, or even a financial setback or divorce, the lesson remains the same: NOW is the time to begin saving.

Compared to people in other careers, physicians are a bit behind the eight ball when it comes to saving because medical training is long and residents and fellows are paid poorly. Consider that attorneys must complete only three years of law school and then get much of their training on the job. If a lawyer is fortunate enough to land a job in a leading corporate law firm, they could be earning in the low six figures right out of law school, in their mid-20s. This would allow them to save significantly early on, while their friends in medical training may not reach that income level for another three to ten years, depending on their specialty.

Six Retirement Tools to Use

A successful plan for retirement means saving money and being tax efficient. Every physician can use some or all of six vehicles to achieve their financial goals. Each has its own tax benefits and some offer protection from lawsuits and liability under state or federal law (which we discuss in Lesson 3). Let's examine all six now.

1. Qualified Retirement Plans for Physician Employees

Physicians who are W-2 employees can often participate in their employer's retirement plan, which allows them to defer income by contributing to the plan.

For example, a 401(k) plan is one type of qualified retirement plan (QRP), and the most common one offered to physician employees of for-profit entities. Government and nonprofit healthcare organizations offer 403(b) plans, which work the same way as 401(k)s. (The pros and cons of QRPs for physicians in private practice who are or will be owners will be discussed later.)

Government-sponsored 457(b) plans are offered by state and local government healthcare organizations. Physicians can defer funds into these plans on a pretax basis in addition to contributing to a 403(b) plan.

Nongovernment organization 457(b) plans, or NGO 457 plans, present a special risk for unwary physicians saving for retirement. While these plans also allow for pretax contributions and tax-deferred growth, they only gain these tax benefits due to a substantial risk of forfeiture imposed by the Internal Revenue Service. Doctors who hold these plans can lose everything if the sponsoring employer goes bankrupt. While account balances from one nongovernment 457(b) can usually be rolled over to another nongovernment 457(b) plan, they cannot be rolled over to an IRA or any other type of plan.

A 401(a) plan is a QRP normally offered by government agencies, educational institutions, and nonprofit organizations rather than by corporations. These plans are usually custom-designed and can be offered to key employees as an incentive to stay with the organization. The employee contribution amounts are normally set by the employer. The employer has a mandate to contribute to the plan as well. Contributions can be pretax or posttax.

2. Tax-Qualified Retirement Plans for Physicians in Private Practice

The term "qualified retirement plan" means that the plan meets the definition of a retirement plan under Department of Labor and Internal Revenue Service rules promulgated under the Employee Retirement and Income Security Act (ERISA). A QRP for a private practice may be in the form of a defined benefit plan, profit-sharing plan, money purchase plan, or 401(k). Properly structured plans offer a variety of benefits: you can fully deduct contributions to a QRP, funds within the QP grow tax-deferred, and (if nonowner employees participate) the funds enjoy superior asset protection.

Despite the benefits QRPs can offer, there are some disadvantages to them that physicians in private practice should understand:

- Mandated maximum annual contributions for defined contribution plans
- Mandatory participation by employees
- Potential liability for management of employee funds in the plan
- Controlled group and affiliated service group restrictions
- Penalties for withdrawal before age 59½
- Required distributions beginning at age 72
- Full ordinary income taxation of distributions from the plan
- Full ordinary income taxation AND estate taxation of plan balances upon death (combined tax rates on these balances can be over 70%)

We discuss such plans further in Chapter 3.4.

In our experience, nearly all physicians in private practice participate in QRPs. The tax deduction is such a strong lure that it often cannot be resisted. For many physician practice owners, however, the cost of contributions for employees, potential liability for mismanagement of employee funds, and the payment of taxes on distributions may outweigh the current tax savings offered by QRPs. These drawbacks suggest that it would make sense to at least investigate another type of plan (that hedges the QRP) as an additional savings vehicle.

This is especially true if you believe that income tax rates, especially the higher marginal rates, will go up over the coming decades. When you use a QRP, you trade today's tax rates on your contribution for the tax rates in the future when you withdraw the money from the plan. If rates rise in the future, the QRP might prove to have not been a good deal at all. While none of us know what the future will bring, we do know that tax rates were much higher than they are today for most of the second half of the twentieth century. Thus, the QRP tax rate bet is one that physicians may be wise to hedge against using retirement savings alternatives such as non-Q plans, which physicians in private practice can implement. Even employed doctors can use hedges such as options 5 and 6 below.

3. Non-Qualified Plans for Physicians in Private Practice

Many private practice physicians want to save significantly for retirement but are limited by the funding rules of QRPs and the employee-related costs. Non-qualified plans (non-Q plans) can be the solution for many doctors. Because they are not subject to QRP rules, non-Q plans do not have to be offered to employees. Further, even within the group of physician owners, there is total flexibility. For example, one doctor could contribute the maximum amount, another could contribute much less, and a third could opt out completely.

The main drawback to non-Q plans is that contributions are never tax-deductible. However, they can be structured for tax-free growth and tax-free access in retirement, like a Roth IRA. In fact, a non-Q plan can be an ideal long-term tax hedge against a QRP. Beyond these general ground rules, there is tremendous flexibility and variation in non-Q plan designs. Consider that they have the following attributes:

- No limitations on contributions (unlike QRPs)
- Implementable in addition to any QRP, such as a practice's 401(k) or profit-sharing plan
- Allowed variation in whether and how much owners and partners can participate
- No requirement of employee participation
- No tax deduction on contributions, but funds can grow tax-free and be accessed tax-free upon withdrawal
- Top asset protection in many states

We discuss such plans further in Chapter 3.6.

4. Benefit Plans for Physicians Who Are Self-Employed

Physicians who receive income reported on Form 1099 (including doctors who "moonlight," work *locum tenens*, or do consulting or speaking in the healthcare industry) and self-employed physicians have other options to help save for retirement.

A SEP IRA is a traditional IRA into which physicians can contribute the lesser of $57,000 or 25% of compensation (under the 2020 limits in place at the time of this book's publication). In addition, physicians with a SEP may also be able to contribute to a separate traditional IRA or Roth IRA. Like other traditional IRAs, account balances can grow tax-deferred and are taxed at ordinary income rates when distributed.

In some states, IRAs and QRPs with only one participant do not offer as much as asset protection as multi-participant QRPs do. Be sure to consult with an expert before establishing such a plan if creditor protection is important to you.

5. After-Tax IRAs

A traditional IRA allows doctors to defer up to $6,000 per year ($7,000 per year if they are 50 or older) into the account (under the 2020 limits in place as we write this). Physicians who are not covered by a workplace retirement plan may deduct pretax contributions; those who are can make non-deductible or partially deductible contributions (depending on their earned income and filing status). The non-deductible portion of the account, also known as the "basis," is tracked with each year's tax return. Account balances can grow tax deferred.

Roth IRA contribution limits are the same as traditional IRA limits, but most physicians earn income at levels exceeding the adjusted gross income limits for Roth IRAs so they are not allowed to contribute directly to a Roth IRA. Doctors can often use a "backdoor Roth IRA" by contributing to a traditional IRA and then converting the traditional IRA to a Roth IRA. (Note: This tactic requires careful planning to avoid unnecessary taxation. Work with an experienced advisor on this.) Roth IRAs can be very beneficial to long-term retirement planning because funds in a Roth IRA grow tax-deferred and come out tax-free.

A spousal IRA is a traditional IRA or Roth IRA that receives contributions on behalf of a nonearning spouse. In order to contribute, the nonearning spouse must meet the ordinary requirements for making an IRA contribution except that they are not required to have earned income. Instead, the earning physician must make enough income to cover the spouse's contribution. Otherwise, the same IRA contribution limits apply to the spousal IRA.

6. Life Insurance as a Retirement Plan

Above, we explained that Roth IRA contributions are after-tax, but then the balance grows tax-free and can be accessed tax-free in the future. Would you be surprised to learn that, managed properly, a permanent life insurance policy behaves the same way? As we described in the previous chapter, "permanent" life insurance means policies like whole life, universal life, variable life, and equity-indexed life policies. Regardless of the type of product, the cash value of such policies grows free of tax and can be accessed free of tax during the insured's life—and this tax treatment has remained stable for over 100 years.

Certainly, there is a lot of noise out there about the strategy of using permanent life insurance and contradictory advice in the marketplace. In fact, you may have heard the saying "buy term and invest the difference," as we have. Our view is that just as physicians have many medicines in their armamentarium, permanent life insurance is a "medicine" with which some "patients" do very well. On the other hand, we recognize that like actual medicine, this "medicine" has ideal applications and side effects and should be managed properly. We urge you to keep an open mind on this subject when we revisit it in more depth in Lesson 4.

Flexibility Is Key. Example: Taxes and Tax Diversification

Regardless of the retirement tools a physician employs to save for retirement, one of the fundamental pillars of any retirement plan should be flexibility to withstand changes in tax rates, income, market performance, and personal health. Here, we will focus only on flexibility with regard to taxes and the importance of tax diversification.

In 2018, we experienced an overhaul of the tax code for the first time in 30+ years. Of course, that doesn't mean that tax rates hadn't changed in those 30 years—in fact, they changed during both previous administrations this century (Obama and Bush II). Moreover, all of the personal tax changes passed in the 2018 tax act are scheduled to *sunset* back to the pre-act provisions in 2025. At least, that is the law at the time we write this in 2020. The bottom line: the tax code is always changing, and even *permanent* tax changes are only permanent until a future Congress and president change them again. See the charts below, which show the highest marginal federal income tax rates over time and the federal capital gains tax rate over time.

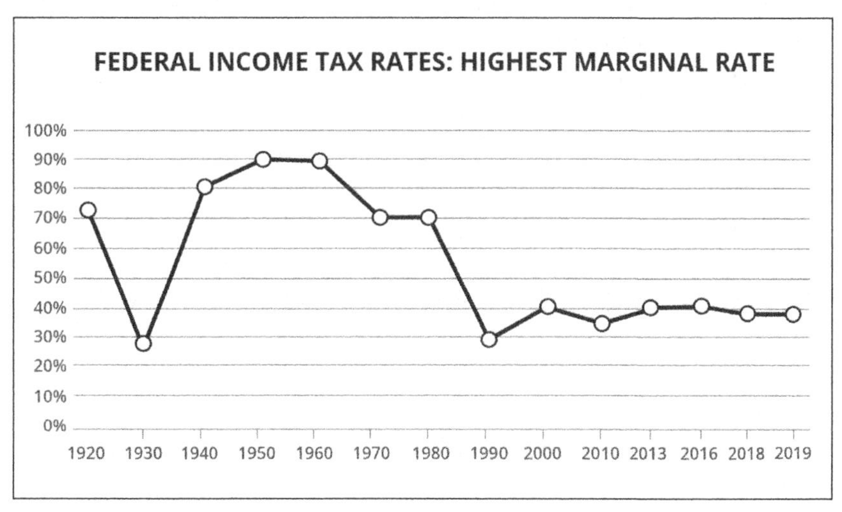

Figure 1.3.2

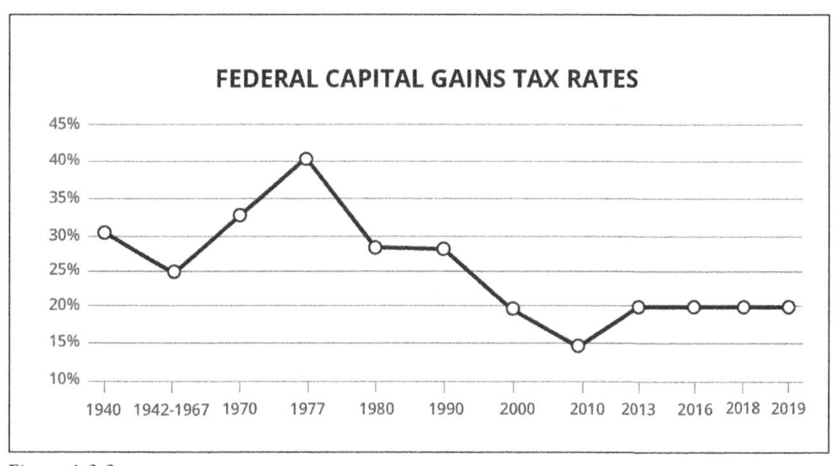

Figure 1.3.3

Examining these charts, it seems quite possible that we could see tax rates continue to rise even more over the long term, regardless of short-term changes that might be made in the next four to eight years. Even if they were to return to the mean rates of the twentieth century, we would experience a sharp increase in at least marginal income tax and capital gains rates. Thus, it makes sense to build in flexibility to account for this possibility.

A tax diversification approach can help alleviate some potential issues. Essentially, this means building up wealth in three "buckets": assets subject to ordinary income tax rates upon distribution in retirement, assets subject to capital gains rates, and assets not subject to tax upon distribution.

While most plans focus on asset class diversification only in the context of investing, we believe it is crucial to layer on top of that attention to diversifying your wealth according to tax rate exposure. As an example, let's return to the six retirement tools discussed above. All options that provide a deduction on the way in (options 1, 2, and 4) will be taxed as ordinary income tax on the way out. Options 3, 5, and 6, conversely, do not allow tax-deductible contributions and are not taxed upon distribution.

The visual below may help you to see the value of having differently taxed "buckets" to draw on when you reach retirement. As the retirement/distribution wealth phase may last for many years, or even multiple decades, being diversified across such tax buckets puts you in a position of strength and gives you options for withdrawing income depending on the tax rates then in effect.

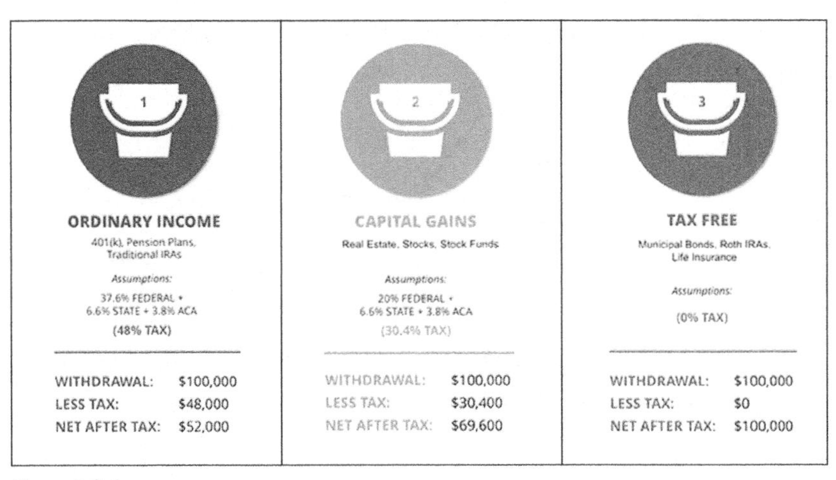

Figure 1.3.4

Here, we assume a marginal top tax bracket in retirement, since many physicians will be in the top two or three tax brackets in retirement and the current rate of 37.6% is not close to an all-time high (see Figure 1.3.2 for a reminder). We also assume a 6.6% state income tax, although many states have rates far exceeding this (see the map in Chapter 1.4 for state income tax rates nationally).

The strategy should be obvious: each year, one can examine tax rates and pull from the appropriate "bucket" to maximize after-tax income. If at the beginning of a physician's retirement (which may last two or three decades) income tax rates are high but capital gains taxes are relatively low, then it may be best to draw from the Bucket #2. If the opposite is true, Bucket #1 may be targeted for "overweight" distributions. Bucket #3 provides the highest level of flexibility, as it can be accessed in any tax environment. An ideal retirement plan calls for physicians to have a significant percentage of their wealth in each bucket; yet in our experience, most physicians have too little wealth in Bucket #3.

TAKEAWAY: For nearly all physicians, getting to retirement on their own terms is the number one financial goal. To reach that goal, doctors should use a range of tax-favored retirement tools. Three keys to success are starting to save early, building flexibility into a retirement plan, and incorporating tax diversification as part of that flexibility.

CHAPTER 1.4

How to Evaluate Career Opportunities Financially and Choose the Right Job

For young physicians finishing medical training, their greatest immediate financial challenge is to evaluate their first job opportunities from a financial perspective. Certainly, the fragmented and often-opaque types of physician compensation arrangements make such a challenge very difficult. Further, most young doctors simply do not have the tools or experience to properly evaluate their job opportunities, and few resources exist to help them.

Not surprisingly, many young physicians become dissatisfied with their initial job choice once they begin living the reality of the position – and financial elements are often part of this job dissatisfaction. As a result, between 50% and 75% of physicians will change jobs during their first five years, with the bulk of those switching after two years of practice. {Smith:2006dm, Mir:2011kb}.

As one can imagine, the decision to pack up and change jobs a second time within a few years can create significant family and personal stress. Moreover, the same lack of accurate financial evaluation that plagued the first job decision is often present in the second job evaluation – if only aided perhaps by the more experienced and jaundiced eye of the doctor.

For these reasons, we think it is imperative that a young physician learn the job evaluation tools outlined in this chapter.

Financial Modeling: The Tool Every Physician Should Use to Evaluate Options

At its core, the technique employs a simple sensitivity analysis, similar to those used by professional analysts, to financially simulate various "what if" scenarios. The purpose of financial modeling is to simplify complex compensation arrangements typically seen in physician employment and identify large discrepancies in compensation and risk to the doctor early in the job search process.

It's Not All About the Money

First, it is important to remember that what a specific job offers financially is not everything. Fresh out of training and loaded with debt, young physicians not uncommonly gravitate toward the highest-paying career opportunity, only to change practices a few years later when financial stresses decrease, or practice conditions and family situations change. It is important to always focus on the big picture during your job search.

Why Understanding the Financial Side Is Important

Although the financial aspects of a particular job are not everything, compensation is often cited as one of the top two reasons that doctors change employers. {Smith:2006dm} Many times, young physicians leave a practice because their income expectations were vastly different than what they end up earning. Contributing to this problem are the incredibly complex compensation formulas, overhead costs, and partnership costs seen in various practice environments in our healthcare system.

What Is Financial Modeling?

In business, financial modeling is the process of creating a summary of a company's expenses and earnings in the form of a spreadsheet that can be used to calculate the impact of a future event or decision. Company executives frequently use this tool to guide decisions and estimate stock prices, relying on the present value of future cash flows that we covered when discussing the importance of using insurance to protect a doctor's future income from disability and death. Despite its seeming complexity, the financial modeling process is relatively straightforward and may be of value to young physicians—executives of a sort guiding their own careers—in their job search.

Financially Modeling Your Future Income

If you know, roughly, what you would earn in a prospective job, as well as various costs, such as your family's living expenses, partnership buy-ins, and taxes, a simple spreadsheet program may be a valuable tool in financially modeling your net worth based on that job opportunity. In some situations, the practice may provide a rough estimate of what partners are taking home as a guide to expected compensation; this is essential information to gather for your evaluation. If you plan to invest your disposable income, it is helpful to estimate living expenses and your desired rate of return in order to see how much you may be able to save and how it will compound over time.

To demonstrate the value of this technique, we offer two hypothetical financial models. Figure 1.4.1 is a spreadsheet designed in Microsoft Excel depicting a hypothetical private practice employment opportunity offering a $350,000 starting salary and a $50,000 partnership buy-in cost during year three. As with many private practice opportunities, income in the partnership is dependent on production, but the practice provided an estimate. Figure 1.4.2 is a spreadsheet based on a second job opportunity with a $450,000 annual salary in a state with higher taxes.

JOB 1		ASSUME $80,000 YEARLY LIVING EXPENES FOR FAMILY; 5% YEARLY RETURN ON INVESTMENTS; 38% EFFECTIVE TAX RATE; $50,000 PARTNERSHIP BUY-IN DURING YEAR 3				
YEAR	YEARLY TAKE HOME	YEARLY AMOUNT SAVED AFTER TAXES, LIVING EXPENSES	AMOUNT SAVED IN EMERGENCY FUND	AMOUNT LEFT OVER FOR SAVING & INVESTING	NON-IRA INVESTMENTS (Growing at 5% Yearly Rate)	JOB 1 NET ASSETS CUMULATIVE SAVINGS WITH INVESTMENTS TOTAL
1	$350.000	$137,000	$50,000	$87,000	$91,350	$141,350
2	$370,000	$149,400	$50,000	$99,400	$195,318	$245,318
3	$495,000	$226,900	$50,000	$176,900	$381,983	$431,983
4	$545,000	$257,900	$50,000	$207,900	$608,983	$658,983
5	$545,000	$257,900	$50,000	$207,900	$874,332	$897,332
6	$545,000	$257,900	$50,000	$207,900	$1,097,598	$1,147,598
7	$545,000	$257,900	$50,000	$207,900	$1,360,378	$1,410,378
8	$545,000	$257,900	$50,000	$207,900	$1,636,297	$1,686,297
9	$545,000	$257,900	$50,000	$207,900	$1,926,012	$1,976,012
10	$545,000	$257,900	$50,000	$207,900	$2,230,213	$2,280,213
11	$545,000	$257,900	$50,000	$207,900	$2,549,623	$2,599,623
12	$545,000	$257,900	$50,000	$207,900	$2,885,004	$2,935,004
13	$545,000	$257,900	$50,000	$207,900	$3,237,155	$3,287,155
14	$545,000	$257,900	$50,000	$207,900	$3,606,912	$3,656,912
15	$545,000	$257,900	$50,000	$207,900	$3,995,158	$4,045,158

Figure 1.4.1 Financial model of hypothetical job offer (Job 1) offering a $350,000 starting salary and a $50,000 partnership buy-in cost during year three with production-based income thereafter.

JOB 2		ASSUME $80,000 YEARLY LIVING EXPENES FOR FAMILY; 5% YEARLY RETURN ON INVESTMENTS; 41.6% EFFECTIVE TAX RATE; NO BUY-IN				
YEAR	YEARLY TAKE HOME	YEARLY AMOUNT SAVED AFTER TAXES, LIVING EXPENSES	AMOUNT SAVED IN EMERGENCY FUND	AMOUNT LEFT OVER FOR SAVING & INVESTING	NON-IRA INVESTMENTS (Growing at 5% Yearly Rate)	JOB 1 NET ASSETS CUMULATIVE SAVINGS WITH INVESTMENTS TOTAL
1	$450.000	$182,800	$50,000	$132,800	$139,440	$189,440
2	$450.000	$182,800	$50,000	$132,800	$279,212	$329,212
3	$450.000	$182,800	$50,000	$132,800	$425,973	$475,973
4	$450.000	$182,800	$50,000	$132,800	$580,071	$630,071
5	$450.000	$182,800	$50,000	$132,800	$741,875	$791,875
6	$450.000	$182,800	$50,000	$132,800	$911,769	$961,769
7	$450.000	$182,800	$50,000	$132,800	$1,090,157	$1,410,157
8	$450.000	$182,800	$50,000	$132,800	$1,277,465	$1,327,465
9	$450.000	$182,800	$50,000	$132,800	$1,474,138	$1,524,138
10	$450.000	$182,800	$50,000	$132,800	$1,680,645	$1,730,645
11	$450.000	$182,800	$50,000	$132,800	$1,897,477	$1,947,477
12	$450.000	$182,800	$50,000	$132,800	$2,125,151	$2,175,151
13	$450.000	$182,800	$50,000	$132,800	$2,364,209	$2,414,209
14	$450.000	$182,800	$50,000	$132,800	$2,615,219	$2,665,219
15	$450.000	$182,800	$50,000	$132,800	$2,878,780	$2,928,780

Figure 1.4.2 Financial model of hypothetical job offer (Job 2) offering a $450,000 annual salary in a state with higher taxes.

If you want to take the analysis a step further, you can graphically depict your net worth based on various job opportunities side by side (Figure 1.4.3). Although this may sound like an overly analytical exercise considering your limited spare time, it may help you better understand your earning potential in alternative jobs. In our example, one can see that although Job 2 has a $100,000 higher starting salary, after three to four years, Job 1 breaks even with Job 2, and Job 1 offers far higher long-term earnings growth. The value of this exercise is that it allows young doctors to easily model a "worst case" and "best case" scenario for each employment offer to better understand its financial risk and reward and consider them in conjunction with practice-specific factors.

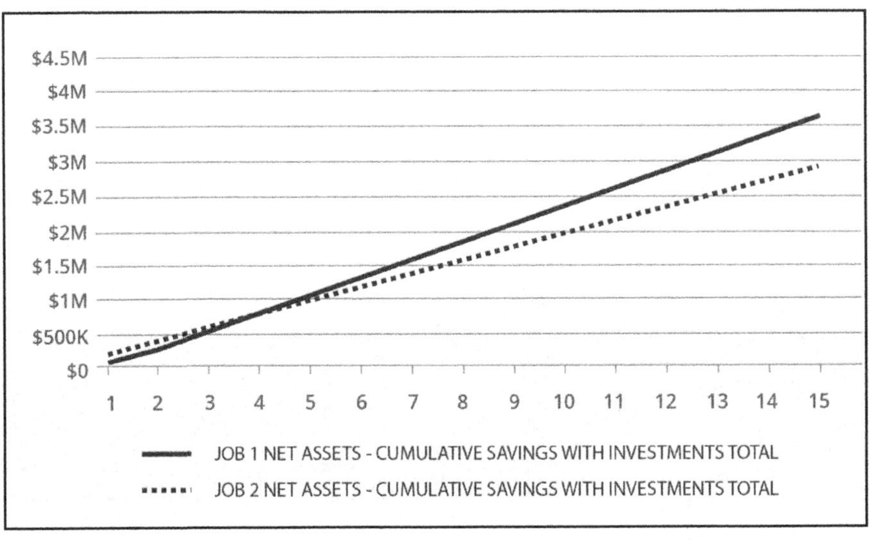

Figure 1.4.3 Comparison of the net worth attained based on both opportunities over a 15-year period. Note that the break-even point occurs between years three and four, with Job 1 having a higher trajectory for growth thereafter.

Taxes as Secondary Financial Factor to Consider

Even in the simple financial models above, we included a rudimentary tax factor. You can see that Job 1 assumed an effective tax rate of 38% and Job 2, 41.6%. This 3.6% difference is much less than the difference one might find in two comparable physician jobs in different states. As you probably know, state income tax rates vary widely across the United States, from 0% in Florida, Nevada, Texas, New Hampshire, and other states up to 13% in California and 12%+ in

New York City when state and city taxes are combined. See the map below from taxfoundation.org showing 2018 income taxes.

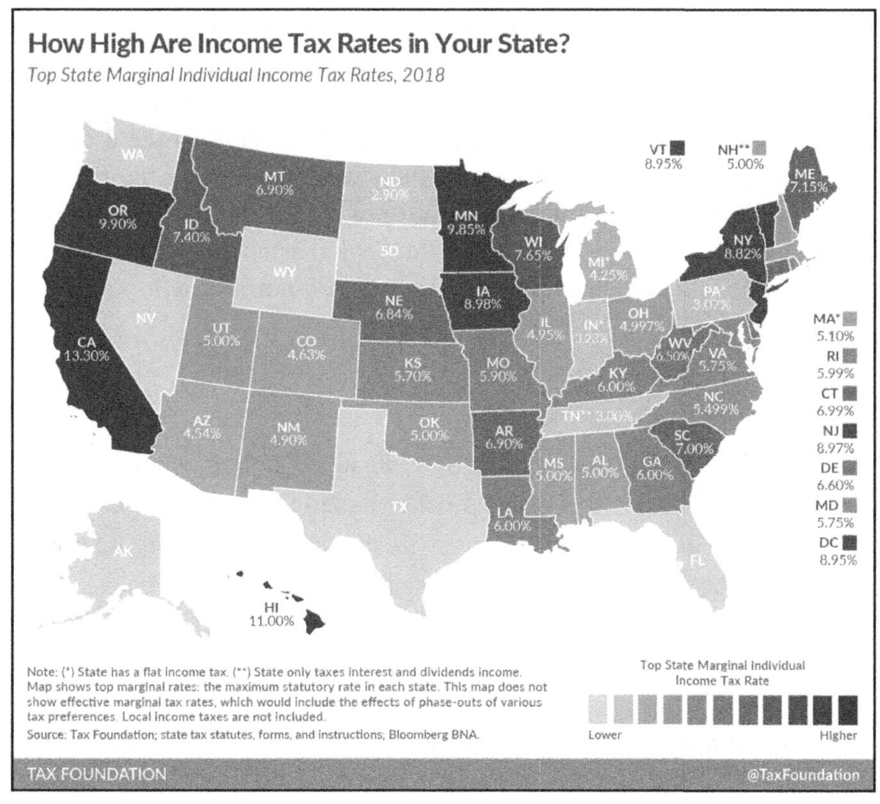

Figure 1.4.4

Applying this reality to job comparisons, as an example, note that taking a position in California rather than one in Nevada offering the same income could result in up to 13.3% less after-tax income each year. Over a career, the difference in retirement savings based on just this one factor can be astounding. Physicians contemplating job options should always factor in state and local taxes.

Benefit Plans as Secondary Financial Factor to Consider

As we describe in other chapters, a physician's proper use of benefit plans can be a significant factor in whether long-term financial and retirement goals are achieved. By "benefit plans," we mean "qualified retirement plans," "non-qualified plans," and even "fringe benefit plans," all of which are described in other chapters. The point here is that all potential jobs are not equal in terms of the quantity and quality of the benefits offered to physicians. Moreover, the long-term financial benefit of such plans can be extremely significant, allowing the doctor who has access to superior plans a more comfortable, or even earlier, retirement. To see a case study demonstrating the power of benefit plans, go to Chapter 3.6. For now, the important point is that physicians looking at different jobs should examine and understand what each position offers in the way of a benefit plan and attempt to quantify the long-term value of each.

TAKEAWAY: Searching for a job as a young or experienced physician is one of the most stressful times in one's career. Although the financial aspects of a job should never be the most important factor in deciding what offer to choose, doctors too often poorly understand what they can expect to earn, which may lead to discontent in the future. Financial modeling is an effective tool that may help physicians simplify the effects of complex compensation arrangements typically seen in physician contracts. Layering in an analysis of secondary financial elements, such as local taxes and available benefit plans, is also well worth the time and effort.

CHAPTER 1.5

Estate Planning Essentials for Physicians of All Ages

In Chapter 1.2, we addressed the importance of using life insurance to protect dependents against a physician's premature death. Certainly, a plan in that area is essential and should be implemented as soon as one has financial dependents. Another related area of wealth management that also should be addressed early (and often with periodic reviews) is estate planning. In fact, this chapter could be repeated in every section of this book—literally from residency to retirement—because a physician's estate planning could require updating every five to seven years, or when major life events occur (marriages, divorces, the births of children or grandchildren, a move to another state, a major change in the estate tax code, etc.).

A common misconception about the term "estate planning" is that many people believe that such planning only concerns what happens after someone dies. Certainly, as we will see in this chapter, estate planning has a broader scope and includes areas that impact physicians while they are still alive. We will discuss three significant parts of estate planning:

- **Incapacitation planning.** Deals with decision-making regarding legal, financial, and medical issues if you are unable to make decisions yourself.
- **Estate distribution planning.** Concerns what happens to assets upon death.
- **Transfer tax planning.** Addresses and plans for the various gift, estate, and other taxes that may be triggered under state and federal law when transferring wealth *during life or at death.*

Incapacitation Planning

Planning for one's own incapacitation (i.e., what happens if you are not able to make decisions for yourself) is never pleasant but always important.

As an example, what happens if you are hospitalized and cannot express your wishes regarding decisions that need to be made about your medical care? Many people assume that their family members would automatically be able to make decisions in this scenario. However, rules vary greatly from state to state. In some cases, decisions are left up to the healthcare providers and institutions in charge of your care. Also consider what may happen if such decisions can be made by your family members but they do not all agree on the best course of action.

There are several key documents that every doctor should have in place, for which the exact names and requirements are controlled by state law and thus will vary. Typically, an estate planning attorney will prepare these at the same time he or she is preparing estate planning documents such as wills and trusts. Such documents might include the following and should be part of every doctor's overall planning:

Living will. A written record of the type of medical care you would want in specific circumstances.

Health care proxy. A document that names someone you trust as your proxy, or agent, to express your wishes and make health care decisions for you if you are unable to speak for yourself.

Advance directive. This term often refers to a combination of the living will and health care proxy documents.

Power of attorney. A document that names someone you trust as your agent to make property, financial, and other legal decisions on your behalf.

Estate Distribution Planning

Before we address the foundational estate planning documents most physicians should employ, consider what occurs if you die without any will or other estate planning document in place. Would you be surprised to know that you already have a will, even if you have never written one or had an attorney draft one? It's true. If you die without a will, then your property will pass under the scheme that your state legislature has written for all of its citizens. This is what is known as dying "intestate."

There are various negative consequences of dying intestate. While the precise rules vary among the fifty states, typically the laws are very rigid and formulaic. Usually, all of your nearest relatives get a piece of your property but no one else does—not friends, cousins, charities, or anyone else. Furthermore, no one gets more than the state-allotted share, even if that seems unfair. Often, this ends up hurting the surviving spouse, if there is one. In this all-too-common scenario, the decedent's grown children may get some of the money meant for the surviving spouse, even if it means the surviving spouse then has too little to live on. In larger estates, this could have the very impractical effect of creating an estate tax payable when the first spouse dies if the children's intestate share of the estate exceeds the federal or state exemption amount. Moreover, intestacy may lead to expensive and lengthy court battles by family members contesting the division of assets.

Perhaps the most upsetting thing about intestacy occurs if you have minor children. In this case, and if both parents die intestate, the courts will decide who becomes the legal guardian of your children. What parents would want to have an unknown judge decide who will care for their children after they pass away? Furthermore, any minor children will receive their share of the estate when they turn 18, rather than at some more appropriate later age that you can specify with proper planning.

The Dangers of Joint Ownership

Before we get to the documents needed to avoid intestacy, we need to examine another more-common estate planning trap that many physicians fall into unknowingly: joint ownership. Not surprisingly, the most common way for married couples to own property is to own it jointly. Though this is typical, it is problematic for many physicians. Not only does this form of titling assets leave your assets unprotected from lawsuits (an issue that we will discuss in Lesson 2) but it also may create estate planning problems.

The risk of owning property jointly with the right of survivorship is that when one joint owner dies, property automatically passes to the surviving joint owner(s). In this way, jointly owned property avoids the probate process, which is good (we discuss probate below). However, it also passes outside of any estate planning documents, like a will or living trust (also discussed below), which could throw an estate plan into chaos, especially one involving second marriages. Consider these stories:

1. William, a man in his late 60s, marries for the second time. Shortly after the wedding, he puts all of his significant property—his home, his winter vacation condominium, and his stock portfolio—into joint ownership with his new wife. Within six months, William dies. The home, the condo, and the stocks all go to William's new wife. His three children and eight grandchildren inherit virtually nothing, even though William had made ample provisions for them in his will.

2. Susan's will bequeathed her property equally to her son and daughter. Because her son lives near her and pays her bills, Susan put her house, her safe deposit box, and her bank account in joint ownership with him. When she dies, Susan's son will get all of the money in the bank account and deposit box, as well as the house, regardless of the will provisions. Unless the son is extremely generous, the daughter will get nothing.

3. Assume the same situation as in the previous paragraph but add the fact that the son has serious debt problems—he has $15,000 in overdue credit card debt and a defaulted loan. His creditors can come after the bank account, the safe deposit box contents, and, likely, the house the moment Susan dies. The only real beneficiaries of Susan's estate may be banks and finance companies.

4. Becky, a single mother in her thirties, is trying to build a college fund for her ten-year-old son, Dylan. Becky has invested some of her excess income by buying

old residential multifamily homes, which she and her partner fix up and rent. While her relationship with her partner has been strained at times, Becky nevertheless takes title to the investment properties in joint ownership with her partner without realizing that, if she dies before they resell the properties, her partner will take them all and leave nothing for Dylan.

Many well-intentioned people get stuck in these predicaments because they do not understand the estate planning consequences of jointly held property. As with intestacy, the negative impact of joint ownership can be planned away. These are some of the reasons that every physician should have valid foundational estate planning documents in place. What are these documents? Again, this depends on the state. In some states, a comprehensive will is enough; in many others, a will with living trust is recommended.

Wills and Living Trusts

While estate planning documentation is completely state-dependent, we can say that in every state, having a will is better than not having a will. However, in many states, with a will alone, your entire estate will be stuck in the probate process. Probate is the court-controlled process by which the state administers your will. In most states, knowledgeable estate planning advisors recommend combining a living trust with a short will called a "pour-over will" because this combination ensures that much of an estate will avoid probate. Before we examine how a living trust works, we must first see why it is so important to avoid probate.

The Pitfalls of Probate

Delays. Probate may take one to two years to complete. During that time, your beneficiaries must wait for their inheritance. Perhaps worse, the representatives of your estate may have to petition the court for permission to conduct transactions involving your estate's assets during this time. This can make it difficult to sell estate property or invest estate assets during the probate process.

Costs. In some states, probate can be very costly. These costs pay for additional legal fees, executor's commissions, and the costs associated with marshalling assets. In some states, these probate fees are assessed on your gross estate, not taking into account any mortgages on your assets! In these states, if you die owning $1 million worth of assets that have mortgages of $800,000, your estate will pay probate fees based on the $1 million fair market value. This is money that could have gone to your beneficiaries rather than to the courts and lawyers.

Privacy. Probate is a public process in all states. Anyone interested in your estate can find out who inherits under your will, how much he or she inherits, the beneficiaries' addresses, and more. While you may not be famous or worried about the newspapers exploiting this information, you should think of your beneficiaries—your surviving family members. They certainly will not appreciate many salespeople calling them with "hot tips" on investments or welcome contact from unscrupulous people who try to take advantage of recent inheritance recipients. These people find beneficiaries by examining probate records. They know who they are and how much "found money" they have to invest.

Control. In probate, the court controls the timing and final say-so on whether or not your will—and the wishes expressed in your will—are followed. Your family must follow the court's orders and pay for the process as well. This can be extremely frustrating.

Double probate. If you own real estate outside your state of residence, your will may need to be probated *again* (in an ancillary proceeding) in each state where real property is located. This becomes very time-consuming and expensive.

You are probably thinking, "Why would anyone choose to use a will for estate planning when probate is this unappealing?" Again, in some states, the rules may be different—this is an overview.

This is why every physician must work with an experienced estate attorney in their state. Often, they will learn that the ideal estate planning documents for them will include both a will and a living trust.

The Living Trust: A Foundational Estate Planning Document

"Living trust" is a common name given to a revocable trust (which, unsurprisingly, is revocable, meaning you can revoke it or amend it anytime during your life). You might also see such a trust called a "family trust" or "revocable family trust."

Regardless of its marketing name, the living trust is a revocable trust that provides direction for the use of your assets both while you are alive and at the time of your death. During your life, the assets transferred to the trust are managed and controlled by you, as the trustee, just as if you owned them in your own name. When you die, these trust assets pass to whomever you designated in the trust, automatically, outside of the probate process. Other benefits of the living trust include the following:

- avoidance of the unintentional disinheritance cause- by joint tenancy
- prevention of court control of assets if you become incapacitated
- protection of beneficiaries with special needs
- the ability to nominate guardians to take care of your children if you are incapacitated (but still alive) or when you die

Funding the Trust

The transfer of assets to the living trust is also known as "funding the trust." If you create a trust with a trust document but don't fund the trust with assets, it is just a useless piece of paper. Just as you must put gas in a car (or charge it up) to use it, if you want to get any benefit from your trust, you must fund it.

Funding the trust is a step you must not forget to take. When you transfer your assets to your living trust while you are alive, you maintain 100% control over these assets as though you still own them in your own name. For your car, stocks, bonds, bank accounts, home, and any other assets, the process of transferring an asset to your living trust is simple. If the asset has a registration or deed, change the name on that document. If the asset is jewelry or artwork that has no official ownership record, use an assignment document to officially transfer ownership to your living trust. Work with your attorney to follow the right process for funding the trust.

These ownership changes will typically transfer the name of the registration or deed to the "John Doe Revocable Living Trust" or to "John Doe, Trustee of John Doe Revocable Living Trust," rather than "John Doe" as it now reads. As sole trustee of the trust, you have the same power to buy, sell, mortgage, or invest as you did before. Furthermore, because the trust is revocable, you can always change beneficiaries, remove or add assets, or even revoke your trust entirely.

Attorneys know that most clients won't be 100% diligent about re-titling existing assets into the name of the trust or titling new assets in the trust name for the rest of their life. This is why most combine the living trust with a short will that, upon death, "pours" all assets titled in the decedent's name into the trust. This is called a "pour-over will" and is a fail-safe for titling assets to the living trust.

Below is a list of some of the valuable benefits of a trust that allow you to achieve important estate planning goals without sacrificing your quality of life:

You may name yourself or someone else as trustee.
You need not name yourself as the trustee of your living trust, although most people do. You could name an adult child, another relative or close friend, or even a corporate trustee, like a local bank or trust company. If you do not like the way the outside trustee is handling the trust, you always have the power to remove that trustee.

When you die or become incapacitated, your successor trustee will take over.
If you are the trustee while you are alive, you will name, in your living trust, an individual (or possibly a corporate trustee) as the successor trustee. That person or entity will take over the trustee duties when you die or

become incapacitated. If you have a co-trustee while you are alive, that person will take over all trustee duties after you have died. These duties involve collecting income or benefits due your estate, paying your remaining debts, making sure the proper tax returns are filed, and distributing your assets according to the Trust instructions. This person or entity acts like an executor for a will. However, unlike with a will, actions taken under a living trust's directions are not generally subject to court interference or supervision.

You decide when your beneficiaries receive their inheritances.

Another significant advantage of a living trust over a will is that you, rather than the court, decide when and how your beneficiaries get their inheritance. Because the court is not involved, the successor trustee can distribute assets right after your final affairs are concluded.

You can choose for assets to not be distributed right away. Instead, you may direct that they stay in your trust, managed by your individual or corporate trustee, until your beneficiaries reach the age(s) at which you want them to inherit. One of the advantages to distributing assets in this manner is that during the time the assets remain in the trust prior to distribution, they are protected from creditors—a feature that may interest you if you have concerns about your heirs' creditors or potential divorces.

The successor trustee must follow your trust instructions.

Your successor trustee (as well as your primary trustee if it is not you) is a fiduciary—a legal term meaning that there is a legal duty to follow the living trust instructions and to act in a reasonably prudent manner. The trustee must treat the living trust as a binding legal contract and must use their "best efforts" to live up to the obligations of the contract. If your successor trustee mismanages the trust by ignoring the instructions in your living trust, they could be legally liable.

Transfer Tax Planning

As mentioned above, the "transfer tax planning" element of estate planning plans for the various gift, estate, and other taxes that may be triggered under state and federal law when transferring wealth during life or at death. In our careers, we have seen the importance of the tax element of estate planning fluctuate widely over the years as the federal government changes the amount exempt from federal transfer taxes. In addition, because we have clients in nearly all fifty states, we see physicians who reside in states with significant state transfer taxes, though many live in states without any such taxes at all.

Four Fundamental Elements of Our Transfer Tax System

For all physicians, it is important to understand four fundamental elements of our transfer tax system in place at the time of publication: the unlimited marital deduction, the unified estate tax credit/ federal estate tax rate, the federal gift tax rate, and any state estate/ inheritance taxes or fees.

The unlimited marital deduction

The unlimited marital deduction rule means that under our federal estate tax system, a decedent can leave an unlimited amount to a surviving spouse without any estate tax (provided that both spouses are U.S. citizens).

The Unified Estate Tax Credit and federal estate tax rate

The unified estate tax credit (UTC) translates into a dollar amount that can be left by a decedent estate free of tax (commonly called the "estate tax exemption"). See Figure 1.5.1, which shows how the per-person UTC has changed over the last 23 years.

YEAR	UTC	TOP ESTATE TAX RATE
1997	$600,000	55%
1998	$600,000	55%
1999	$650,000	55%
2000	$675,000	55%
2001	$675,000	55%
2002	$1,000,000	50%
2003	$1,000,000	49%
2004	$1,500,000	48%
2005	$1,500,000	47%
2006	$2,000,000	46%
2007	$2,000,000	45%
2008	$2,000,000	45%
2009	$3,500,000	45%
2010	$5,000,000 or $0	35% or 0%
2011	$5,000,000	35%
2012	$5,120,000	35%
2013	$5,250,000	40%
2014	$5,340,000	40%
2015	$5,430,000	40%
2016	$5,450,000	40%
2017	$5,490,000	40%
2018	$11,180,000	40%
2019	$11,400,000	40%

Figure 1.5.1

The federal gift tax rates

Because ours is a "transfer tax" system, one cannot avoid taxes by gifting assets to beneficiaries during one's life just to avoid the estate taxes that would be owed if those same assets were left to beneficiaries at death. Thus, estate and gift taxes are intertwined in our tax system. See Figure 1.5.2 for the changing federal gift tax exemption and tax rates in this century.

YEAR	GIFT TAX EXEMPTION	TOP GIFT TAX RATE
2000	$675,000	55%
2001	$675,000	55%
2002	$1,000,000	50%
2003	$1,000,000	49%
2004	$1,000,000	48%
2005	$1,000,000	47%
2006	$1,000,000	46%
2007	$1,000,000	45%
2008	$1,000,000	45%
2009	$1,000,000	45%
2010	$1,000,000	35% or 0%
2011	$5,000,000	35%
2012	$5,120,000	35%
2013	$5,250,000	40%
2014	$5,340,000	40%
2015	$5,430,000	40%
2016	$5,450,000	40%
2017	$5,490,000	40%
2018	$11,180,000	40%
2019	$11,400,000	40%

Figure 1.5.2

State Transfer Taxes

States vary significantly in their taxation of estates through either an "estate tax" or "inheritance tax." Some levy no tax at all, others tie into the federal tax, and still others levy a completely separate and possibly significant tax. Because states are constantly changing how they deal with this issue, it is imperative that physicians get advice from a local expert.

Transfer Tax Planning

Physicians—like all of us—do not know (1) when they (or their spouse) will die or (2) what UTC or federal estate tax rates will be in effect at that time. Also, many are not 100% sure what state they will be residing in when they die. For these reasons, and the probability that most clients will live to their actuarial life expectancies, it becomes clear that estate tax planning must not only reflect what rules exist *today* but also allow flexibility for when things inevitably change in the near and not-so-near future. In sum, transfer tax management is a moving target. As such, it should be considered by physicians repeatedly over time as they accumulate assets.

Rather than spend pages here outlining various strategies that might be applicable for a physician's estate tax management, we have decided to include a short chapter on this in Lesson 6. Please continue there if this subject is of interest.

TAKEAWAY: Every physician should have incapacitation and estate planning documents in place. Transfer tax management is a moving target but should be considered by physicians as they accumulate assets.

Protecting Assets from Potential Liability

In our litigious society, asset protection planning is an integral part of any physician's comprehensive wealth plan. Obviously, medical malpractice liability is the leading concern in most physicians' minds. Perhaps this is because they hear about multimillion-dollar judgments against colleagues or see them on the news occasionally and wonder, "What if that were me?" This awareness only grows as a doctor gains more experience in practice and—not surprisingly—accumulates more assets that need protection.

While medical malpractice is the most visible litigation risk, there are others. In fact, physicians should also consider the potential for vicarious liability for negligent acts of employees and for liability for claims by employees (alleging discrimination, for example), claims due to slips or falls at the practice, claims by renters or visitors involved in accidents at other properties they own, and claims arising from car accidents caused by either their teenage children or themselves. Regardless of the type of claim, physicians should come to this conclusion: "If there are effective ways to minimize my exposure, I should explore them." In other words, aim for the best, plan for the worst. This is where asset protection planning comes into play.

The goal of asset protection planning is simple: positioning a client's assets so that is it difficult, costly, and sometimes impossible for creditors and lawsuits to reach them. Asset protection requires expertise from several disciplines and must be managed on an ongoing basis to be successful. As a physician's situation or asset mix changes, so too will the plan need to change to adequately protect their wealth.

In this Lesson, we will begin by explaining the importance of asset protection, the sliding scale of asset protection, and common asset protection myths. Then, we will explain several tools and strategies that have helped doctors protect their assets, including the following:

- Business and personal insurance
- Assets that are exempt from collection under state and federal laws
- Family limited partnerships and limited liability companies
- Various types of trusts
- Strategies for protecting your home
- Strategies for protecting against divorce

To see which tools work best for protecting your assets, you will have to work with your advisory team; make sure there is at least one asset protection specialist in the group.

CHAPTER 2.1
The Importance of Asset Protection

Until the last part of the twentieth century, it might have seemed excessive to be concerned with protecting assets from potential lawsuits. Lawsuits were not particularly common and jury awards were reasonable. In the 1980s, the number of lawsuits in the United States skyrocketed and outrageous jury awards became commonplace. This has been especially the case in employment and medical malpractice claims—two areas where physicians are specifically targeted. Thus, doctors have realized that protecting their assets from lawsuits needs to be the focus of any financial plan.

The Proliferation of Lawsuits

Why are there so many more lawsuits today? It may be because many Americans see a lawsuit as a way to "get rich quick" rather than as a way to be made whole and ultimately achieve justice for being wronged by another. In our society, many people believe that misfortune is an opportunity to place blame and seek financial reparations—even if the targeted person wasn't at fault for the misfortune. Unfortunately, juries routinely adopt the idea that someone must pay for alleged wrongdoing and often disregard the facts of the case when reaching a verdict. Through emotion and bias, juries sometimes give away large sums of money to unfortunate victims, even when the defendants were not to blame for the misfortune.

To illustrate this point, let's consider the decisions reached in some cases you may have read about in your daily newspaper:

Claim: A woman sues a franchise eatery because the coffee she spilled in her lap was too hot.
Decision: Woman receives $2.6 million.

Claim: A trespasser is injured while burglarizing a home.
Decision: Burglar receives thousands of dollars.

Claim: A Pennsylvania woman sues a physician, claiming to have lost her psychic powers during a routine set of tests.
Decision: Woman receives a jury award for $690,000.

After reading about the large sums these ordinary people received, it seems rational that other people would begin to ask themselves, "Why not me?" The more press these cases receive, the greater the reinforcement of this belief. The greater the number of people who try to work the system, the greater the number of people who will eventually succeed. Each new outrageous success gains more press, and the vicious cycle of lawsuits continues.

Knowledgeable doctors realize that this lawsuit trend cannot be ignored. They insist on having their advisors create financial plans that address the protection of their assets. They realize that they have something to lose if they are sued and that the plaintiff often has nothing to lose. This is especially true in the United States legal system.

American Rule of Legal Fees

Did you know that in virtually every other legal system in the world, a plaintiff who sues unsuccessfully must pay the defendant's legal bills? That is correct. This rule, called the "British rule," effectively keeps people from suing others unless they truly think they have a case with merit. If a plaintiff does not have a very good case, he risks paying not only his own attorney's fees but also the defendant's.

This is obviously not the situation in the United States. In U.S. courts, we follow the "American rule," which dictates that each side pays their own legal fees regardless of the outcome of the case. This rule was originally created so that people wouldn't be discouraged from suing big businesses. Though this rule may have had some positive impact, it has created two negative consequences:

1. As a plaintiff, you have a lot less to lose if you bring a meritless case. In fact, with the prevalence of contingency fee attorneys, plaintiffs are literally in a no-lose situation because they have no skin in the game. This is because contingency-fee attorneys do not charge their clients hourly fees. Their only compensation is a percentage of the settlement or judgment in the cases they win.

2. As a defendant, a winning outcome is still a losing proposition. We say this because a successful defense of a lawsuit results in significant out-of-pocket legal fees and other defense costs. In addition, a legal defense causes time out of work and an unquantifiable amount of stress.

It is clear that the American rule of legal fees encourages civil lawsuits. Proponents of the rule claim that it gives the poor access to the legal system and is a method allowing Americans to redress injustices. They may be right. Nonetheless, an unwanted side effect of this rule is that it also allows thousands, if not millions, of frivolous and dubious lawsuits to be filed each year.

TAKEAWAY: The American legal system operates in a way that encourages civil litigation. Physicians can be targets of litigation in many contexts, including as medical providers, employers, drivers, property owners and lessors, and parents. As a result, asset protection planning should be part of every physician's wealth management planning.

CHAPTER 2.2

The Sliding Scale of Asset Protection

The most common misconception among physicians regarding asset protection is the idea that an asset is either protected or unprotected. This black-or-white analysis is no more accurate in the field of asset protection than it is in the field of medicine. In fact, asset protection advisors approach clients very similarly to how physicians approach patients. In this chapter, we will discuss the way in which advisors categorize a client's assets using a sliding scale. Then we will suggest ways in which doctors can protect assets, avoid high-risk assets, and achieve a high level of protection.

The Three Objectives of Asset Protection Planning

There are three objectives of asset protection planning:

1. **Discouragement.** Owning assets in protected rather than exposed positions on the scale may discourage a claim from the outset, as it may appear to a potential claimant that it will be too difficult or costly to pursue you and your assets.

2. **Settlement.** If a claim does arise, the costs and uncertainty involved in pursuing assets in protected positions will often encourage a claimant to settle with you on favorable terms rather than pursue a lawsuit to a judgment.

3. **Protection.** If the claimant does pursue litigation to get a judgment against you, they will have fewer rights (in some cases, no rights) to assets, depending on their position.

The Sliding Scale and Scores

To categorize the assets of a client, advisors use a sliding scale that indicates the client's "good" and "bad" financial habits. Like doctors, asset protection professionals will first try to get a client to avoid bad habits. For a medical patient, bad habits might mean smoking, drinking too much, or maintaining a poor diet. For a client of ours, bad habits might include owning property in their own name, owning property jointly with a spouse, or failing to maximize the percentage of exempt assets in an investment portfolio.

Like a doctor who judges the severity of a patient's illness, asset protection specialists use a rating system to determine the protection or vulnerability of a client's particular asset. The sliding scale runs from (-5) (totally vulnerable) to (+5) (superior protection). As you have probably already guessed, our goal is to bring a physician's score closer to (+5) for each of their assets.

When most clients initially come to see us, their asset planning scores are overwhelmingly on the negative side of the scale. The reason for this varies. Typically, personal assets are owned jointly (-3) or in their individual name (-5). Both ownership forms provide little protection from lawsuits and may also have negative tax- and estate-planning implications.

Many medical practices also have asset-planning scores that are overwhelming negative. For practices, the worst way to operate a business or title assets is as a general partnership (-5). For all other business entities, liability from operations is always a concern. For this reason, owning any business assets within an operating business is extremely unwise (-5).

Before asset protection specialists can achieve a high level of protection for their clients, they must first eliminate the high-risk assets. There are many ways to protect assets, but the most efficient way to avoid owning high-risk assets and achieve a high level of protection is to use exempt assets. This is mentioned briefly in the next section and discussed in greater detail in Chapter 2.6.

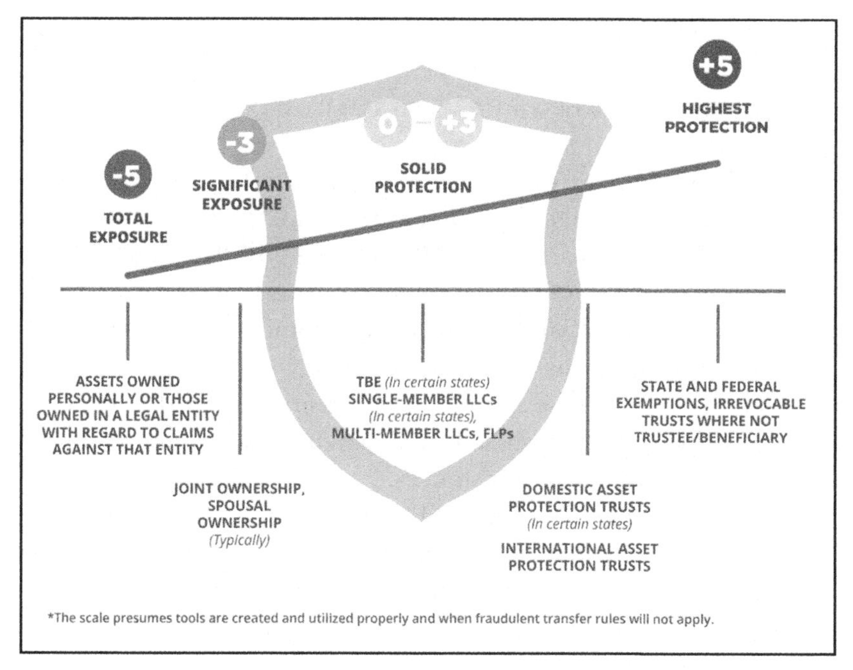

Figure 2.2.1

The Best Protection: Federal and State Exempt Assets

Each state has laws that identify assets that are absolutely exempt from creditor claims in that state. Federal law also exempts certain assets. Because these assets are inherently protected by law, they enjoy the highest level of protection, a +5 score on the sliding scale.

Good examples of how state laws can protect assets are found in Texas and Florida, where homestead exemption values are unlimited for personal residences (within certain geographic and other limitations) and the cash value in life insurance policies is completely protected. At the federal level, bankruptcy law affords +5 protection for ERISA-qualified retirement plans like pensions and 401(k) plans.

Basic Domestic Legal Tools

In many states, the state exemptions are not very generous. Even in those states where the exemptions are broad, we need to make sure that asset protection goals are balanced with wealth-accumulation and investment goals. For these reasons, there will almost always be nonexempt assets in a client's asset mix. For these assets, we must use other protection tools.

The basic asset protection tools are family limited partnerships (FLPs), limited liability companies (LLCs) and, in some states, domestic asset protection trusts (DAPTs). FLPs and LLCs provide good protection of assets against future lawsuits, allow you to maintain control, and can provide income and estate tax benefits in certain situations. For these reasons, we call FLPs and LLCs the building blocks of a basic asset protection plan. FLPs and LLCs afford asset protection scores somewhere between (+1) and (+3), depending on the circumstances.

Regarding DAPTs, as of this edition of the book, about eighteen states have statutes authorizing a DAPT, also called a "self-settled asset protection trust" statute. This type of statute allows you to set up an irrevocable trust in that state and be a beneficiary of the trust. When there is no concern about lawsuits, you can get to the trust assets as beneficiary, but if you have lawsuit claimants after you, the trust can be written so that the trustee cannot make distributions to you because you are "under duress." In this way, a DAPT can allow you both access to the trust assets when the coast is clear and protection when lawsuits and creditors are baying.

Thus, a DAPT can be very attractive for clients who live and practice in a state with DAPT legislation. In such states, we would consider such a trust at least a (+4) tool—the only reservation is that these statutes are relatively new (the first DAPT statute was in Alaska in 1999 – and many states have statutes that are less than 10 years old), so they have not been tested like older state exemption statutes.

Some doctors may consider using a DAPT in a foreign state if their home state does not allow DAPTs. In our view, there is significant risk to this approach. At the time of this writing, there is no guarantee that a court in your home state will recognize the protections of an out-of-state DAPT when the state in which you live and likely will be sued has not passed such legislation. Certainly, some attorneys advocate out-of-state DAPTs for clients, but we advise clients to ask questions about experience with such protections working in their home state before moving forward. Often, the more conservative approach in these cases is to use a "hybrid" DAPT concept that uses a trust that elements of a DAPT but also more closely resembles trusts in the client's home state.

Other Protection Strategies

Most doctors can achieve much of their asset protection planning with a combination of insurance coverages, exempt assets, and legal tools (like FLPs, LLCs, and trusts). However, physicians with higher levels of income, assets, or exposure may want to access advanced strategies to help them protect their assets, such as debt shields, nonqualified plans, and captive insurance arrangements (for a practice).

> **TAKEAWAY:** Asset protection planning, like any sophisticated multidisciplinary effort, is a matter of degree. We use a (-5) to (+5) sliding scale to give context to an asset's exposure and potential protection. For most physicians, the goal is to move as much of their exposed negative-score wealth as possible into positive-score states of protection.

CHAPTER 2.3

Asset Protection Myths

Every day, we speak to doctors about how they can achieve the protection they desire in order to maintain their wealth. In these conversations, we hear many common myths. Perhaps you too hold some of these false beliefs. Here are five of them:

- "I own my assets jointly with my spouse, so I'm okay."
- "My assets are owned by my spouse, so I'm okay."
- "I am insured, so I'm covered."
- "I can just give assets away if I get into trouble."
- "My living trust (or family trust) provides asset protection."

These myths are dangerous because they lull the individual or family into a false sense of financial security. This, in turn, may prevent the physician from taking the steps necessary to truly protect assets. Let's examine each of these common myths and dispel them.

Myth #1: "I Own My Assets Jointly with My Spouse, So I'm Okay."

Most married doctors hold their homes and other property in joint ownership. Unfortunately, this ownership structure provides little asset protection in most states.

In community property states, community assets will be exposed to community debts regardless of title. Community debts include any debt that arises during marriage as the result of an act that helped the community (that is, the married couple). Certainly, any claims resulting from a medical practice, income-producing property (e.g., rental real estate), or auto accident would be included.

Even in non-community-property states—which is most states—joint property is typically at least 50% vulnerable to claims against either spouse. There are many other problems associated with joint property as well, including the disinheritance risk that we discussed in Chapter 1.5. The exception is in states that have tenancy by the entirety (TBE), which we discuss later.

Myth #2: "My Assets Are Owned by My Spouse, So I'm Okay."

One of the most common misconceptions about asset protection is that assets in your spouse's name cannot be touched by your creditors. We cannot tell you how many doctors have come to us with their assets in the name of one spouse, assuming that those assets were protected from claims against the other. This often happens when one spouse has significant exposure as a physician, and the other does not.

Unfortunately, transferring title of an asset to the non-vulnerable spouse does not protect the asset in most states. The creditor is often able to seize assets owned by the spouse of the debtor by proving that the income or funds of the debtor were used to purchase the asset. To determine if this is the case, three questions can be asked:

- Whose income was used to purchase the asset?
- Has the vulnerable spouse used the asset at any time?
- Does this spouse have any control over the asset?

If the answer is "yes" to any of these questions, then the creditor may be able to reach the asset.

Myth #3: "I Am Insured, So I'm Covered."

While we strongly advocate in favor of insurance as a first line of defense and a crucial part of any asset protection plan, an insurance policy is fifty pages long for a reason. Within those numerous pages are a variety of exclusions and limitations that most people never take the time to read, let alone understand. Even if you have insurance and the policy covers the risk in question, underinsurance, strict liability, or bankruptcy of the insurance company could leave you with substantial or sole financial responsibility for the loss. Moreover, if your policy pays a claim, you may see your future premiums go up significantly.

Myth #4: "I Can Just Give Assets Away if I Get in Trouble."

Another common misconception regarding asset protection is that you can simply give away or transfer your assets if you ever get sued. If that were the case, you could just hide your assets when necessary. You wouldn't need an asset protection specialist. You would only need a shovel and some good map-making skills so you could find your buried treasure later.

In recognition of the possibility that people may try to give away their assets if they get into trouble, there are laws prohibiting "fraudulent transfers" (also called "fraudulent conveyances" or "voidable transfers"). In a nutshell, if you make an asset transfer after an incident takes place (whether you knew about a pending lawsuit or not), the judge has the power to rule the transfer a fraudulent conveyance and order that the asset be returned to the transferor, thereby subjecting it to the claims of the creditor. The law can even allow such a result if the transfer was made *before* the incident giving rise to liability if liability was reasonably foreseeable. An example: a transfer that you made knowing that you might soon default on a loan.

If you suspect that you may be sued, there are other ways you can protect yourself. Typically, reactive strategies are not very effective and may be much more expensive than the highly successful strategies that can be implemented when there is no "reasonably foreseeable" claim.

Myth #5: "My Living Trust (or Family Trust) Provides Asset Protection."

Countless times, clients have come to us under the impression that their revocable living trust provides asset protection. While you are alive, this is simply not true. As we described in Chapter 1.5, revocable trust assets are fully attachable by any creditor because the trust is a grantor trust. In Chapter 2.8, you will read about irrevocable trusts and how they provide varying levels of asset protection for you and your heirs in addition to the estate planning they are primarily designed to achieve. A living trust may provide some asset protection, but that protection does not exist until one spouse dies.

> **TAKEAWAY:** Many doctors develop a false sense of security as a result of believing dangerous asset protection myths. With the myths dispelled, you can follow the proper steps to implement the asset protection plan that is right for you.

CHAPTER 2.4

The Best Asset Protection Is NOT Asset Protection

Too many physicians with whom we've consulted over the last 25 years have sought cookie-cutter asset protection plans to give them some "peace of mind." While we admire these doctors' commitment to proactively managing their risk, we have to remind them that all "asset protection plans" are not created equal. In fact, many of these "plans" will not work if they are ever tested. Why is this? Essentially, it is because of a basic tenet of asset protection: for any asset protection plan to truly stand up to a challenge, it *must have economic substance.*

Looking at it from a different viewpoint, superior asset protection planning involves tools that are primarily used by people for purposes other than asset protection. That is, the best asset protection plan involves tools typically not thought of as asset protection tools; instead, they are business planning tools. Stated another way, the best asset protection is not asset protection.

Similar to Tax Planning

While few physicians are aware of this crucial fact of asset protection planning, leading attorneys in the field know it quite well. In fact, we are not alone, as tax attorneys and CPAs know this adage is just as true when it comes to tax planning.

Simply put, when determining whether a particular transaction with significant tax benefits was an illegitimate tax shelter, the IRS or tax court typically uses a simple test: "Would a taxpayer have done this deal if not for the tax benefit?" In other words, they are asking whether this transaction was done just to save taxes or if it had another economic purpose. If there was such a purpose, the transaction stands. If the transaction was solely tax-motivated, it fails to achieve its tax-savings purpose.

This same test applies when evaluating whether a credit protection tactic will be upheld if challenged. Here, the question is, "Did this transaction have an economic purpose, or was it done only for asset protection purposes?" If you are using tools that millions of Americans use on a daily basis for non-asset-protection purposes, you can convincingly answer, "It had an economic purpose."

Why This Is So Important

Over the last decade, many courts throughout the United States have become increasingly frustrated with "asset protection planning." Reading judges' decisions in this area, it is obvious what has created their frustration: the prevalence of firms marketing themselves as "asset protection" experts and promoting the idea that the judgments of U.S. courts can be frustrated by their planning. Is this surprising? No. Of course judges are not going to be happy about an area of planning that is designed to circumvent the execution of judgments that their courts rendered and prevent successful plaintiffs from getting paid.

The courts' frustration is most severe when the defendant has made transfers or engaged in transactions that seem "fishy," even if the conduct was well before the beginning of the lawsuit. If the transaction comes too late, the judges can resort to remedies to undo "fraudulent transfers." However, even in cases where the transaction occurred well before any plaintiff's action, we have seen judges strain to circumvent the asset protection planning.

In fact, there are certain cases where courts have given more credence than one might expect to a claim of fraudulent transfer based on a "foreseeability" argument. Under the logic of one particularly noteworthy case, a medical malpractice claim could always be seen as foreseeable. Taken to its logical conclusion, this position could support the argument that a doctor who does procedures daily is always aware of the possibility of mistakes and any transfer is suspect. If this were true, a plaintiff suing a doctor could attack asset protection transfers made years earlier.

If you use "non-asset-protection" asset protection, you will not be as vulnerable to this emerging trend in the law. The techniques explained in this chapter do not involve "transfers" at all. Given this, and "non-asset-protection" techniques with tangible and concrete economic substance, these tools and tactics are among the strongest protection you can implement for the long term.

Asset Protection That Isn't

The best asset protection tools were not created as asset protection tools. They are tools that have other primary benefits and offer outstanding creditor protection as a secondary benefit. Which asset protection tools are not asset protection tools? Let's examine a few of them briefly here. They will all be developed further in other parts of the book.

Qualified Retirement Plans

A qualified retirement plan (QRP) is one that complies with certain Department of Labor and Internal Revenue Service rules. You might know such plans by their specific type, including pension plans, profit-sharing plans, money purchase plans, 401(k)s, and 403(b)s. Properly structured plans offer a variety of real economic benefits: you can fully deduct contributions to these plans, and funds within them grow tax-deferred. Most medical practices sponsor QRPs because of these benefits. We further discuss QRPs in Chapters 1.3 and 3.4.

What you may not know is that under federal bankruptcy law and nearly every state's law, these plans are protected against lawsuits and creditor claims, enjoying (+5) protection status if they meet ERISA rules. Yet the overwhelming majority of the millions of Americans who use qualified plans are not using them for asset protection purposes. This, then, is a great example of an attractive economic tool that just so happens to have tremendous asset protection benefits as well.

Non-Qualified Plans

Non-qualified plans are relatively unknown to physicians, even though most Fortune 1000 companies make non-qualified plans available to their executives. These types of plans should be very attractive to physicians, as employees are not required to participate and allowable contributions are much higher than with qualified plans (although not deductible). Once again, non-qualified plans are generally not used for asset protection purposes, but they may have such benefits. Read more about them in Chapter 3.6.

Captive Insurance Companies

Captive insurance companies (CICs) are used by many of the Fortune 1000 for a host of strategic reasons. This technique involves the owners of a medical practice or hospital or group of physicians in a particular geographic area creating their own properly licensed insurance company to insure risks of the hospital/practice/practices. These can be economic risks (reimbursements drop), business risks (electronic medical records are destroyed), or litigation risks (medical malpractice claims, harassment claims, or HCFA audits). If it is created and maintained properly, the CIC is an insurance company, established in a real economic arrangement with its insured. Also, CICs typically enjoy outside creditor protection under state law.

Cash Value Life Insurance

Cash value life insurance (CVLI) policies are purchased by millions of Americans each year for their tax benefits (generally, tax-free growth, tax-free access, and payment of income tax-free to heirs), for family protection, and for estate planning purposes. See Chapters 4.2, 4.3 and 4.4 for more on CVLI policies. Nonetheless, in many states the cash value can enjoy the top (+5) protections. In this way, a physician can purchase a product as part of a financial plan and easily enjoy (+5) protections.

TAKEAWAY: The best asset protection techniques are those that have significant non-protection uses and benefits, such as tax reduction, risk management, and retirement savings. If you can use such tools, your protection plan will be significantly stronger.

CHAPTER 2.5

The Mixed Blessing of Property and Casualty Insurance

We see property and casualty (P&C) insurance as an important part of any asset protection plan—both for the practice and for personal assets. In fact, we make it part of our comprehensive review process for our clients, using a national firm with access to the largest P&C insurers and even Lloyd's of London and other syndicates when cost-effective insurance is difficult to find. In this chapter, we will define P&C insurance coverage and discuss its uses and limitations in the context of asset protection planning.

What Is P&C Insurance?

There are two categories of insurance: life and health (L&H) and property and casualty (P&C). L&H insurance includes all life insurance and health insurance as well as disability insurance and long-term care insurance. P&C insurance is designed to protect against property and casualty losses. Often, P&C insurance is referred to as "property and liability" insurance because it protects people from all types of liabilities. Examples of P&C coverage include automobile, homeowners' and renters', umbrella liability, professional liability, medical malpractice, general liability, flood, earthquake, premises liability, errors and omissions, and products liability.

P&C insurance is designed to "indemnify" the insured. The insurance industry's definition of "indemnify" is "to make whole" or restore the status quo. In other words, if you suffer a loss and have P&C coverage, you will be "put back" into the same financial place you were in before the loss (minus any applicable deductibles or co-payments). Thus, P&C coverage will cover your legal bills and other loss adjustment expenses as well as the actual loss. Such other expenses may include the costs of adjusters, estimates, expert testimony, and other associated costs.

P&C insurance coverage is very important given today's litigious society and the "American Rule" of legal fees. As mentioned before, there is no out-of-pocket cost (or deterrent) to the plaintiff under this system, yet the defendant is responsible for the actual loss and associated fees. Therefore, if you won the case against you but didn't have P&C insurance, you might owe tens—if not hundreds—of thousands of dollars in legal fees and expenses. For this reason, it is usually worth buying insurance just to avoid these costs and inconvenience and aggravation, let alone the potential judgment or loss.

Best Uses of P&C Insurance

As we mentioned above, there are various types of P&C insurance. The most common types of P&C insurance are homeowners' (or renters') and automobile insurance. Clients generally have these forms of coverage because they have a mortgage on their home and a loan or lease on a car, which require collateral—buyers must insure the asset while they are paying for it. Once the debt on a home or car is paid off, there is no bank or finance company requiring insurance protection. Of course, we would never recommend dropping all insurance on a home. The odds of a house fire or burglary occurring are very slim, but the cost of insurance is very small relative to what clients could lose.

Another common type of P&C insurance is the umbrella liability policy. For a very reasonable premium, you can get an additional one to five million dollars of excess liability insurance on top of the liability protection you have from your homeowners' or auto policies. You should seriously consider an umbrella policy.

Other popular P&C coverage includes professional liability insurance and premises and products liability insurance. For physicians, medical malpractice insurance, premises liability insurance, and other overhead insurances are wise options, if not requirements.

Four Limitations of P&C Insurance

While some P&C insurance always makes sense as part of a doctor's asset planning, there are limitations to this tool. That is why we typically recommend using the other asset protection tools we describe in this Lesson in addition to insurance. Let's examine the limitations of insurance individually.

1. **Policy exclusions**
   We often find that clients are completely unaware of the "fine print" P&C exclusions and policy limitations. Unfortunately, they sometimes become aware of such exclusions after it is too late. For example, many clients fail to realize that their umbrella policy only applies if certain underlying insurance coverage amounts are in effect.

   If your liability limits on your homeowner's policy or auto policy are too low, then you'll have to pay out of pocket before the umbrella coverage pays anything.

Case Study: Andy's Daughter's Car Accident

Andy was sued for more than $150,000 when his teenage daughter was involved in a car accident while using his car. Andy was certain that his insurance policy covered his daughter. Only then did his insurance agent tell Andy that the policy no longer covered his daughter since she had recently moved out of the house. There was an exclusion from coverage for child drivers if they did not reside in the same residence as their parents. Andy faced a lawsuit that cost him over $150,000.

The lesson to be learned from Andy's story is simple: know your policy and the limitations contained therein!

2. **Inadequate policy limits**
   Even if your insurance policy does cover you in a particular lawsuit, the coverage limits may be well below what a jury will award. You must pay any excess judg-

ment out of your own pocket. If you were hit by a large judgment, would your policy cover you completely?

3. **Insurance forces you to lose control of the defense**
   Even if your insurance policy covers you against a specific claim, you must consider the consequences of filing a claim. You will lose negotiating power because your insurance company will dictate when the case is settled and how much the settlement will be. While this may not matter with a personal injury car accident lawsuit, a case against you professionally is another matter. You may not want to admit liability and settle a malpractice case even if your insurance company does.

   On the other hand, if the claim implicates your professional reputation, you may want to settle the case out of court and away from the public view. There is no guarantee that your insurer will see things the same way. In these situations, if you rely solely on insurance, you lose all ability to negotiate effectively.

4. **Claims bring ever-higher premiums**
   An additional consequence of relying solely on insurance to protect you from lawsuits is that once you make claims under the policy, your premiums rise. Given the dismal statistics, you will probably endure a number of lawsuits over your time, and your insurance costs will rise with every claim, even if you are not at fault.

Recommendations to Manage Limitations

To manage the four limitations of P&C insurance outlined above, we recommend the following preventive measures:

1. Know your policy
2. Don't skimp on coverage
3. Consider an umbrella policy
4. Use other asset protection tools

TAKEAWAY: Like every tool discussed in this book, property & casualty insurance has its place in a doctor's comprehensive financial plan. Certain types of coverage, such as homeowners', auto, umbrella, and medical malpractice for physicians, are compulsory. However, because of its limitations, we caution physicians not to rely solely on insurance for protection.

CHAPTER 2.6

Maximizing Exempt Assets

In the following chapters, we will explain several legal entities and techniques that can be used to protect the assets of physicians. This chapter on maximizing exempt assets is first because, in our view, physicians should always reasonably maximize their use of exempt assets before moving on to legal tools and other techniques. Why? The answer is simple: exempt assets are the highest level of protection one can get (+5).

Despite their superiority to other asset protection strategies, exempt assets are not effectively used by most doctors. This chapter will explain why many advisors don't recommend exempt assets as often as they should. Then we will discuss all of the exempt assets that can be valuable components of a comprehensive financial plan. Throughout the book, you will revisit many of these exempt assets as they provide additional benefits outside of asset protection. For now, let's begin discussing why exempt assets are considered the best asset protection tool and then discuss the reasons they remain underutilized in asset protection planning.

Exempt Assets: The Best Asset Protection Tools

We consider exempt assets to be the best asset protection tool for the following reasons:

1. **No legal/accounting fees**
   Most of the tools in subsequent chapters involve the creation of legal entities that require setup and ongoing legal fees, state fees, accounting fees, and even additional taxes. Using exempt assets involves *none*

of these significant costs and affords better protection as well.

2. **No loss of ownership or control**
   The legal tools of the following chapters typically require giving up some level of ownership or control to family members or even third-party trustees. *By using exempt assets, you can own and access the asset at any time while enjoying the highest (+5) level of protection.*

3. **Superior Protection**
   The legal tools explained later offer protection that ranges from (+1) to (+5). *Exempt assets always enjoy the top (+5) protection up to their exempt amount.*

Why Exempt Assets Are Underutilized

Given the clear benefits of exempt assets, one would think that exempt assets would be preferred over other tools in an asset protection plan. Surprisingly, this is often not the case. The reason for this may be that most asset protection planning is implemented by an attorney who is not familiar with the financial tools a multidisciplinary team could offer.

There are various planning pitfalls that can arise when you do not have the benefit of a coordinated multidisciplinary team to help implement your plan. Attorneys generally do not understand many of the exempt asset classes, such as cash value life insurance, annuities, and qualified plans like 401(k)s and defined-benefit plans. You cannot expect an advisor to recommend something he or she doesn't understand.

This doesn't mean that one attorney could not recommend an adequate asset protection plan. What it does mean is that the plan created by one attorney may not be efficient because the plan may be limited to legal solutions. If you were more skeptical, you might point out that attorneys are generally not licensed to sell financial products. Is it unrealistic to expect an attorney to have a bias against the use of exempt assets for asset protection, which does not require any legal work?

Is it unreasonable to expect attorneys to focus their asset

protection recommendations on the use of legal documents that may generate thousands of dollars in legal fees? This is not a conspiracy against, nor is it an indictment of, attorneys—we, as an author group, include several attorneys. However, we are attorneys who appreciate multidisciplinary planning and recognize the value of financial, as well as legal, solutions. *The reason we wrote this through the OJM Group is that we believe 100% in a multidisciplinary approach to asset protection planning.*

The lesson here is simple. Your asset protection plan, like the rest of your financial plan, must be handled by a coordinated multidisciplinary team that carefully considers all planning options to help you efficiently achieve your goals. The absence of exempt assets in a plan is always a warning sign that the planning is not coordinated.

Federally Exempt Assets

Federally exempt assets are those assets that are protected under federal bankruptcy law. Federal law protects certain assets from creditors and lawsuits if the defendant is willing to file bankruptcy to eliminate the creditor. In a Chapter 7 bankruptcy, the debtor will be able to keep any assets that federal law deems exempt. The two significant asset classes that federal law protects are qualified retirement plans (QRPs) and IRAs. A "qualified" retirement plan is one that complies with certain Department of Labor and Internal Revenue Service rules. For the protection to apply, the plan should also comply with the Employee Retirement Income Security Act (ERISA). Most plans with non-owner employees will—but be sure to check your plan.

You might know such plans by their specific type, including profit-sharing plans, money purchase plans, 401(k)s, and 403(b)s. IRAs are very similar to such plans, though there are several technical differences, and are now given exempt status under federal law as well.

While this protection is (+5), you must recognize that this protection applies only if you are in bankruptcy and have access to the federal exemptions. The amount of value in the QRP or IRA that would be protected outside of bankruptcy, as with an ordinary lawsuit and creditor action, would be governed by your state law.

State Exempt Assets

State exemption leveraging is a fundamental part of a financial plan and one that every doctor should take seriously. The most significant state exemptions are the following:

- Qualified retirement plans (QRPs) and individual retirement accounts (IRAs)
- Primary residence (or homestead)
- Life insurance
- Annuities

Important note: We will make general comments regarding state exemptions below. They are *not* meant to be accurate for any particular state.

Qualified Retirement Plans and IRAs

Nearly all states have significant (+5) exemptions for qualified retirements plans and IRAs. Some states protect only a certain amount in such asset classes or protect qualified plans more significantly than they do IRAs. It is crucial that a doctor understand the exemptions for such assets in their state and build their wealth accordingly.

Primary Residence: Homestead

Many physicians consider the home to be the family's most valuable asset. You might think that you know the laws that protect your home. Perhaps you have previously heard the term "homestead" and assume that you could never lose your home to bad debts or other liabilities because of homestead protection. The reality is that few states provide a total (+5) shield for the home.

Most states protect only between $10,000 and $60,000 of the homestead's equity. Some states, such as New Jersey, provide no protection, while other states, such as Florida and Texas, generally provide unlimited protection (with some restrictions). Given today's real estate values and the equity that many doctors have in their home, it is clear that most states' homestead exemptions provide inadequate protection.

To determine how well a homestead law protects your home, you should compare the protected value to the equity. In order to do so, subtract the value of any mortgages from the fair market value of your home. For example, if you live in a home with a $300,000 fair market value and have a $150,000 mortgage, then your equity is $150,000. If your state protects only $20,000 through its homestead law, then you still have $130,000 ($150,000 of equity – $20,000 homestead) of vulnerable equity.

Homestead protection is often automatic, but it may require additional action in some cases. Each state has specific requirements for claiming homestead status. In some states, you must file a declaration of homestead in a public office. Other states set a time requirement for residency before homestead protection is granted. Never assume that your home is protected. You may be wrong, and your inaction could cost you the protection you deserve. Your asset protection advisor can show you how to comply with the formalities in your state.

Life Insurance: Protected Everywhere

All fifty states have laws that protect varying amounts of life insurance.

For example:

- Many states shield the entire policy proceeds from the policyholder's creditors. Some also protect against the beneficiary's creditors.
- States that do not protect the entire policy proceeds set amounts above which the creditor can take proceeds.
- Many states protect the policy proceeds only if the policy beneficiaries are the policyholder's spouse, children, or other dependents.
- Some states protect a policy's cash surrender value in addition to the policy proceeds. This can be the most valuable exemption opportunity.
- If the policy is purchased as part of a fraudulent transfer, a court can undo the policy, as it can any other fraudulent transfer.

One of the reasons for the underutilization of life insurance as an exempt asset is that most physicians—and their advisors—do not understand cash value, also called "permanent" life insurance. We cover this subject in more depth in Chapters 4.2, 4.3, and 4.4.

Annuities: Shielded in Many States

Another exempt asset in many states is the annuity. Annuities are insurance contracts that offer the upside of investment appreciation, tax-deferred growth, and principal protection. This diverse list of benefits makes annuities important components of asset protection and wealth accumulation plans.

Quasi-Exemption: Tenancy by the Entirety

Tenancy by the entirety (TBE) is not a (+5) exempt asset, but it is a state law-controlled form of joint ownership that can provide total protection against claims against one spouse. TBE is available in about twenty states, but its effectiveness is diminishing. In some states, TBE protects only real estate; in others, both real estate and personal property (such as bank accounts) can be effectively shielded by TBE. In those states that protect it, assets held in TBE cannot be taken by a party with a claim against only one spouse. These assets are immune to such a claim.

As such, TBE can be a very cost-effective tool for married physicians in the states where TBE is an effective shield. This is especially true where state case law continues to support the protections and where the married couple has few joint exposures.

While this is a very powerful benefit, there are some risks with TBE, including the following:

1. **Joint claim risk**
   TBE provides no shield whatsoever against joint risks, including lawsuits that arise from your jointly owned real estate or acts of minor children.

2. **Divorce risk**
   If you get divorced before or during a lawsuit, you lose all protections from TBE.

3. **Survivor risk**

If one spouse dies before or during a lawsuit, you lose all protections from TBE.

TAKEAWAY: The easiest way to achieve the highest level of asset protection is to use (+5) exempt assets and, for married physicians in some states, the "quasi-exempt" ownership form of tenancy by the entirety. It makes sense that every doctor who is interested in asset protection should attempt to maximize his or her use of exempt assets.

CHAPTER 2.7

Family Limited Partnerships and Limited Liability Companies

While (+5) exempt assets may be the most effective asset protection tools, most clients will need to go beyond the use of exempt assets in their quest to protect assets. They will make use of legal tools as well. Of all the legal tools used to shield assets, two of the most popular are family limited partnerships (FLPs) and limited liability companies (LLCs).

Of course, having family members play a role in these tools is common—that's why we use the "F" in front of the "LP." However, using family members in this way is *not* required. Whether you use family members or non-family members, these entities can give you solid asset protection. In this chapter we will discuss the similarities of the two tools, how they protect assets, and three tactics doctors should use to incorporate FLPs and LLCs into their plans to build and preserve wealth.

FLPs and LLCs: Similarities and Differences

We have combined FLPs and LLCs in this chapter because they are very similar. You can think of them as closely related, like brothers and sisters, as they share many of their best characteristics. In fact, unless we make the point otherwise, we will use these tools interchangeably—if a case study refers to an FLP, you can generally assume that an LLC could have been used, and vice versa. Similarities of the FLP and LLC include the following:

1. **They are both legal entities certified under state law**
   Both FLPs and LLCs are legal entities governed by the law of the state in which the entity is formed.

Many states have identical laws, as they are modeled after the Uniform Limited Partnership Act and Limited Liability Company Act, which have been adopted at least partially by every state. As state-certified legal entities, state fees must be paid each year to keep an FLP or LLC valid.

2. **They both have two levels of ownership**

   FLPs and LLCs allow for two levels of ownership. We'll call one ownership level "active ownership"—that is, the active owners have 100% control of the entity and its assets. In the FLP, the active owners are called "general partners," while in the LLC the active owners are called "managing members" or "managers." (Note: managers of LLCs do not have to be "owners.")

   As you may have already guessed, the second ownership level is "passive ownership"—the passive owners have little control over the entity and only limited rights. The passive owners are called "limited partners" in the FLP and "members" in the LLC.

   This bi-level ownership structure allows for a host of planning possibilities because clients can use FLPs and LLCs to share ownership with family members without having to give away any practical control of the assets inside the structures.

3. **They both can elect pass-through tax treatment**

   Both tools can elect "pass-through" taxation, meaning neither the FLP nor the LLC is liable for income taxes. Rather, the tax liability for any and all income or capital gains on FLP/LLC assets "passes through" to the owners (partners or members). Also, as discussed in the income tax and estate planning Lessons, both entities allow the participants to take advantage of "income sharing" and "discounting" techniques in the same ways.

4. **They both have the beneficial "charging order" asset protection benefit**

   While state laws vary, those based on the Uniform Acts provide "charging order" protections to FLP and LLC owners. The "charging order" will be discussed later in this chapter.

Two Differences between the FLP and the LLC

1. **Only the LLC can be used for a single owner**
   Most states now allow single-member (owner) LLCs, while in every state a limited partnership must have at least two owners. Thus, for single clients, the LLC is often the only option.

2. **The FLP's general partner has liability for the FLP**
   While a general partner has personal liability for the acts and debts of the FLP, a managing member has no such liability for his or her LLC. For this reason alone, asset protection experts always recommend using an LLC rather than an FLP when the entity will own "dangerous" assets; i.e., those likely to lead to lawsuits.

"Safe" assets, conversely, are those that are unlikely to lead to lawsuits. Common safe assets include cash, stocks, bonds, mutual funds, CDs, life insurance policies, checking and savings accounts, antiques, artwork, jewelry, licenses, copyrights, trademarks, and patents.

"Dangerous" assets are those that have a relatively high likelihood of creating liability. Common dangerous assets include real estate (especially rental real estate), cars, RVs, trucks, boats, airplanes, and interests in closely held businesses. Since FLP general partners have liability exposure and LLC managing members do not, it usually makes sense to use an LLC rather than an FLP to own dangerous assets.

How FLPs and LLCs Protect Assets

In order to understand how FLPs and LLCs provide protection, we must first examine both "inside risks" and "outside risks."

"Inside risks" are those that threaten the business and its assets from the inside. These are risks that the business faces because of its activity. Examples of inside risks are lawsuits against the business by its customers for product liability, by its patients for malpractice, or by its employees for wrongful termination. Neither the FLP nor the LLC can shield the business itself from such inside claims. The only way to protect the business from inside claims is to protect the assets and cash flow of the business from potential business creditors. At a minimum, protection can be achieved through the proper P&C insurance coverages, as noted in previous pages.

We just wrote that "neither the FLP nor the LLC can shield the business itself from such inside claims," but what about the *owners* of the business? In other words, if there is a claim against the business for, as an example, product liability, are the business owners' assets vulnerable? As we explained above, this is a big difference between the LLC and the FLP. In the LLC, none of the members are liable for the debts of the business, whereas with an FLP, the general partner is liable. This is why active businesses or dangerous assets should never be owned through an FLP with a human general partner.

"Outside risks" are potential claims against the owners' interests in the business. As an example, an outside claim might be a successful car accident lawsuit against the owner of the business that has led to the plaintiff now wanting to get to the assets of the business to satisfy the judgment. For outside risks, FLPs and LLCs are asset protectors because the law gives a very specific and limited remedy to creditors coming after assets in either type of entity. When a personal creditor pursues you and your assets are owned by an FLP or LLC, the creditor cannot seize the assets in the FLP/LLC. Under the Uniform Act provisions, a creditor of a partner (or LLC member) cannot reach into the FLP/ LLC and take specific partnership assets.

If the creditor cannot seize FLP/LLC assets, what can the creditor get? The law normally allows for only one remedy: the "charging order." The charging order is something a creditor can be granted by a court against a debtor's interest in an FLP or LLC.

Essentially, this order allows the creditor to get distributions.

In other words, the creditor must legally be paid any distributions that would have been paid to the debtor. The charging order is meant to allow the entity to continue operating without interruption and provide a remedy for creditors. However, as you will see, the charging order is generally a very weak remedy.

Of course, this discussion assumes that, in transferring assets to an FLP or LLC, the owners do not run afoul of fraudulent transfer laws. We introduced the concept of these laws earlier in this Lesson. It also assumes that the owners remain in compliance with state laws and do not use the FLP/LLC as the "alter ego" of their personal affairs.

The Limitations of the Charging Order

As mentioned earlier, the charging order is a court order that instructs the FLP/LLC to pay the debtor's share of distributions to his or her creditor until the creditor's judgment is paid in full. Importantly, *everything we will describe below assumes that your FLP or LLC operating agreement is properly drafted and all formalities are followed*. If so, the charging order does not

- give the creditor FLP/LLC voting rights,
- give the creditor FLP/LLC management rights, or
- force the FLP general partner or LLC manager to pay out any distributions to partners/members.

While the charging order may seem like a powerful remedy, you do need to consider its limitations. It is a temporary interest that may have to be renewed. In addition:

1. **It is available only after a successful lawsuit**
   First, the charging order is available only after the creditor has successfully sued you and won a judgment. Only then can your creditor ask the court for the charging order.

2. **It does not afford voting rights—so you stay in complete control**
   Despite the charging order, you remain the general

partner of your FLP (or managing member/manager of the LLC). You make all decisions about whether the FLP/LLC buys assets, distributes earnings to its partners or members, shifts ownership interests, and so forth. Judgment creditors cannot vote you out because they cannot vote your shares. Thus, even after creditors have a judgment against you, you still make all decisions concerning the FLP/LLC, including whether to pay distributions to the owners.

3. **The creditor may have to pay the tax bill**
   One element of advanced FLP/LLC planning is how the charging order may backfire on creditors for income tax purposes. Because taxes on FLP/LLC income are passed through to the parties who are entitled to the income, the FLP/LLC does not pay tax. Each partner/member is responsible for his or her share of the FLP/LLC income. This income is taxable regardless of whether the income is actually paid out.

If a creditor with a charging order against an FLP partner or LLC member goes to the step of "foreclosing" on the charging order, the creditor's interest will then become permanent. With the proper provisions in the FLP partnership agreement or LLC operating agreement, this may have the effect of making the creditor liable for all of the income attributable to the charged interest. At this point, the creditor "steps into your shoes" for income tax purposes with respect to the FLP/LLC interest—and thus receives your tax bill for income taxes on your share of the FLP/LLC income. This tax liability will exist even though the creditor will likely never receive any income. Once this occurs, creditors will be very motivated to settle—as they have swallowed the tax "poison pill" without even realizing it.

Case Study: William and Donna Are Protected by FLPs

Let's examine spouses William and Donna. Assume that William is an oncologist. After two years of employment, William's assistant, Maribel, sues William for sexual harassment and wins an award of $750,000. William's general business insurance package does not cover this type of lawsuit. Once Maribel discovers, through a debtor's examination, that William and Donna's assets are owned by their LLCs, what can she do?

She cannot seize the portfolio owned by the LLCs. State law provisions prohibit that. She also has no fraudulent transfer claim to cling to in an attempt to undo transfers to the LLCs because all transfers were accomplished well in advance of her claim. She can get a charging order on William's 39% share of the LLCs, but William and Donna would still control the LLCs. Maribel would probably not receive any distributed profits, but she may receive a tax bill on dividends paid out by the stocks that William and Donna never distributed. This charging order will not sound too inviting to Maribel, will it?

You may wonder why we have such protective laws for limited partnerships and limited liability companies. The charging order law, which can be traced back to the English Partnership Act of 1890, is aimed at achieving a particular public policy objective: business activities of a partnership should not be disrupted because of non-partnership-related debts of the individual partners. The rationale for this objective is that if non-debtor partners and the partnership were not at fault, why should the entire partnership suffer? American law has followed this policy for over 100 years, culminating in the charging order law of the Uniform Limited Partnership and Uniform Limited Liability Company Acts.

Three Tactics for Maximizing FLP/LLC Protection

You now understand the basic strategy for using FLPs/LLCs: you put your assets into the FLP/LLC and they will be protected from personal creditors. This is basic "outside" asset protection. Beyond this, consider these three basic rules:

1. **Don't put all your eggs in one basket**
   One never knows when a court of law is going to make a surprise departure or deviation from accepted legal norms or precedents. One never knows when an asset within a single FLP/LLC could cause a lawsuit. Life is full of uncertainties. Because our clients understand that they cannot control court decisions or the litigious nature of society, they protect their assets by using multiple FLP/LLC arrangements (among other tools discussed in this Lesson) in different states to title their assets. Titling your assets in different legal entities makes it more difficult for any creditor to come after your entire wealth because they may have to conduct more investigations, file more motions with the court, and perhaps even travel to different states. The more entities used, the more difficult it will be for your creditors to attack your wealth. As a result, creditors will be more likely to negotiate more favorable settlements.

2. **Segregate the dangerous eggs from the safe ones**
   Separating safe assets from dangerous assets increases the "inside" asset protection for the safe assets. In other words, since no dangerous assets are within the same entity as the safe assets, a lawsuit arising from a dangerous asset will not threaten the safe assets if the safe assets are in their own LLC. As we explained in the beginning of the chapter, dangerous assets should be owned by an LLC rather than by an FLP because LLCs give better "inside" protection. The general partner of an FLP can be personally liable for acts within an FLP but the managing member of an LLC cannot be personally liable for the acts within the LLC.

3. **If possible, use LLCs or FLPs in the most protective states**
   Not all LLCs and FLPs are created equal. It is true that LLCs and FLPs vary greatly in their asset protection, estate, and tax benefits based on the experience and

expertise of the attorney drafting the operating agreement. However, the point here is that some states have much more protective language in their LLC or FLP statutes.

For some assets, like investment accounts, you may have the option to use LLCs or FLPs in states that are more protective than your own. As an example, states like Nevada, Ohio, and Delaware have passed extremely restrictive LLC statutes designed to provide the highest level of protection for entities established in their state. In theory, this is no different than the reason Delaware is where so many Fortune 500 companies are based—the laws there are the most protective of corporate officers and boards.

Today, many doctors use an investment firm based outside of their own state to manage their assets. Many assets managed by these firms are actually held by a large custodian (like Schwab or TD Ameritrade) in a third state. Investment assets, as opposed to real estate, which always sits in one fixed place, may be suitable for ownership in an LLC outside of your home state. This type of "jurisdiction shopping" is found in numerous areas of the law, from estate planning to tax planning and regulatory planning.

As an example, you might live in State X and set up an LLC in Ohio for its top-level protection laws. Still, your litigation risk still resides in your home state, where you live and practice medicine. Certainly, if you were ever sued, it would likely be in your home state, and if your LLC were attacked by a plaintiff in your home state, a court overseeing that lawsuit may be inclined to apply local law even with respect to an Ohio LLC. Nonetheless, if the costs of using a "better LLC state" like Ohio are not much more than setting up an LLC in your home State X (or even are less), then we generally recommend it, as you can save costs and perhaps avail yourself of better protection rules. In essence, if it doesn't cost you a lot more to use a more protective state, there is really no reason not to so do.

Thus, physicians can use legal entities domiciled in jurisdictions that offer the best law and should make sure that a member of their team is an asset protection expert, who will keep an eye on developments in the field so that they can switch state domiciles if necessary.

Beware of Single-Member LLCs

As explained above, the origin of the charging order protections goes back to partnership law in England where the policy goal was to keep the business activities of a partnership from being disrupted because of non-partnership-related debts of the individual partners. The goal underlying this policy was to protect innocent partners from being injured because of one liable partner. Interrupting the partnership business to satisfy the claim against one liable partner for a debt unrelated to the partnership was judged to be unfair to the innocent partners.

This has been adopted here in the United States and applies to both FLPs and LLCs. With FLPs, you must have at least two partners, so, in theory, the same policy goal applies. However, what about a single-owner LLC? If you own 100% of an LLC and then have creditor issues, why shouldn't that creditor be able to execute against the assets of the LLC, as there are no innocent partners/LLC members who would be harmed?

This exact question has been raised by plaintiffs attacking single-member LLCs—and they have been successful in a number of high-profile asset protection cases, including the *Olmstead* case in Florida and the *Albright* case in Colorado. These courts allowed penetration of single-member LLCs essentially because they had no innocent owners. In response to these cases, a number of state legislatures amended their LLC statutes specifically to prevent this from happening to single-member LLCs in their states.

What does this mean for doctors who are single? At a minimum, it means that they should, when feasible, form LLCs in states where the statutes specifically forbid such treatment of single-member LLCs. However, even married clients should be concerned when living in or using LLCs in states where single-member LLCs appear to be vulnerable. A court might view an LLC owned 100% by a married couple as, in substance, a single-member LLC.

Perhaps this risk is even more pronounced in community property states like many of those in the West. *The bottom line: unless you live in a state with a clearly protective single-member LLC statute and are using an LLC formed in such a state, it makes sense to discuss with your asset protection advisor the value of an ongoing gifting program of LLC interests to children or other family members. The farther you are from a single-member LLC in form and in substance, the better position your entity will be in against outside claims.*

TAKEAWAY: Since exempt assets generally can't protect 100% of a physician's assets at the top (+5) level, we have to find other techniques to fill the gap. FLPs and LLCs are two of the asset protection tools used most frequently use to manage the wealth of doctors and their families.

CHAPTER 2.8

Using Trusts to Shield Wealth

In addition to exempt assets, FLPs, and LLCs, a trust is another tool that can be used to protect doctors' assets and maintain their wealth. A trust is a legal entity that is often misunderstood. In this chapter, we will explain what a trust is and the asset protection role trusts play in planning for physicians.

What Is a Trust?

A trust is essentially a legal arrangement where one person holds property for the benefit of another. The person who holds the property is the trustee. He or she "holds" the property for the benefit of the beneficiary or beneficiaries. A trust is created by a trust document that specifies that the trustee holds property owned by the trust for the benefit of the beneficiary of the trust. The trust document also establishes the terms of how the trust should be administered and how the trust assets should be distributed during the lifetime of the trust as well as after the trust is terminated.

The following definitions and classifications should help you understand a trust and how it functions:

- **Grantor.** The grantor is the person who sets up the trust. He or she is usually the person who transfers property into the trust. A grantor may also be called the trustor or settlor.
- **Trustee.** The trustee is the legal owner of the trust property. The trustee is responsible for administering and carrying out the terms of the trust. He or she owes

a fiduciary duty to the beneficiaries—a duty to use the utmost care to follow the terms of the trust document and manage the trust property properly. A trustee may be a person, such as a family member or trusted friend. The trustee can also be an institution, such as a professional trust company or the trust department of a bank. When there is more than one trustee, they are called co-trustees.

The trustee is the legal owner of any assets owned by the trust and has "legal title" to the assets owned by the trust. For example, assume that Dad wants to set up a trust for his children, Son and Daughter. Dad wants his brother, Uncle, to serve as trustee. If Dad transfers his house into the trust, the title to that house will be with "Uncle, as trustee of the Dad Trust."

- **Beneficiary.** The beneficiary (or beneficiaries) is the person (or people) for whom the trust was set up. (In the example discussed above, the beneficiaries would be Son and Daughter.) While the trustee has legal title to assets owned by the trust, the beneficiary has *equitable title*, or the right to the trust property. The beneficiary can sue the trustee if the trustee mismanages the trust property or disobeys specific instructions in the trust. The beneficiary may be the same person as the grantor and may be the same person as the trustee. For asset protection purposes, the trustee, beneficiary, and grantor, though, cannot all be the same person.
- **Funding.** Funding the trust means transferring assets to the trust. A trust that is "unfunded" has no property transferred to it. It is completely ineffective. You must title assets to the trust if you want trust protection, as with any other legal entity/ asset protection tool discussed previously. To title real estate to the trust, you must execute and record a deed to the property to the trust. Bank and brokerage accounts can be transferred by simply changing the name on the accounts. Registered stocks and bonds are changed by notifying the transfer agent or issuing company and requesting that

the certificates be reissued to the trust. Other assets, such as household items, furniture, jewelry, artwork, etc., are transferred by a simple legal document called an assignment or bill of sale. Your asset protection specialist can transfer assets simply and quickly. Of course, depending on the type of trust, there may be tax consequences to such transfers, so professional advice is required.

Revocable Living Trusts: Illusory Asset Protection

As we described in Chapter 1.5, revocable living trusts (also called "family trusts" or "A-B trusts") allow the grantor of the living trust the flexibility to make changes to an estate plan and to avoid unnecessary probate expenses. Revocable living trusts can also effectively sidestep the hidden dangers of joint tenancy. However, many people mistakenly assume that these trusts provide asset protection benefits.

During your lifetime, living trusts provide absolutely no asset protection. This is because living trusts are revocable. While revocability and flexibility are valuable characteristics for almost all financial planning tools, these characteristics render the revocable trust useless for asset protection purposes. Remember this simple rule: *revocable trusts are vulnerable to creditors.* Let's explore the main reason that revocable trusts offer no protection.

Creditors Can "Step into Your Shoes," Revoke the Living Trust, and Seize Trust Assets

Revocable trusts are useless for asset protection because revocable trusts allow the grantor to undo the trust. If you wanted to unwind a revocable trust and use the funds for yourself, you could do so. Therefore, a creditor can essentially force the grantor of the trust to do this. If the grantor's creditors want to seize assets owned by a revocable trust, they need only petition the court to "step into the shoes" of the grantor and direct the funds of the trust back to the debtor. The trust assets will no longer be owned by the trust, but by the debtor personally. The creditors then have rights and privileges to seize these assets now owned by the debtor.

Irrevocable Trusts: The Asset Protectors

While revocable trusts offer no asset protection, irrevocable trusts are outstanding for asset protection. Once you establish an irrevocable trust, you forever abandon the ability to undo the trust and reclaim property transferred to the trust. With an irrevocable trust, you lose both control of the trust assets and ownership.

Of course, this discussion assumes that in transferring assets to any irrevocable trust, you do not run afoul of fraudulent transfer laws. Now, let's discuss why and how irrevocable trusts can protect assets.

Why Irrevocable Trusts Protect Your Assets

Irrevocable trusts protect assets for the same reason that revocable trusts do not. As mentioned earlier, revocable living trusts do not provide asset protection because creditors can "step into your shoes" and undo such a trust. The logic here is that if you have the power to undo your trust, so do your creditors.

An irrevocable trust results in the opposite. Because an established irrevocable trust cannot be altered or undone, your creditors cannot "step into your shoes" and undo the trust any more than you can. Assets in an irrevocable trust are immune from creditor attack, lawsuits, and other threats against the grantor (the person who created the trust).

Two Clauses Your Irrevocable Trust Should Have

There are two clauses that are extremely important for an irrevocable trust to include so that you can properly protect your assets. These clauses are not necessarily important to protect the trust creator but rather work to shield the beneficiaries from their creditors.

Spendthrift Clause

The spendthrift clause allows the trustee to withhold income and principal—which would ordinarily be paid to the beneficiary—if the trustee feels that the money could or would be wasted or seized by the beneficiary's creditors. This clause accomplishes two goals. First, it prevents a wasteful beneficiary from spending trust funds or wasting trust assets. This is especially important to many doctors who set up trusts with their children as beneficiaries. If you worry that money in trust for your children would be wasted if not controlled, then use a spendthrift clause. The trustee can then stop payments if your child spends too quickly or unwisely.

Second, the spendthrift clause protects trust assets from creditors of the beneficiaries. Beneficiaries may be young now, but as adults they will face the same risks that we all do: lawsuits, debt problems, divorce, failing businesses, etc. The spendthrift clause protects trust assets from your children's creditors by granting the trustee the authority to withhold payments to a beneficiary who has an outstanding creditor. If the beneficiary and trustee are at "arm's length," the creditor has no power to force the trustee to pay the beneficiary. The creditor only has a right to payments actually paid by the trustee; he cannot force the trustee to make disbursements.

Anti-Alienation Clause

The anti-alienation clause also protects trust assets from the beneficiary's creditors. Specifically, the anti-alienation clause prohibits the trustee from transferring trust assets to anyone other than the beneficiary. This, of course, includes creditors of the trust beneficiary. Thus, while the spendthrift clause allows the trustee to withhold payments if a creditor lurks, the anti-alienation clause goes one step further—it prohibits the trustee from paying trust income or principal to anyone but the named beneficiary.

Domestic Asset Protection Trusts

As discussed in Chapter 2.2, domestic asset protection trusts (DAPTs) are unique irrevocable trusts in that you can be both the settlor establishing the trust and a beneficiary of the trust. When there is no lawsuit concern, you can get to the trust assets as beneficiary—but if you have lawsuit claimants after you, the trust can be written so that the trustee cannot make distributions to you, as you are "under duress." In this way, a DAPT can allow you both access to the trust assets when the "coast is clear" and protection when lawsuits and creditors are baying. As such, it can be very attractive for clients who live and practice in a state with DAPT trust legislation. In such states, we would consider such a trust at least a (+4) type of tool—the only reservation is that these statutes are relatively new (the first DAPT statute was enacted in Alaska in 1999, and many states' laws ae less than ten years old) so they have not been tested in court as much as older state exemption statutes.

Some doctors may consider using a DAPT in a foreign state if their home state does not allow DAPTs. In our view, there is significant risk to this approach. There is no guarantee that a court in one's home state will recognize the protections of the out-of-state DAPT when the state in which you were sued has not passed such legislation. Certainly, some attorneys recommend out-of-state DAPTs for clients, but we advise clients to ask questions about the experience of such protections working in their home state before moving forward. Often, the more conservative approach in these cases is to use a "hybrid" DAPT concept that uses a trust that elements of a DAPT but also more closely resembles trusts in the client's home state.

TAKEAWAY: Once doctors have maximized their use of exempt assets, they move on to FLPs, LLCs, and trusts. Since the only trusts that protect assets are irrevocable, they are much stronger "medicine" than FLPs and LLCs and should be contemplated thoroughly before being employed. For doctors who live in states where DAPT legislation has passed, this tool becomes much more attractive, as you can "have your cake and eat it too."

CHAPTER 2.9

Protecting Your Home

Along with retirement accounts, the family home is often a doctor's most valuable asset. Beyond its purely financial value, the home has great *psychological* value as well. In fact, we find that most of our clients who engage in asset protection planning begin with the question, "How can I protect my home?" That's why we thought it important to dedicate an entire chapter to discussing this asset and how to protect it from outside threats.

This chapter will discuss the pros and cons of state homestead laws, LLCs/FLPs, and the debt shield. You may be surprised to find out that something you've always been afraid of could be your ally in your quest to protect your most valuable asset.

State Homestead Law

As you learned earlier, every state has some type of homestead protection law. In a few states, homestead laws protect an unlimited value, although there may be some geographic limitations (Texas and Florida are examples). In many states, from Illinois to New York to California, the value that homestead rules protect is very low when compared to what real estate is worth. On average, state homestead laws protect about $30,000–$50,000 of equity—typically much less than the value of most doctors' homes. In those states, additional protection options must be examined.

Tenancy by the Entirety

Described earlier as a "quasi-exempt" asset class, tenancy by the entirety (TBE) is a form of joint ownership for married couples that is available in a number of states. In essence, in the states that protect real estate well through TBE, the home will not be subject to any claims against one spouse. This can be very valuable to a married couple when one spouse has significant exposure and the other does not. Inherent in TBE, however, are a number of risks. These include the following:

1. **Joint Risk**
   TBE provides no shield whatsoever against joint risks, including lawsuits that arise from your jointly owned real estate or acts of your minor children.

2. **Divorce Risk**
   If you get divorced before or during a lawsuit, you lose all protections from TBE.

3. **Liability Risk**
   If one spouse dies before or during a lawsuit, you lose all protections from TBE.

4. **Death Risk**
   TBE is a poor ownership form for estate planning purposes because at the death of the first spouse, the entire value of the home will automatically go into the surviving spouse's taxable estate.

LLCs and FLPs

LLCs and FLPs are two tools that theoretically could protect a primary residence. However, the drawbacks of these methods are perfect examples of why multidisciplinary planning is a necessity for doctors. Let's look at some of the problems with doing asset protection planning in a vacuum with respect to the home.

Drawbacks of LLCs and FLPs for the Home

In Chapter 2.7, we discussed LLCs and FLPs in detail. We will assume that this is fresh in your mind, so you can see why owning real estate in an LLC would be attractive. However, when it comes to the primary residence, these entities are not common choices for homeowners.

The family home has unique tax attributes—most notably, the deductibility of the mortgage interest to a certain level and the $250,000-per-person ($500,000-per-couple) capital gains tax exemption upon the sale of a home (as of this writing). Owning the home within an LLC or an FLP could cause both of these tax benefits to be lost. This could mean hundreds of thousands of dollars of additional taxes owed by certain clients.

Also, many advisors in the field do not think that the LLC/FLP protections described above would stand up if challenged with respect to the ownership of such a personal asset as a home. If you are considering such a tactic, make sure you are guided by an asset protection expert familiar with your state.

Qualified Personal Residence Trusts

When using a qualified personal residence trust (QPRT), the owner transfers ownership of the home to the QPRT irrevocably. While this is effective for both asset protection and estate planning purposes, it comes with a significant cost—you no longer own your home. In fact, when the term of years is up (the typical range of years for a QPRT is five to twenty years), you have to pay rent to the trust just to live in the home. Also, homes with mortgages on them present tax difficulties. For these reasons, while the QPRT is a strong asset protection tool, we typically do not advise using it for most younger clients whose main concern is asset protection, not estate planning. Nonetheless, if it can be implemented correctly, a QPRT receives a rating of (+4) or (+5) level of protection.

The Debt Shield Concept

The debt shield can be the most effective way to shield the equity of the home. Essentially, using a debt shield means getting a loan against the equity in your home. For many clients, this is counterintuitive—they want to pay down the mortgage as much as possible. While doing so may have an emotional appeal, for asset protection purposes it is the exact opposite of what you want to do in states where home equity is exposed and homestead protections are minimal.

For some doctor clients, using a debt shield does not mean

taking a new loan on their home at all—rather, it may mean not following a strategy of paying the mortgage down quicker than what is required. Here, the decision on whether (or to what extent) to pay down a mortgage they already have is examined from the asset protection perspective (could the funds be invested in another better-protected asset?) and the wealth accumulation perspective (could the funds be invested in another better-performing asset?). When getting a new loan is involved, the analysis is identical.

From an asset protection perspective, the transaction is simple—use the debt shield to move the equity from the vulnerable asset (the home) to a better-protected asset (exempt asset, LLC, FLP, etc.).

From an economic perspective, too, the transaction is simple—consider whether the cost of the equity move (the after-tax interest cost) is higher or lower than the return that the ultimate repository asset of the loan proceeds can generate and how "safe" what you are investing in with the loan proceeds is.

TAKEAWAY: For most doctors, there is no more financially valuable and psychologically important asset than the family residence. Some states offer great homestead protection, but most provide an inadequate shield. Potential options include TBE, trusts, or some type of debt shield strategy.

CHAPTER 2.10
Divorce Protection

Of all the risks to doctors, the most common threat to long-term financial security may be divorce.

Divorce protection is not about hiding assets from a soon-to-be-former spouse. Nor is it about cheating or lying to keep your wealth. Rather, it concerns resolving issues of property ownership and distribution before things go sour. By agreeing in advance what will be yours and what will be your spouse's, you save money, time, and emotional distress in the long run. In fact, this type of asset protection planning inevitably benefits all parties, except divorce lawyers of course.

Divorce planning is also about shielding family assets from the potential divorces of children and grandchildren. Given the statistics, it is almost a certainty that either a child or grandchild of yours will get divorced. Thus, for purposes of intergenerational financial planning, this is a crucial topic unless you want to give half of your legacy to the ex-spouses of your heirs. This is a lesson that wealthy families have known, and addressed, for decades. Wealthy families *do* not know the secret to avoiding divorce. Wealthy families do know the secret to avoiding the financial losses that can be associated with inevitable divorces. This chapter will discuss why divorce can be so financially devastating, the pros and cons of prenuptial agreements, irrevocable trusts, and ways to protect your children from financial loss due to divorce.

Community Property States

Many of the country's western states have community property law. Community property law stipulates that in a divorce, if there is no valid pre- or post-marital agreement, the court will equally divide any property acquired during the marriage other than inheritances or gifts to one spouse. Even the appreciation of one spouse's separate property can be divided if the other spouse expended effort on that property during the marriage and the property appreciated concurrently with or after the effort being expended. From these facts, it is obvious that how the asset is titled does not control who will receive it in a divorce. Rather, when the asset was acquired and how it was treated are far more important factors.

Equitable Distribution States

Non-community-property states are called "equitable distribution" states because courts in these states have total discretion to divide property "equitably," or fairly. The court will normally consider a number of factors in deciding what is "equitable," including the length of the marriage, the ages and conduct of the parties, and the present earnings and future earning potential of each former spouse. The danger of equitable divorces is that courts often distribute both non-marital assets (those acquired before the marriage) and marital assets (those acquired during marriage) in order to create a "fair" arrangement. In this way, courts often split up property in ways that the ex-spouses never wanted or expected.

Can a "Pre-Nup" Protect You?

A premarital agreement (also known as a prenuptial agreement, premarital contract, or antenuptial agreement) is the foundation of divorce-related financial protection. The premarital agreement is a written contract between the spouses. It specifies the division of property and income upon divorce, including disposition of specific personal property, such as family heirlooms. It also states the responsibilities of each party with regard to their children after divorce. Finally, these agreements lay out the parties' responsibilities during marriage, such as the financial support each spouse can expect or the religion in which any children will be raised. The agreement cannot limit child support because the right to child support lies with the child and not the parent.

Irrevocable Spendthrift Trusts: Ideal Tools for Keeping Assets in the Family

As mentioned earlier, irrevocable trusts are very effective asset protection tools because the grantor no longer owns the assets in the trust. In other words, the grantor has transferred the property with no strings attached. Because the grantor neither owns nor controls the property, future creditors, including an ex-spouse, cannot claim the property. Moreover, the grantor can make children, grandchildren, and even future great-grandchildren beneficiaries of an irrevocable trust. At the same time, the trust document can be drafted such that these descendants' creditors, including ex-spouses, cannot get to trust assets.

Nonetheless, using an irrevocable trust should not be taken lightly. Giving away assets forever with no strings attached can prove to have serious consequences when protecting against divorce, lawsuits, or other threats. When would such a strategy make sense? In circumstances where you would have inevitably given away the assets to certain beneficiaries anyway. For example, the trust might be used for assets that (1) you will leave to your children or grandchildren when you die and (2) you do not need for your own financial security. For a more detailed example, consider Irving's case study.

Case Study: Irving's Trust Protects His Summer Home

Irving, a plastic surgeon, bought a summer home in Malibu. He and his first wife had three small children. Unfortunately, they divorced about six years into their marriage. In the settlement, he received the summer home.

Fifteen years later, Irving was ready to marry again, now in Santa Fe. Both he and his prospective spouse had been married before and understood divorce. Irving considered a premarital agreement to keep the summer home as his separate property. He had planned to give it to his three children but wondered whether working on the home would jeopardize this plan if he later divorced.

continued...

After speaking with Irving, we noted three important points:

1. Irving's handiwork on the home might make it marital property;
2. Irving's children and their families used the home throughout the year; and
3. Irving was involved in a lawsuit from a failed real estate venture.

Given these points, it was clear that the best strategy for Irving was to have an irrevocable trust own the summer home, which would give his three children equal beneficial interests in the home.

By transferring the summer home to an irrevocable trust, Irving protected the home against possible future divorce and also shielded it from other creditors and lawsuits. By including spendthrift provisions, Irving protected the home from his children's creditors, as well. This will ensure that the summer house stays in the family for generations.

Protect Your Children from Divorce

When your children or grandchildren come to you giddy with exciting news about their engagements, the last thing they want to hear you ask is, "Are you going to sign a prenuptial agreement?" In fact, if you weren't paying for the wedding, you might lose your invitation for making such a suggestion!

As you learned earlier, the secret to protecting assets from divorce is keeping them "separate property" and not commingling them with community or marital property. You can't trust your children to do this, so you are going to do it for them—without their consent or that of their future (or current) spouses being required.

By leaving assets to your children's irrevocable trusts with the appropriate spendthrift provisions, rather than to them personally, you can achieve this goal. Of course, if the children take money out of the trust and use it to buy a home or other property, that property will be subject to the rules of their state. To illustrate this point, let's look at the example of Rob and Janelle.

Case Study: Janelle's Divorce and Her Inheritance

Rob and Janelle were college sweethearts who got married right after graduation. Within a few years, their romance turned sour and Rob could no longer handle the physical and emotional abuse. However, during their three-year marriage, Janelle had received a sizeable inheritance from her grandparents and used it to pay off the couple's mortgage on their home. In their divorce, Rob's attorney successfully argued that his time and labor on the house, and the fact that he lived in it except when Janelle occasionally kicked him out and he had to stay at his mother's, made half of the equity in the home ($100,000) Rob's fair share. Though Rob and all of his friends will argue that the $100,000 was small consolation for what he endured, Janelle's grandparents certainly didn't intend for Rob to receive what they left to Janelle.

What could have been done differently to ensure that Janelle's assets were protected? Her grandparents could have left her the inheritance through an irrevocable trust that allowed her to take out only so much money per year. She could have used the interest from the inheritance to pay the mortgage down each month. The inheritance itself would have remained separate property and would not have been part of the divorce settlement. In the short three years of their marriage, Janelle and Rob would have had next to no equity in their home and Rob would have left the marriage with what he brought into it and his wounded pride—but none of Janelle's grandparents' life savings. It is left to the reader to determine what is equitable—we aren't marriage counselors; we are only trying to help you reach your desired objectives.

In a nutshell, a little proactive financial planning can go a long way toward making sure that a divorce doesn't completely disrupt a family's financial situation.

TAKEAWAY: Divorce is one of the most common risks to the long-term financial security of a physician. To manage this risk, premarital planning, the use of irrevocable trusts, and planning for future generations are all tactics to consider.

LESSON 3

Tax Planning When in Practice

Nearly every practicing physician we have spoken with in our combined careers wants to reduce their taxes in legally permissible ways. This Lesson covers this topic. We start with an overview of our tax system and some history. We then discuss tactics that an employed physician can use to reduce taxes. Next are a few chapters geared to doctors in private practice, where we describe the difference tax treatment choices for practice entities (S vs C corporations), as well as options for reducing taxes through qualified retirement plans, non-qualified benefit plans, and even captive insurance companies. We also dedicate some time to discussing how to stay out of trouble, especially with qualified plans and captives.

CHAPTER 3.1
Tax Planning: An Overview and Background

Having worked with more than a thousand physicians, we can confidently say that reducing taxes is the number one short-term financial goal of most physicians (their top long-term goal being to reach a comfortable retirement on their terms). Of course, you don't have to be a doctor to want to legally reduce your taxes. As Judge Learned Hand once said, "Anyone may arrange his affairs so that his taxes shall be as low as possible. . . There is not even a patriotic duty to increase one's taxes." The difference between moderately successful and highly successful physicians is that the latter consider the tax impact of everything they do.

Doctors should understand that taxes permeate all areas of their financial lives. First, every dollar earned will be subject to federal, state, and possibly local income taxes. These taxes can add up to 50% or more of your earnings, depending on your income level and where you live.

When you work to grow your net worth, you will run into the capital gains tax. This is a federal tax on the sale of appreciated assets (as opposed to earned income). Typically, states do not have a capital gains tax; they treat such gains as income subject to their regular income tax rates.

Finally, when you gift assets to family members, heirs, or others, the gift and estate tax system comes into play.

In this Lesson, we will address income and capital gains taxes and suggest tactics and strategies that many physicians can use to reduce or delay tax burdens, whether they are employees or practice owners. We will leave a discussion of estate taxes and planning to Chapters 1.5 and 6.3.

Before we delve into solutions, we want to set out the ground rules with an overview of our tax system and the recent (2017) tax overhaul passed by the federal government.

Income Taxes

Every citizen pays income taxes on salaries and other income. Do you know exactly how income taxes are computed? Many people believe that they move from income tax bracket to income tax bracket, increasing the percentage they pay on all dollars earned as they move up to the next bracket. They believe that they are worse off when they earn more because it puts them in a higher tax bracket. This is incorrect.

As a taxpayer's income crosses a threshold into the next tax bracket, *only the dollars earned within that bracket* are taxed at the higher rate. Hence, moving into a higher tax bracket will never make anyone worse off. Figure 3.1.1 illustrates how federal income taxes are calculated in 2020 (the publication date of this book).

IF TAXABLE INCOME IS:	THEN INCOME TAX EQUALS:
SINGLE INDIVIDUALS	
NOT OVER $9,700	10% OF THE TAXABLE INCOME
OVER $9,700 BUT NOT OVER $39,475	$970.00 PLUS 12% OF THE EXCESS OVER $9,700
OVER $39,476 BUT NOT OVER $84,200	$4,543.00 PLUS 22% OF THE EXCESS OVER $39,475
OVER $84,201 BUT NOT OVER $160,725	$14,382.50 PLUS 24% OF THE EXCESS OVER $84,200
OVER $160,726 BUT NOT OVER $204,100	$32,748.50 PLUS 32% OF THE EXCESS OVER $160,725
OVER $204,101 BUT NOT OVER $510,300	$46,628.50 PLUS 35% OF THE EXCESS OVER $204,100
OVER $510,301	$153,798.50 PLUS 37% OF THE EXCESS OVER $510,300
MARRIED INDIVIDUALS FILING JOINT RETURNS AND SURVIVING SPOUSES	
NOT OVER $19,400	10% OF THE TAXABLE INCOME
OVER $19,401 BUT NOT OVER $78,950	$1,940 PLUS 12% OF THE EXCESS OVER $19,400
OVER $78,951 BUT NOT OVER $168,400	$9,086 PLUS 22% OF THE EXCESS OVER $78,950
OVER $168,401 BUT NOT OVER $321,450	$28,765 PLUS 24% OF THE EXCESS OVER $168,400
OVER $321,451 BUT NOT OVER $408,200	$65,497 PLUS 32% OF THE EXCESS OVER $321,450
OVER $408,201 BUT NOT OVER $612,350	$93,257 PLUS 35% OF THE EXCESS OVER $408,200
OVER $612,351	$164,709.50 PLUS 37% OF THE EXCESS OVER $612,350

Figure 3.1.1

To better understand how income tax is tabulated, let's look at the example of Mike and Gina.

Mike and Gina are married and file jointly. Mike makes $240,000 per year, while Gina runs an in-home business that generates $10,000 per year. For simplicity, we assume they have no deductions and live in a state with no state income tax. They have $250,000 of total taxable income that generates federal income tax liabilities of $48,349. Mike and Gina are in the 24% marginal tax bracket with a 19% effective tax rate.

"Marginal tax bracket" means the highest rate an income earner pays on income that exceeds their highest tax bracket. In Mike and Gina's case, the 24% rate is their marginal tax bracket. This is determined by examining the relevant tax rate chart (married, filing jointly) and finding the rate where their income tops out.

Contrast "marginal tax bracket" with "effective tax rate," which is the average rate one pays over all brackets, calculated by dividing total tax paid by total taxable income.

History of the Highest Marginal Federal Tax Rate

As we write this book, federal income tax rates are at one of the lowest points in the history of the U.S. income tax. (See Figure 1.3.2 in Chapter 1.3.)

It becomes obvious that our highest federal marginal rate today is quite low from a historical perspective—37% is less than half of the highest rate in most periods between 1940 and 1980. While few high-income taxpayers reached the 80% or 90% marginal rates in those days, we present this chart as a reminder that rates are now relatively low. Could pressure to raise marginal rates on high-income earners like physicians be politically expedient at some point? With a record level of national debt that seems to rise with each passing year, such a scenario is not hard to imagine.

Taxes on Investments

Once you earn money and pay income taxes, you aren't finished with tax payments. You will spend money on consumer goods and have to pay sales tax, and you may buy real estate and pay annual property taxes. Another possibility is that you might save money and put it in some type of investment, such as real estate, public securities, commodities, or interests in closely held businesses.

Most investments can generally be classified as either income or growth vehicles. In some cases, an investment may be both. Income investments are those that offer some type of regular return (income) to the investor. Your bank accounts, CDs, and money market accounts earn interest. If you own traditional bonds, you receive a coupon every six months or year. If you own rental real estate, you collect rental income. All of these—interest payments, bond coupon payments, and rent checks—are added to your income for the purpose of calculating taxable income. If you are in a 32% marginal federal income tax bracket, you will have to pay federal tax of 32% on this investment income. If you are in a 35% marginal tax bracket, then you will pay 35% of the investment gain in taxes on that investment income. Of course, if, like most people, you are not in an income tax–free state, you could pay up to 13% in state income taxes as well.

Not all investors require immediate income from their investments. When you don't need current income from your investments, you can afford riskier investments in search of greater long-term appreciation.

When you invest in a company by buying stock, your money is used to help grow that business. The company will reinvest the proceeds and potentially increase the net worth (value) of the company. As the value of the company increases, the value of your shares in the company will also increase. You do not receive a regular check from the company. Rather, you have the right to sell your shares of the company. If you realize this type of profit on your investment, you are responsible for taxes on your "capital gains."

For tax purposes, capital gains are categorized as long-term or short-term. *Short term* is defined as realized (sold) appreciation of an asset that you owned for less than one year. If you have a short-term gain, it is treated exactly the same way (for tax purposes) as the interest, coupons, and rental income mentioned above. If your income puts you in a marginal federal tax bracket of 32%, your short-term capital gains would be taxed at 32% (plus any applicable state income taxes).

If you hold an asset for more than one year, the federal government gives you a benefit: your taxes are based on long-term capital gains tax rates on your realized appreciation. As we write this in 2020, these rates are 20% for taxpayers in the highest tax bracket and 15% for those in other tax brackets. This benefit is an incentive to investors to keep their funds invested. This stability is much better than constant buying and selling, which could significantly disrupt business. This tax incentive also acts as a deterrent to potentially unethical short-term trading.

In addition, investors with adjusted gross income above $250,000 must pay a 3.8% net investment income tax on these gains under the Affordable Care Act. Finally, as mentioned, states will treat such gains as income and tax them at applicable state income tax rate. Back to the example of Mike and Gina, our happily married couple who filed jointly. Let's say that Mike and Gina invest $70,000 in a 5% money market account. This generates a $3,500 interest payment annually. They must add this $3,500 to their income on both their federal and state income tax returns.

Like federal marginal income tax rates, it is clear that federal capital gains rates are low now and could easily become much higher in the future. Since wealth planning is a long-term endeavor, one must take the high probability of an increased capital gains tax rate into account.

2017 Tax Cuts and Jobs Act: What You Need to Know

At the end of 2017, Congress enacted sweeping tax reform that had widespread effects on both individuals and medical practices, with many changes taking effect January 1, 2018. This was the most significant change to the tax code in years.

Taxes at the Individual Level

For individuals, first and foremost were changes to the tax rates and brackets. There are now seven tax brackets, with a top marginal rate of 37%, down from 39.6%. Capital gains and dividend rates remained unchanged.

In addition to rate and bracket changes, several other aspects of the law affected individuals. The standard deduction nearly doubled, from what would have been $6,500 in 2018 for single taxpayers and $13,000 for married taxpayers filing jointly to $12,000 and $24,000, respectively. There is no longer a deduction for personal or dependency exemptions. These had previously been reduced or eliminated for many high-income taxpayers.

While the alternative minimum tax (AMT) was not repealed for individuals, the exemption amounts increased to $70,300 for single taxpayers and $109,400 for married taxpayers filing jointly, and the exemption phaseout now will not begin until $500,000 for single taxpayers and $1,000,000 for married filers.

Many changes to itemized deductions for individual taxpayers affected physicians in significant ways. The deduction for state and local income, sales, and property taxes was capped at $10,000 for married and single taxpayers and $5,000 for head-of-household filers. Most miscellaneous itemized deductions were eliminated, including tax preparation fees, investment fees, and unreimbursed employee business expenses.

For mortgages taken out after December 16, 2017, interest is deductible for a principal residence and for a second residence on a loan principal of $750,000 (previously the loan limitation was $1,000,000). Mortgages in place before that date were grandfathered in at the $1,000,000 amount. Refinancing of grandfathered mortgages is also grandfathered, but not beyond the term and amount of the original mortgage. In addition, interest on home equity loans is no longer deductible unless it is shown that the loan proceeds were used to purchase or substantially improve the home.

The limit for charitable contributions to public charities increased to 60% of AGI from the previous 50%; however, the deduction for contributions made in exchange for college athletic event seating rights is no longer allowed. The law also eliminated PEASE limitations, which reduced itemized deductions for higher-income taxpayers.

Taxes at the Practice Level

Business taxpayers have also seen many changes. Perhaps most notable was the new flat 21% corporate tax rate for corporation tax years beginning after December 31, 2017. The alternative minimum tax was repealed for corporations. There was also a provision for immediate 100% expensing for the purchase of business equipment placed in service after September 27, 2017 and before January 1, 2023. The depreciation cap on luxury autos was raised, and the limitation for Section 179 expensing was set at $1,000,000. The deduction for net interest expenses is now limited to 30% of adjusted taxable income. Net operating loss carryforwards is limited to 80% of taxable income, and Section 1031 like-kind exchanges are limited to real property. The deduction for any activity deemed entertainment, amusement, or recreation (including club membership dues) was repealed, but 50% of the cost of business meals is still deductible.

What may be the greatest failure of "tax simplification" are the new provisions for pass-through business income, including that from S corporations, partnerships, and sole proprietorships, which means that most medical practices are affected.

There is now a 20% deduction against qualified business income of these pass-through entities. The deduction amount will be the lesser of the following:

- 20% of the taxpayer's qualified business income, or
- The greater of (1) 50% of W2 wages paid with respect to the business or (2) the sum of 25% of W2 wages paid plus 2.5% of the unadjusted basis of all qualified property

The deduction is further limited to the net of the taxpayer's taxable income less the taxpayer's net capital gain. The wage limitation does not apply to married taxpayers with taxable income under $321,400 ($160,700 for single taxpayers) in 2020.

However, specified service businesses (accountants, attorneys, doctors, etc.) are excluded from the deduction unless they are under the $321,400/$160,700 taxable income thresholds.

The Importance of Tax Diversification

What tax rates will be in place during your retirement, which may last ten to thirty years or more? Obviously, you do not know, even if you are already retired, and neither do we. Because nobody knows what the tax rates, rules on deductions, and other tax-related laws will be in the future, we think it is crucial for holistic wealth management to include a *tax diversification* strategy.

As we discussed in Chapter 1.3, *tax diversification* means building up wealth in three "buckets": assets subject to ordinary income tax rates upon distribution in retirement, assets subject to capital gains rates, and assets not subject to any tax upon distribution. While most plans focus on asset class diversification only in the context of investing, we believe it is fundamental to also include diversification of your wealth based on tax-rate exposure.

Figure 1.3.4 in Chapter 1.3 illustrates the value of having differently taxed buckets to draw on when you reach retirement. As your retirement/wealth distribution phase may last for many years or even decades, being diversified across tax buckets puts you in a position of strength and gives you options for where to draw income from depending on the tax rates then in effect.

Let's look at the examples of cardiologist Cathy and gastroenterologist Gary. Cathy and Gary are both presently 45 years old and plan on retiring at age 65, as do their spouses, who are also currently 45. At this point, both couples have a joint life expectancy of age 91, meaning that, according to the actuaries, at least one spouse in each couple should live until age 91. With a planned retirement age of 65, these couples will need to rely on their assets and other sources of income (for example, social security) to provide them with income for 26 years.

While numerous financial, investment and planning factors are essential for Cathy and Gary, let's concentrate just on the tax planning issue here. Both couples will begin drawing down assets in 20 years and stop doing so 46 years from now. During that period of time, tax rates may be very different than they are today and may change several times.

Let's assume that Cathy and Gary have the same overall net worth, but their asset mix is very different. Cathy has her net worth in all three buckets—some in a qualified retirement plan (QRP), some in after-tax brokerage accounts and real estate, and some in a Roth IRA and a permanent life insurance policy. Gary has nearly all his net worth in his home and 401(k) QRP. They both qualify for social security.

Cathy is much better positioned than Gary to maximize her post-tax retirement income. Most of Gary's retirement income will come from his QRP and social security, both of which are subject to ordinary federal and state income tax. If income tax rates are high,

Gary has little flexibility to take income from other sources unless he is willing to sell his home, which he may be reluctant to do, especially in his first decade of retirement. (Also, he can't sell only part of his home, like Cathy can do with her brokerage accounts. Further, it may be difficult for him to get favorable loans against his home equity in retirement when he will have no income.)

Cathy, on the other hand, is well positioned if income tax rates are high—she can draw down her brokerage account if capital gains taxes have remained lower than income taxes. Moreover, she can take income from her Roth IRA or access life insurance cash values, both completely tax-free. Further, Cathy is much better positioned to alter her income plan if tax rates change over her retirement. Gary does not have this flexibility. It is not difficult to understand that, despite their equal net worth, Cathy may net out much greater after-tax retirement income than Gary.

TAKEAWAY: Reducing taxes is the leading short-term planning goal for most physicians. This is not surprising when you look at how much the typical physician pays today in income taxes and will pay, in the future, in capital gains and estate and gift taxes. Understanding how taxes work and implementing a long-term plan of tax diversification are two important steps in tax planning.

CHAPTER 3.2
Tax Planning for Employed Physicians

After advising physicians for the last twenty-five years, we are well aware of the recent and growing trend of physicians becoming employed by others. With the emergence of supergroups, hospital acquisitions, and private equity practice ownership, an increasing number of physicians well along in their practices are becoming non-owner employees for the first time in their careers. Additionally, many younger physicians whose first jobs are as employees will likely remain employees throughout their careers.

Employed physicians have fewer significant tax-saving opportunities as compared to their colleagues who are partners in private practices. This Lesson reflects that fact—we have written several chapters about planning options for private practice owners but just this one for employed doctors.

The message to employed physicians is simple: maximize what is available to you and don't worry about what is not. We have written this chapter, in fact, along those lines, focusing on leveraging the tax-advantaged plans that you can use, tax-savvy investing and college education funding, and the use of charitable strategies when applicable.

Note 1: If you are an employed physician but you earn independent income through moonlighting, *locums* work, speaking, or any non-medical business, be sure to read other chapters in this Lesson as well. We certainly have clients who are able to do some valuable tax planning with their "outside" income, even though most of their earnings are as employed doctors.

Note 2: If you read Lesson 1 on Financial Planning Basics, you may see much of the descriptions of retirement planning options repeated here. Either read on to brush up on the topic, or move on to the "Tax-Efficient Investor" discussion. Your choice!

Leverage Tax-Advantaged Plans

Maximize Contributions to Employer's Qualified Retirement Plan

Physicians who are W-2 employees often can participate in their employer's retirement plan, which allows them to defer income by contributing to the plan.

For example, a 401(k) plan is one type of qualified retirement plan (QRP), and it is the most common one offered to physician employees of for-profit entities. Governmental entities and non-profit healthcare organizations offer 403(b) plans, which work the same way as 401(k)s. (The pros and cons of QRPs for physicians in private practice who are or will be owners will be discussed later.)

Government-sponsored 457(b) plans are offered by state and local government healthcare organizations. Physicians can defer funds into these plans on a pretax basis in addition to contributing to a 403(b) plan.

Nongovernmental organization 457(b) plans, or NGO 457(b) plans, present a special risk for unwary physicians saving for retirement. While these plans, like 401(k) plans, allow for pretax contributions and tax-deferred growth, they gain these tax benefits only due to a substantial risk of forfeiture imposed by the Internal Revenue Service. Doctors who hold these plans can lose everything in them if the sponsoring employer goes bankrupt. While account balances from one nongovernmental 457(b) can usually be rolled over to another nongovernmental 457(b) plan, they cannot be rolled over to an IRA or any other type of plan.

A 401(a) plan is a QRP normally offered by government agencies, educational institutions, and nonprofit organizations rather than by corporations. These plans are usually custom-designed and can be offered to key employees as an incentive to stay with the organization. The employee contribution amounts are normally set by the employer. The employer must contribute to the plan as well. Contributions can be pretax or post tax.

Use After-Tax IRAs When You Can

A traditional IRA allows doctors to defer up to $6,000 per year ($7,000 per year if they are 50 or older) into the account (under the 2020 limits in effect as we write this). Physicians who are not covered by a workplace retirement plan may deduct pretax contributions; all others can make nondeductible or partially deductible contributions (depending on their earned income and filing status). The nondeductible portion of the account, also known as the "basis," is tracked with each year's tax return. Account balances can grow tax deferred.

Roth IRA contribution limits are the same as traditional IRA limits, but most physicians earn more than the adjusted gross income limits for Roth IRAs so they are not allowed to contribute directly to a Roth IRA. Doctors can often use a "backdoor" Roth IRA by contributing to a traditional IRA and then converting the traditional IRA to a Roth IRA. (Note: This tactic requires careful planning to avoid unnecessary taxation. Work with an experienced advisor.) Roth IRAs can be very beneficial in long-term retirement planning because funds in a Roth IRA grow tax-deferred and are tax-free when they are withdrawn from the account. As we discussed in the last chapter, "tax diversification" is fundamental to long-term tax planning, and a Roth IRA can be part of the tax-free bucket—assets that are distributed tax-free in retirement.

A spousal IRA is a traditional IRA or Roth IRA that receives contributions on behalf of a nonearning spouse. In order to contribute, the nonearning spouse must meet the ordinary requirements for making an IRA contribution except that they are not required to have earned income. Instead, the earning physician must make enough income to cover the spouse's contribution. The normal IRA contribution limits apply to the spousal IRA.

Use Life Insurance as Part of Your Retirement Plan, When Appropriate

We explained above that Roth IRA contributions are after-tax, but then the balance grows tax-free and can be accessed tax-free in the future. Would you be surprised to learn that, managed properly, a permanent life insurance policy behaves the same way? As we described in Lesson 1, "permanent" life insurance means whole life, universal life, variable life, equity-indexed life, and similar policies. Regardless of the type of product, the cash value of such policies grows free of tax and can be accessed free of tax during the insured's life—and this tax treatment has remained stable for over a hundred years.

Certainly, there is a lot of noise out there about the strategy of using permanent life insurance, and there is contradictory advice in the marketplace. In fact, you may have heard people say to buy term and invest the difference, as we have. Our view is that just as physicians have many medicines in their armamentarium, permanent life insurance is a "medicine" with which some "patients" do very well. On the other hand, we recognize that like actual medicine, this medicine has ideal applications and side effects and should be managed properly. We urge you to keep an open mind on this subject when we revisit it in more depth in Chapters 4.2, 4.3, and 4.4.

Be a Tax-Efficient Investor

Beyond investing within tax-efficient vehicles, it is also important to invest personal assets tax efficiently—and this is especially true for employed physicians who do not have the deduction options afforded to practice owners. Consider the following tactics to invest tax efficiently:

Recognize that Asset Location Matters

Leveraging asset location, part of the overall tax diversification strategy discussed in the last chapter, is an important tactic. If one has investments in various structures, each of which is taxed differently, it makes sense to create an overall allocation across asset locations and then place the appropriate assets in the tax-maximized location. For example, if Physician Phil's overall allocation to municipal bonds will be 5%, it makes tax sense to hold that part of his portfolio in his name or a tax-neutral account (like a limited liability company for asset-protection purposes, if taxed as a partnership or disregarded entity). On the other hand, Phil may select a 10% allocation to dividend-yielding large cap stocks. Since Phil is years from needing those dividends in retirement, it likely makes sense for him to hold such stocks in a tax-deferred account, such as a QRP or IRA, thereby avoiding a tax hit on current dividends. These are a couple of examples of how one might construct a portfolio from an investment perspective and then locate it within the available tax structures for minimum tax impact.

Be Cognizant of Holding Periods

As mentioned in the last chapter, long-term capital gains rates are much more favorable than short-term rates. Holding a security for a period of twelve months presents an opportunity to save nearly 20% on the taxation of an appreciated position. For example, an initial investment of $50,000 that grows to $100,000 represents a $50,000 unrealized gain. If an investor in the highest tax bracket simply delays liquidation of the position (assuming the security price does not change), the tax savings in this scenario would be $8,500. Although being aware of the holding period of a security would appear to be a basic principle of investing, many mutual funds and managed accounts are *not* designed for tax sensitivity. Therefore, it is generally advantageous to seek the advice of a financial professional who is aware of holding periods and has experience executing an appropriate exit strategy.

Use Tax Loss Harvesting

One benefit of diversifying across asset classes is that if the portfolio is structured properly, the securities typically will not move in tandem. This divergence of returns among asset classes not only reduces portfolio volatility, it also creates a tax-planning opportunity. For example, at the time of this writing (2020), domestic equities have experienced a consistent upward trend from the depths of the financial crisis in March 2009; however, international stocks, commodities, and multiple fixed income investments have experienced down years. Astute advisors were presented with the opportunity to save clients thousands of dollars in taxes by performing strategic tax swaps before the year's end. It is important to understand the rules relating to wash sales when executing such tactics.

The laws are confusing, and if a mistake is made your loss could be disallowed. Make certain your advisor is well versed in using tax offsets.

Employ a Tax-Focused Wealth Management Firm

As we discuss in Lesson 5 and in our book *Wealth Management Made Simple*, it is certainly possible for physicians to manage their own investments and be successful. It is even possible, although less likely, for them to successfully tax-manage their portfolio. It is not surprising, though, that most doctors choose to work with a licensed and experienced professional or firm. Ideally, such a firm has in-house tax expertise and experience in helping clients reduce the tax impact on their portfolios using tactics like asset location and tax loss harvesting.

Use the Right College Savings Vehicle(s)

If you have children or grandchildren who might go to college, graduate school, medical school, or law school, there are tax-efficient ways to save for this future expense. Here is the short list of potential tax-efficient investment options:

- 529 college savings plans
- 529 prepaid tuition plans
- Uniform Gifts to Minors Act/Uniform Transfers to Minors Act (UGMA/UTMA) Trusts
- Coverdell plans (formerly education IRAs)

Because the Coverdell plan's contribution limits are $2,000 per year and that amount is completely inadequate for high-income earners like physicians, we will exclude it from our analysis. To compare and contrast the first four plans, we want to consider each of them across a number of metrics. Then, we will offer a qualitative discussion about the contribution limits, tax benefits, accessibility, and flexibility of each plan to help you understand why physicians should use some plans more than others.

To do so, let's consider the following table.

COMPARISION OF TAX-EFFICIENT EDUCATIONAL FUNDING OPTIONS			
	529 SAVINGS PLAN	529 PREPAID PLAN	UGMA / UT
INCOME LIMITATIONS	NONE	NONE	NONE
MAXIMUM YEARLY CONTRIBUTION PER BENEFICIARY (ALL NUMBERS DOUBLE WHEN GIFTS COME FROM TWO PARENTS OR GRAND- PARENTS)	ANNUAL FEDERAL GIFT TAX EXCLUSION (UP TO 5 YEARS IN ADVANCE)	ANNUAL FEDERAL GIFT TAX EXCLUSION (UP TO 5 YEARS IN ADVANCE)	ANNUAL FEDERAL GIFT TAX EXCLUSION
ACCOUNT EARNINGS	TAX-FREE, IF USED FOR QUALIFIED EXPENSES	TAX-FREE, IF USED FOR QUALIFIED EXPENSES	TAXABLE
ABILITY TO CHANGE BENEFICIARIES	YES	YES	NO
CONTROL OF WITHDRAWALS	OWNER OF ACCOUNT	OWNER OF ACCOUNT	TRANSFERS TO CHILD WHEN CHILD REACHES LEGAL AGE
INVESTMENT OPTIONS	READY-MADE PORTFOLIOS OF MUTUAL FUNDS	TUITION UNITS GUARANTEED TO MATCH TUITION INFLATION	WIDE RANGE OF SECURITIES
STATE-TAX-DEDUCTIBLE CONTRIBUTIONS	VARIES BY STATE	VARIES BY STATE	NO
QUALIFIED USE OF PROCEEDS	ANY ACCREDITED POST-SECONDARY SCHOOL IN THE US	VARIES BY STATE	UNLIMITED
PENALTIES FOR NONQUALIFIED WITHDRAWALS	10% PENALTY WITHHELD ON EARNINGS	10% PENALTY WITHHELD ON EARNINGS	NO
TAXATION OF QUALIFIED WITHDRAWALS	TAX-FREE	TAX-FREE	A PORTION MAY BE EXEMPT; INCOME MAY BE TAXED AT CHILD'S RATE OR AT TRUST TAX RATE
OWNERSHIP OF ASSETS FOR FINANCIAL AID PURPOSES (MAY VARY BY INSTITUTION)	ACCOUNT OWNER	STUDENT	STUDENT

Figure 3.2.1

Basics of 529 Plans

Under a 529 plan, you can make annual tax-free "gifts" of up to $15,000 to any person. A couple can make such gifts of up to $30,000 per year to each child. With the 529 college savings plan, an individual can make five years' worth of gifts in advance. Total benefits include the following:

- Contributions over $30,000 for a married couple (and $15,000 for an individual) are allowed—gift tax free.
- You, the donor, control the withdrawals.
- You may change the beneficiaries.
- You receive any tax benefits.
- You direct the type of investments (from a short list of choices).
- The money grows tax free.

Contributions Over $30,000 May Be Allowed—Gift Tax Free

You may already know that an individual can make annual tax-free "gifts" of $15,000 to any person and that a couple can make such gifts of up to $30,000. With the 529 college savings plan, you can make five years' worth of gifts in one year without paying a gift tax. The 529 Plan allows you to allocate those gifts over the next five years. Thus, a couple can gift $150,000 tax-free in one year to a 529 plan for each child or grandchild. If this option is chosen, another tax-free gift cannot be made for the next four years to that beneficiary.

The total balance (including principal and earnings) in a 529 plan is capped at an amount that differs from state to state. Caps range from $235,000 to over $500,000 and can change annually. This means that a set of parents could gift $150,000 to a 529 plan *and* a set of grandparents could gift an additional $150,000 to the same child's 529 plan, as long as the total balance in the plan remains under the capped amount.

When you compare the 529 plan to the educational IRA (now called a Coverdell plan), whose annual contribution limit is $2,000, there is no question as to which is the better choice.

You Control the Withdrawals and Beneficiaries

Unlike with an UGMA account or Coverdell, you control the withdrawals from and may change the beneficiaries of a 529 plan. If one child doesn't go to college or receives a scholarship, you may change the plan to benefit someone else. You can make these changes as often as you like, as long as the beneficiaries are related. In fact, you can even name yourself the beneficiary if you plan to go back to school.

If you change your mind and want to withdraw the funds and use them yourself, you may do so. The only downside is that you must pay a 10% penalty in addition to ordinary income taxes on any growth of the funds in the plan.

You Receive the Tax Benefits

The funds in a 529 plan grow on a tax-free basis. Because annual capital gains and dividends are not taxed in the 529 plan, the account balance has the potential to grow faster than if it were invested in comparable taxable investments. If you consider that dividends and short-term capital gains are taxed at rates that may be as high as 42% in some states, the 529 plan could grow twice as quickly as a UGMA or UTMA account that offers no real tax-deferral benefit.

You Direct the Type of Investments

Some 529 plans allow you to invest in a variety of stock, bond, and money market funds. You may have a choice of a growth portfolio or a balanced portfolio. There are even "age-based portfolios" that focus on growth in the child's early years and automatically rebalance every few years to focus more on capital preservation as college approaches.

Use Charitable Planning, When Applicable

The desire to give is strong in many people. As a society, we cherish the right to give to the charitable institutions of our choice. The desire to give is what we refer to as "charitable intent." Often, the biggest hurdles to giving are that we do not know how to give, or we assume that our family will suffer as a result of our giving. In Chapter 6.3, we will discuss charitable planning in more depth.

Here, we will focus on a few tools under the charitable planning umbrella that physicians primarily use for income tax reduction, not estate planning.

Direct Gifts

Direct gifts are gifts that are made to a charitable organization for immediate use. The federal tax code provides for current income tax deductions for gifts to charities that have qualified under 501(c)(3) as a charitable organization. The tax rules governing charitable giving are rather complex. Our explanation will be rather simplistic but should give you a basic understanding.

The IRS distinguishes between "public charities" (universities, hospitals, churches, etc.) and "private charities" (private family foundations are the most common). What's the difference? If the gift is given to a public charity, you can deduct the amount of the gift against your adjusted gross income (AGI) up to a maximum of 60% of your AGI. If the gift exceeds this amount, you can apply the excess as deductions against future years' income for five additional years.

If the gift is to a private charity, then you can deduct only a maximum of 30% of your AGI, but this too can be carried forward five years. Let's see how public and private charities differ in the case study of Charitable Chris.

Charitable Chris: Give to Foundation or Alma Mater

Chris is a retired cardiologist who created a small private family foundation a few years ago to give something back to the community. He involved his children in the foundation and realized some significant tax benefits. Now Chris has $60,000 worth of highly appreciated stock he doesn't need to support his retirement needs. As a result, he would like to make a gift to charity. His annual AGI is only $30,000 per year from the consulting work he does. Chris is considering gifting the stock either to his family foundation or to his alma mater, where he sits on the board.

If he gifts the stock to the foundation, he will be able to deduct only $9,000 per year on his tax return (30% of AGI). If he gifts to the university, he will be able to deduct $18,000 (60% of his AGI). Because he can carry the deduction forward only five years, he'll be able to apply only $54,000 worth of deductions (six years x $9,000) using the family foundation, but he'll be able to use all $60,000 worth of deductions (three years x $18,000 and one year x $6,000) if he gifts to the university.

Indirect Gifts

Indirect gifts are often called "split interest" or "planned" gifts because some of the benefit of the assets being gifted goes to the charitable organization and some of it will be retained by the grantor (or donor) and their family. The real beauty of charitable giving from the family perspective is that the IRS allows tremendous tax benefits for "indirect" gifts—those left to charity through a trust or annuity. In fact, the IRS also allows deductions for indirect gifts through irrevocable charitable remainder or lead trusts and through charitable gift annuities, which provide lifetime income to the donor as guaranteed by the charity and monitored by the state. Using an indirect gift, charitable planning can truly be a win-win-win situation: you win, your family wins, and your favorite charities win.

TAKEAWAY: Employed physicians have fewer tax-reduction tactics available to them than do those who own private practices and, therefore, should be even more focused on leveraging the ones that are available. Maximizing the use of tax-advantaged benefit plans, tax-savvy investing and college education planning, and charitable planning are among the leading tools employed physicians can use for tax reduction today and in the future.

CHAPTER 3.3

The Best Tax Treatment for a Medical Practice: S Corp or C Corp in the Post-TCJA World?

Choosing the tax treatment of one's medical practice is an important decision. Historically, many advisors to medical practices felt that avoiding potential double taxation made the S corporation the logical choice. This conventional wisdom often overlooked the benefits that a C corporation offers. For many practices, the C corporation was the superior structure.

After passage of the Tax Cuts and Jobs Act (TCJA) at the end of 2017, an advisor's determination became even more complex, as tax rates for C corporations fell to a flat rate of 21% and the new Section 199A created a confusing qualified business income (QBI) deduction for pass-through entities such as S corporations.

In this chapter, we will outline the basics of C and S corporations and how they can be used by medical practices in the post-TCJA world.

The Basics of Corporations

First, let's assume that your practice is either a C or S corporation. There is little reason for a solo practice to operate as a sole proprietorship; that choice of entity can result in unnecessary lawsuit risk as well as the inability to take advantage of many valuable tax-deductible business expenses mentioned in this Lesson. The general partnership legal structure is also very problematic with respect to asset protection because it leaves each partner's personal assets at risk in the event of any act or omission by the practice or any partner that creates liability. Nonetheless, partnership tax treatment can be beneficial because it allows partners to specially allocate expenses or have unequal distributions. For this reason, limited liability companies (LLCs) are often taxed as partnerships, and this is especially common when the company owns medical practice real estate or valuable equipment.

In this Lesson, we will focus on comparing C corporations and S corporations.

All businesses that incorporate are automatically C corporations absent an election to become an S corporation. A practice organized as an LLC can choose to be taxed as a corporation, which defaults to taxation as a C corporation unless an additional election is made to be taxed as an S corporation. Both C and S corporations have their own tax ID numbers and are required to file tax returns with federal and appropriate state tax agencies. Both entities have shareholders and can be created in any state in the country.

C Corporations

When a C corporation earns profit, it must pay tax at the corporate level. Profit, of course, is the difference between income and expenses. Compensation paid to physicians, as long as it is reasonable, is deductible by the corporation on its tax return (and is therefore not taxable to the corporation). The owner's salary is taxable to the owner as wages. After the C corporation pays taxes, distributions of earnings already taxed at the corporate level can be paid to the physician owners in the form of dividends. These are generally taxed to the physician owners as qualified dividends, creating "double taxation" of such earnings. Qualified dividends are currently taxed at long-term capital gains rates—15% for persons not in the highest tax bracket and 20% for those in the highest individual income tax bracket. Therefore, a C corporation physician owner will pay 21% corporate tax on net profits of the practice plus either 15% or 20% tax on the dividends distributed by the corporation. This results in up to a 41% federal tax on profits.

S Corporations

An S corporation is also a separate entity that must file a tax return. However, the S corporation is a "pass-through" entity. Rather than being taxed at the corporate level, all income and deductions pass through to the shareholders and the shareholders must pay tax on any S corporation income at their individual rates. Whether an S corporation's income is paid to the physician owners as salary or distributions does not affect the federal or state income tax rates on that income. There is never any tax to the corporation; therefore, there is no "double taxation."

When an S corporation owner provides services to the entity—such as a physician owner practicing medicine—the owner must be paid reasonable compensation in the form of W-2 wages. These wages are a deductible expense to the corporation and are also taxable on the owner's individual income tax return at his or her individual income tax rate.

Planning Within Your Entity

Many physicians think of C and S corporations as having exactly the same benefits. Since the C corporation tax treatment creates the potential for double taxation, many doctors and their advisors make an S election to avoid this problem. Others think a C corporation must be the answer in the post-TCJA world because of the new lower 21% flat tax rate.

The double taxation problem in a C corporation can often be avoided by reducing practice profits to zero, or close to zero, at the end of the year by paying reasonable compensation and bonuses to the physician owner. Also, a C corporation enjoys a full deduction for the cost of employees' (including owner employees') health insurance, group term life insurance of up to $50,000 per employee, and even long-term care premiums without regard to age-based limitations. The C corporation can also deduct the costs of a medical reimbursement plan.

If one has a small corporation and a lot of medical expenses that aren't covered by insurance, the C corporation can establish a plan that results in all of those expenses being tax-deductible. Fringe benefits such as employer-provided vehicles and public transportation passes are also deductible. If the practice has rental activity, a C corporation has the advantage of allowing rental losses to offset operating income. In addition, under the TCJA, C corporations avoid alternative minimum tax. However, all salary and bonuses paid to the physician owner as compensation are subject to the Medicare tax (as high as 3.8%).

In contrast, health insurance paid by an S corporation for a more-than-2% shareholder is not deductible by the corporation. The shareholder must generally take a self-employed health insurance deduction on his or her personal return. Long-term care insurance premiums paid through an S corporation for shareholders are also not deductible. The shareholders must deduct them personally, which makes them subject to age-based limitations. Shareholders of an S corporation must treat rental losses as a passive activity subject to the passive-loss and at-risk rules. An S corporation owner, however, may be able to take some compensation in the form of reasonable W-2 wages and take a profit distribution from the S corporation, which is not subject to the Medicare tax, potentially saving thousands of dollars.

Under the TCJA, a qualified business income deduction of up to 20% was established by the new Internal Revenue Code section 199A. While medical practices are considered to be a "specified service trade or business" and thus excluded from this deduction, individual taxpayers whose taxable income falls below certain thresholds may take advantage of the 20% QBI deduction on income from their pass-through entities. See Chapter 3.5 to learn more about how private practice physicians close to the income thresholds may be able to reduce taxable income enough to qualify for the powerful 199A deduction.

Get the Best of Both Worlds – Why Not Use Both?

Many practices can take advantage of both C corporation and S corporation benefits by setting up two distinct entities to operate different aspects of the practice. Perhaps the S corporation will be used for the operating side of the practice (the professional practice of medicine) while the C corporation will be used for management functions (billing and administration) or for a retail function such as sale of dermatology products or eyewear—or vice versa. In this way, the practice as a whole can take advantage of both the tax deductions afforded a C corporation and the flow-through advantages of an S corporation. The combination of the two entities may also provide some additional asset protection. As long as all formalities of incorporation are followed and rules for employee participation in all benefit plans are complied with, medical practices can benefit from this dual corporate structure.

TAKEAWAY: Choosing the tax treatment of one's medical practice is an important decision, as it affects the tax paid by every physician owner. Careful consideration of the pros and cons of C and S corporation tax treatment is necessary, especially in the post-TCJA world.

CHAPTER 3.4

Tax-Advantaged Benefit Plans for Practice Owners

As we said in Chapter 3.2, in our experience, the number one financial goal for nearly all physicians is to get to a financially secure retirement on their terms, including each doctor's unique timeline and lifestyle goals. It is not surprising that data from national physician surveys confirm this as the top financial objective.

In this chapter, we will provide an overview of tax-favored benefit plans that can help private practice physicians reach their retirement goals. In later chapters in this Lesson, we will delve deeper into a few types of benefit plans.

Note: If you read Lesson 1 on Financial Planning Basics, you may see much of the descriptions of retirement planning options repeated here. Either read on to brush up on the topic or move to the next chapter. Your choice!

Tax-Qualified Retirement Plans for Physicians in Private Practice

The term "qualified retirement plan" (QRP) means that the plan meets the definition of a retirement plan under tax rules, Department of Labor regulations, and the Employee Retirement and Income Security Act (ERISA). A QRP for a private practice may be in the form of a defined benefit plan, profit-sharing plan, money purchase plan, or 401(k). Properly structured plans offer a variety of benefits: you can fully deduct contributions to a traditional QRP, funds within the QRP grow tax-deferred, and (if non-owner employees participate) the funds within a QRP enjoy superior asset protection. Despite the benefits QRPs can offer, though, there are some disadvantages to QRPs that physicians in private practice should understand:

- Mandated maximum annual contributions for defined contribution plans
- Mandatory inclusion of employees who wish to participate
- Potential liability for management of employee funds in the plan
- Controlled group and affiliated service group restrictions
- Penalties for withdrawal before age 59½
- Required distributions beginning at age 72 for traditional plans
- Full ordinary income taxation of distributions from the traditional plan
- Full ordinary income taxation *and* estate taxation of plan balances upon death

In our experience, nearly all physicians in private practice participate in QRPs. The tax deduction is such a strong lure that it often cannot be resisted. For many physician practice owners, however, the cost of contributions for employees and the potential liability for mismanagement of employee funds, as well as the ultimate tax costs on distributions, may outweigh the current tax savings offered by QRPs. If these drawbacks don't convince you to not participate in a QRP, they at least suggest that it would make sense to investigate another type of plan that hedges the QRP as an additional savings vehicle.

This is especially true if you believe that income tax rates, especially the higher marginal rates, will go up over the coming decades. When you use a QRP, you trade today's tax rates on your contribution for the tax rates in effect when you withdraw money from the plan. If rates rise, the QRP might prove not to be a good deal at all. While none of us knows what the future will bring, we do know history: tax rates were much higher than they are today for most of the second half of the twentieth century. Thus, the QRP tax-rate bet is one that it may be wise to hedge against using retirement savings alternatives such as non-qualified plans, which physicians in private practice can implement.

Types of QRPs

Defined contribution plans. The government defines the maximum amount you can contribute each year to a defined contribution plan (you can always contribute less). This provides maximum flexibility. Once your account is funded, it will be up to you to decide how to invest your money. But while the money in that plan is yours, there are strict rules regarding the timing of withdrawals. Typically, you'll face a stiff penalty if you withdraw funds before age 59½ (though there are a few exceptions). The most popular defined contribution plans for medical practices are 401(k)s and profit-sharing plans. In 2020 (the year of publication), the rules allow contributions up to $19,500 for 401(k)s and up to a total of $57,000 for profit-sharing plans for participants under age 50. People age 50 and older can make an additional $6,500 catch-up contribution.

Defined benefit plans. With a defined benefit plan, an actuarial calculation is made to determine the amount of the contribution into the plan based on the benefit that is to be available in retirement. This calculation involves each employee's or owner's current age, planned retirement age, income, and other information. Using such calculations, defined benefit plans often allow much greater annual contributions than defined contribution plans—some physicians are able to contribute $225,000 annually to defined benefit plans.

The price of larger contributions is that, typically, contributions for employees must also be larger. In addition, there is less funding flexibility with these types of plans than with 401(k)s and profit-sharing plans. Nonetheless, structured properly, defined benefit plans can be very valuable for many medical practices. We will delve deeply into one type of plan—a cash balance plan—in the next chapter.

Non-Qualified Plans for Physicians in Private Practice

Many private practice physicians want to save significantly for retirement but are limited by the funding rules and employee costs of QRPs. Non-qualified plans (non-Q plans) can be the solution for many doctors. Because these plans are not subject to QRP rules, non-Q plans do not have to be offered to any employees. Further, even among the physician–owners, there is total flexibility. For example, one doctor could contribute the maximum amount, the next partner could contribute much less, and a third physician could opt out completely.

The main drawback to non-Q plans is that contributions are not tax-deductible. However, they can be structured for tax-free growth and tax-free access in retirement, like a Roth IRA. In fact, a non-Q plan can be an ideal long-term tax hedge against a QRP. Non-Q plans for an employee generally allow a tax deduction at the time the employee has taxable compensation from the plan.

We discuss such plans further in Chapter 3.6.

Benefit Plans for Self-Employed Physicians/Outside Businesses

Physicians who receive income reported on Form 1099 (including doctors who moonlight, work *locum tenens*, or do consulting/speaking in the healthcare industry) and self-employed physicians have other options to help save for retirement.

A SEP IRA is a traditional IRA established under a self-employed pension plan document (often Form 5305-SEP). Physicians can contribute the lesser of $57,000 or 25% of compensation (under the 2020 limits in place at this book's publication). In addition, physicians with a SEP may still be able to contribute to a separate traditional IRA or Roth IRA. As with other traditional IRAs, account balances can grow tax-deferred and are taxed at ordinary income rates when distributed.

In some states, IRAs and QRPs with only one participant are not as well protected from creditors as multi-participant QRPs are. Be sure to consult with an expert before establishing such a plan if asset protection is important to you.

After-Tax IRAs

A traditional IRA allows doctors to defer up to $6,000 per year ($7,000 per year if age 50 plus) into the account (under the 2020 limits in place as we write this). Physicians who are not covered by a workplace retirement plan may deduct pre-tax contributions, while those covered at work can make non-deductible or partially deductible contributions, depending on their earned income and filing status. The non-deductible portion of the account, also known as its "basis," is tracked with each year's tax return on Form 8606. Account balances can grow tax deferred. Qualified withdrawals (excluding the basis) are subject to ordinary income tax while non-qualified withdrawals generally result in a penalty.

Roth IRA contribution limits are the same as traditional IRA limits. Most physicians, however, earn income at levels exceeding adjusted gross income limitations so they are not allowed to contribute directly to a Roth IRA. Doctors can often do a "backdoor" Roth IRA by first contributing to a traditional IRA and then converting the traditional IRA to a Roth IRA. (Note: This tactic requires careful planning to avoid unnecessary taxation. Work with an experienced advisor on this.) Roth IRAs can be very beneficial to long-term retirement planning because funds in a Roth IRA grow tax-deferred and come out tax-free.

A spousal IRA is a traditional IRA or Roth IRA that receives contributions on behalf of a nonearning spouse. In order to contribute, the nonearning spouse must meet the ordinary requirements for making an IRA contribution, but they are not required to have earned income. Instead, the earning physician must make enough income to cover the spouse's contribution. Otherwise, the same IRA contribution limits apply to the spousal IRA.

Life Insurance as a Retirement Plan

Previously, we explained that Roth IRA contributions are made after tax, but then the balances grow tax-free and can be accessed tax-free in the future. Would you be surprised to learn that, if managed properly, a permanent life insurance policy can act the same way? As we described in Chapter 1.2, "permanent" life insurance means policies like whole life, universal life, variable life, and equity indexed life policies. Regardless of the type of product, the cash value of such policies grows tax-free and can be accessed tax-free during the insured's life—and this tax treatment has remained stable for over 100 years.

Certainly, there is a lot of noise and contradictory advice in the marketplace about the strategy of using permanent life insurance. You may have heard people say, "buy term and invest the difference," as we have. Just as physicians with many medicines in their armamentarium, we see permanent life insurance as a "financial medicine" with which some "patients" do very well. On the other hand, we recognize that this "medicine," like actual medicine, has ideal applications and side effects and should be managed properly. We urge you to keep an open mind on this subject as we revisit it in more depth in Chapters 4.2, 4.3 and 4.4.

TAKEAWAY: For nearly all physicians, including those in private practice, getting to retirement on their financial terms is the number one financial goal. To reach that goal, doctors in private practice can leverage a number of tax-favored retirement tools. Each has a role in a wealth management plan.

CHAPTER 3.5

Getting Larger Deductions in Private Practices with Cash Balance Plans

As we said earlier in this Lesson, in our experience, the leading short-term planning goal for most physicians in private practice is to reduce their income taxes. This is not surprising because (1) *everyone* wants to reduce their taxes and (2) exerting some control over tax planning options is one of the reasons physicians want to remain in private practice and resist W-2 employment.

In the last chapter, we provided an overview of all types of benefit plans that physicians can implement in their private practices. This included a discussion of qualified retirement plans (QRPs) that encompassed both defined contribution plans and defined benefit plans. In this chapter, we will discuss cash balance plans (CBPs), a form of defined benefit QRPs. They are a very powerful tax planning tool that many private medical practices have yet to consider.

Cash Balance Plans: Modern Retirement Plans

We refer to CBPs as "modern retirement plans" because their use has been growing rapidly in closely held businesses, including medical practices, in recent years as high-income business/practice owners have looked for tools that can give them large short-term tax deductions along with strong long-term economics.

With the new tax code expressly carving out physicians (along with attorneys, consultants, CPAs, and others) from its most powerful tax benefits, we would not be surprised to see medical practices seek to implement CBPs even more in the coming decade. CBPs are truly one of the few remaining significant tax tools for physicians in 2020 and beyond.

Main Benefits of CBPs for Physician Practice–Owners

There are four leading reasons why physicians in private practice are interested in CBPs:

1.Significantly Increased Deductions for Plan Contributions

As we noted in the previous chapter, 401(k)s are subject to a 2020 maximum deductible contribution limit of $19,500, with the profit-sharing plan limit at $57,000. These limits will increase slightly each year. Properly structured CBPs, on the other hand, allow physicians to make tax-deductible contributions of $200,000 or more, saving them $80,000 to more than $100,000 in taxes annually.

2. Additional Costs That Are Much Less than Additional Tax Savings

CBPs involve higher annual administration costs and, typically, higher employer contribution amounts for employees than 401(k)s or profit-sharing plans. But the tax savings for physicians typically dwarf these additional expenses, making the CBP extremely attractive for many medical practices.

3. A Possible Second Level of Deductibility

For physicians whose income puts them above the new tax code's QBI limits, a CBP can be a tool to reduce taxable income enough to allow them to qualify for the QBI deductions as well—creating one deduction leads to a second deduction. We will further discuss this later in the chapter..

4. Greater Access to the Top (+5) Asset Protection Level

As we explained in Lesson 2, ERISA-qualified QRPs, as exempt assets under federal law and most state laws, are protected at the highest (+5) level. Unless a CBP is put in place for only one physician owner with no other employees, this ERISA protection will generally apply to the CBP as well. With larger contribution levels allowed in the CBP, this means more wealth can be protected in the CBP than in most other QRPs.

Cash Balance Plan Basics

With a CBP, a participating employee will have access to a specified sum upon reaching retirement. We'll use $100,000 as an example. In order get to $100,000 at retirement, the plan assumes a combination of employer contributions and compound interest over time. When the employee retires, they can take the $100,000 either as a lump sum or as an annuity that pays a portion of the $100,000 in periodic payments.

Each participant's account grows annually in two ways:

A benefit credit. The benefit credit is a percentage of pay or a flat dollar amount that is specified in the plan document. The credit is often class-based so that higher dollar or percentage amounts accrue to owners/partners and lower dollar or percentage amounts to staff. This, as one would expect, makes the CBP ideally suited for medical practices—the physicians or partners can be a separate class.

An interest credit. The interest credit is a guaranteed rate of return specified in the plan document and is typically tied to federal long-term interest rates or set at a fixed rate around 5%. The interest credit is not dependent on the plan's actual investment performance, but the plan's investment portfolio should be structured to attempt to perform in line with the anticipated crediting rate.

How Cash Balance Plans Are Similar to and Different from 401(k)s

A CBP is similar to a 401(k) or other QRP in many respects, including rules on employee eligibility, nondiscrimination regulations, timing of deductible contributions, eligibility to roll over into an IRA, and early withdrawal penalties that apply for accessing funds before age 59½.

A CBP is also different from a 401(k) in a number of ways. With a 401(k), an employee makes contributions to a retirement plan. The employer sponsoring the 401(k) may or may not make matching or profit-sharing contributions.

With a 401(k), the amount that the employee will have in retirement is not "defined." Instead, the employee's retirement benefits depend on the performance of their funds in the plan. With a cash balance plan, on the other hand, the amount of money an employee can expect in retirement is "defined." That's what makes it a defined benefit plan! The employer, not the employee, bears the risk of market fluctuations. Also, participation in a CBP does not depend on employees contributing part of their compensation to the plan—contributions by employees are not permitted.

It is certainly costlier to establish and administer a CBP than a 401(k) or profit-sharing plan, the types of plans that most medical practices have in place. This is because the plan's funding must be certified by an actuary each year. However, the tax benefits of the CBP will often significantly exceed the additional cost—this can be modeled out on a case-by-case basis before implementing any new plan.

How Cash Balance Plans Are Similar to and Different from Traditional Defined Benefit Plans

CBPs are similar to traditional defined benefit plans with respect to funding and reporting requirements. Minimum funding standards apply—there is a minimum annual employer contribution that is reported on a CBP's tax Form 5500. An actuary is required to calculate this contribution amount using a reasonable actuarial funding method and actuarial assumptions specified by the IRS. The employer can decide to contribute an amount between the minimum funding requirement and the maximum permitted deduction but should attempt to fund to the actuary's recommended contribution level in order to meet the plan's current benefit liability.

On the other hand, CBPs are different from traditional defined benefit plans that promise a specified monthly benefit amount at retirement (e.g., 3% of pay per year of employment, payable at retirement age of 67). CBPs define benefits in the form of an account balance rather than a periodic amount. This can be helpful because employees always understand what they are entitled to under the CBP—it is a specific amount. Owners and employees both know what is going into the plan on their behalf and what will come out when they leave.

Cash Balance Plans Work Well with 401(k)s

CBPs and 401(k)s are not mutually exclusive. A medical practice can use both types of plans simultaneously. In fact, because so many medical practices already have 401(k) plans in place, physician owners often consider "layering in" a CBP on top of their existing 401(k). Typically, this can be done.

Ideal Practices for a CBP

In general, any medical practice whose physician owners are looking for a tool that provides greater deductible contributions—and that has the necessary cash flow—is a good candidate for a CBP. It is not difficult to model CBP economics for any medical practice. Consequently, we think it makes sense for almost any practice to at least see what the financial model shows.

Beyond this generalization, there are a few situations where a CBP goes from being a home run to a grand slam (yes, baseball analogies!). Examples are practices with older physicians and younger staff, reasonable ratios of physicians to employees, and physicians who have outside business income from moonlighting, speaking, or working with industry.

How a Cash Balance Plan Can Create Two Deductions for the Price of One

Earlier in the chapter we mentioned that for physicians whose income puts them above the new tax code's QBI limits, CBPs can be tools to reduce taxable income enough to qualify for the QBI deductions. In other words, the CBP can create one deduction that leads to a second deduction.

As an example, a physician practice with taxable income above the QBI threshold amount might make a CBP contribution of $200,000 or more, which is deductible from practice taxable income. This reduced practice taxable income could, in turn, reduce the physician's personal taxable income in such a way that it would fall below the threshold amount, so specified service business rules would not apply. The result would be that the physician could take the 20%QBI deduction against net practice income. The tax savings from the combination of CBP deduction and QBI deduction can help pay for the cost of the CBP.

How a CBP Can Create Tax-Free Retirement Income and/or Medical Expense Payments

As we discussed at the outset of this Lesson, tax diversification is fundamental to savvy long-term tax management. Also, as you likely recall, all QRPs are in "Bucket #1," meaning that they are subject to the highest ordinary income tax rates (as opposed to capital gains rates) when they are accessed by the participant. As a QRP, CBPs are subject to this high tax rate upon distribution as well. In that same discussion on tax diversification, we also noted that permanent life insurance is one of the asset classes that provides tax-free accumulation and tax-free access (Bucket #3).

There is a way to use a CBP and permanent life insurance together to achieve a powerful result for the physician. By having some of the funds in the CBP invested in permanent life insurance and then exchanging the policy for cash outside the CBP at the appropriate time, the two tools can be used to give the physician a method for enjoying tax-free accumulation and tax-free access in retirement. This, too, can be modeled at the outset of the plan so appropriate decisions can be made.

In addition to using permanent life insurance with a CBP to provide tax-free retirement income, a portion of CBP funds can be designated to fund a 401(h) account. These accounts are appealing because distributions from them are tax-free when used for qualified healthcare expenses. In this way, part of the CBP can come out tax-free (after a tax deduction and tax-deferred growth) if structured and used properly.

TAKEAWAY: Cash balance plans (CBPs) are powerful planning tools that allow larger contributions than the plans most medical practices are using. CBPs are special types of defined benefit QRPs and may be attractive to practice owners who are looking for larger tax deductions, asset protection, and superior retirement income.

CHAPTER 3.6

Why Many Physicians Should Consider Using Non-Qualified Plans to Reach Retirement Goals

As we have observed, the number one financial goal of nearly all physicians is to get to a financially secure retirement on their own terms, based on their unique timeline and lifestyle goals.

What is surprising (to us anyway) is how many private practice physicians attempt to reach this goal using one tool available to them at the practice—qualified retirement plans (QRPs)—while being completely unaware of another tool they could be using—non-qualified plans (Non-Q plans). In Chapter 3.4, we delved deeply into QRPs; here, we will discuss Non-Q plans.

Qualified Retirement Plan Drawbacks: Why Non-Q Plans Should Be Attractive

While we consider QRPs to be tools that most physicians should implement, they do have a number of significant drawbacks:

- Mandated maximum annual contributions
- Mandatory participation by eligible employees
- Potential liability for management of employee funds in the plan
- Controlled group and affiliated service group restrictions
- Penalties for withdrawal before age 59½
- Required distributions beginning at age 72
- Full ordinary income taxation of distributions

- Full ordinary income taxation *and* estate taxation of plan balances upon death (combined tax rates on these balances can be over 70%)

All of these drawbacks can be avoided with a Non-Q plan as long as a current deduction for contributions is not permitted.

Non-Qualified Plan Basics

Non-Q plans are not used by physicians nearly as much as by corporate executives. This is unfortunate because they could be valuable retirement tools for many doctors. Because they are not subject to QRP rules, Non-Q plans do not have to be offered to any employees. Further, even within the group of physician owners there is total flexibility. For example, one doctor could contribute a maximum amount, the next partner could contribute much less, and a third could opt out entirely.

The main drawback to Non-Q plans is that contributions are never tax deductible. However, they can be structured for tax-free growth and tax-free access in retirement, like a Roth IRA. Ask yourself this: how much would you put in a Roth IRA if there were no funding limitations? If you think you would fund such a vehicle, then a Non-Q plan could be very attractive to you.

In fact, a Non-Q plan can be an ideal long-term tax hedge against a QRP. Beyond these general ground rules, there is tremendous flexibility and variation with Non-Q plan designs. Consider that they have the following attributes:

- No limitations on contributions, unlike QRPs
- Can be implemented in addition to any QRP (such as a 401k or profit-sharing plan)
- Owners/partners can independently choose whether to participate and, if they do, how much they contribute
- Employee participation is not required
- No tax deduction for contributions, but funds can grow tax-free and be accessed tax-free upon withdrawal
- Top asset protection in many states

What Goes into Establishing a Non-Q Plan?

There are several elements that go into the creation of a Non-Q plan for a medical practice:

1. Planning/Modeling/Choosing Funding Vehicle
This is where most of the work in putting a plan together is done. Because each physician has a choice about whether to participate and at what contribution level, each physician essentially can map out their own game plan. This will include choosing the type of product they want to fund their plan into, what type of contributions they plan on making, how many years they will make contributions, how they will build flexibility into their funding schedule, and when they plan to take distributions.

It should be noted that a practice can set up a Non-Q plan that has "golden handcuffs" elements: the practice itself owns the assets in the plan and the executive participant needs to stay at the practice for a term of years or achieve some business results in order to vest into their benefit. If they do not vest, the practice keeps the benefit. This type of "golden handcuffs" plan may make sense for a non-physician, non-owner executive, such as the practice manager or CEO. To incentivize them to lead the practice to certain benchmarks, a Non-Q plan can be much more effective and tax-efficient than a simple bonus plan. However, this is not the type of plan we are describing here.

In a Non-Q plan for physicians, assets are owned individually; that is, each physician owns their plan assets separately from the practice and their other owners.

The amount of money that funds a physician's Non-Q plan comes out of their cash compensation and is treated as if it were paid to them directly. If a physician leaves, they take their plan assets with them as they would any other personally owned asset. There is no vesting or any circumstance where the practice has any rights to any physician's plan assets—they are the physician's from day one.

Many immediate-compensation Non-Q plans for physicians, which we are describing here, fund into a permanent life insurance policy because of its tax treatment. The policy is the funding vehicle and all investment gains grow within the policy. As you will read in Chapters 4.2, 4.3, and 4.4, investments held within such policies can grow tax free and, if managed properly, accessed tax free as well. Understanding how such policies work is crucial to understanding the economics of Non-Q plans that use them. We encourage you to read these chapters if Non-Q plans are of interest.

2. Agreement

Once each physician has modeled out their contribution level, time horizon, product choice, and other factors—or decided to opt out of the plan—then a simple agreement needs to be in place at the practice.

This agreement will spell out the roles of the employee and the employer. It will describe any fees associated with the plan and how and by whom those fees will be covered, and it will lay out the practicalities of how contributions are handled through payroll.

3. Funding

Each physician will determine their contribution schedule. For some, it may be monthly or bi-weekly, while others could decide to make contributions to their plan once a year. Often, contributions go directly from the practice into the funding vehicle as a "forced" savings system, similar to how many practices handle physicians' QRP contributions.

4. Regular Reviews

Unlike a QRP, which should be reviewed regularly at both the practice level (for fees and potential liability traps and conflicts as described in Chapter 3.7) and personal level (for individual investment performance), Non-Q plan reviews are done by each physician with their advisor to look at their specific Non-Q plan assets and performance. Typically, no employees other than physicians participate, and each doctor has an individually owned policy that does not affect other physicians. Further, because all contributions come out of the physician's compensation, the practice itself has no investment whatsoever. Nevertheless, for the individual physician, annual reviews of the policy's performance are crucial for all of the reasons we describe in Chapter 4.4 in relation to permanent life insurance.

Non-Q Plans as a Hedge for QRPs

At the outset of this Lesson, we described the importance of tax diversification to long-term wealth management. This focus on diversification is important for all physicians, especially those who believe that income tax rates, especially the higher marginal rates, will go up over the coming decades. When you use a QRP, you trade today's tax rates on your contribution for the tax rates in the future when you withdraw money from the plan. If rates rise in the future, the QRP balances are worth less to you in retirement than if rates remain the same. Therefore, it may be wise to hedge against the QRP "tax rate trade" using retirement savings alternatives such as Non-Q plans, which can be designed to grow tax-free and be accessed tax-free in retirement.

Case Study: A 20-Doctor Multi-Specialty Group Considers a Non-Q Plan

We were approached by a 20-physician multi-specialty group after they read one of our books for a review of their tax planning, from their corporate structure to their QRP to tools that they had yet to consider. One of those tools was the Non-Q plan. After we presented the concept to the group, five to seven of the physicians were very interested in participating in such a plan. Because the annual administrative costs for the plan were low (around $1,000 per year), as long as one or two physicians participated there would be absolutely no cost for the non-participating physicians. The practice was in favor of moving forward with a Non-Q plan since it cost the non-participating doctors nothing and each physician who wanted to participate funded it out of their income and paid a fraction of the deductible plan expense each year (a few hundred dollars).

For illustrative purposes, we will show what the financial proposals for a few of the physicians looked like, including comparisons of a Non-Q plan and the type of investment they already had in place. In other words, we compared "doing the plan" with each physician's *status quo* on their post-tax investment plans.

We have chosen three doctors of different ages, participation levels, genders, and investment risk tolerances. This will give you a good overview of how a Non-Q plan can be beneficial for a range of physicians. All three physicians were proposed a permanent life insurance policy from a top-rated mutual insurance carrier. For more on what this means, including why mutual carriers may be more attractive than stock companies, see Chapter 4.4.

Doctor 1: 52-year old man

This physician planned to contribute $100,000 annually to the plan and was a conservative investor. He told us that if he didn't go forward with the plan he would allocate the funds to a conservative portfolio where he expected to generate a 6% annual return. On the conservative portfolio, he paid his investment advisor 100 basis points (bps) (1%), the underlying funds had a 50-bps fee, and it generated about a 100-bps tax drag. Also, as one of the higher-income physicians in the practice, his income tax rate was around 40% when both federal and state taxes were considered.

Given his conservative investment outlook, Doctor 1 opted for a whole life policy. As you can read more about in Chapter 4.2, whole life is the most conservative of the permanent life insurance policy structures because it grows with the general account of the insurance company, which is highly regulated and invested primarily in bonds and mortgages. For Doctor 1, this type of policy most closely matched his conservative portfolio.

Assuming that he either contributed $100,000 each year for ten years into his conservative portfolio or this policy through the with a Non-Q plan since it cost the non-participating doctors nothing and each physician who wanted to participate funded it out of their income and paid a fraction of the deductible plan expense each year (a few hundred dollars). Non-Q plan, and assuming the conservative portfolio's 6% return and the whole life policy's current growth rate (called "dividend rate") of 6.1%, we then compared the income each option would generate for retirement, specifically from ages 65 to 84.

While the doctor's conservative portfolio would spin off $57,585 of annual after-tax income, the whole policy within the Non-Q plan would generate $68,096 annually. This equated to an 18% improvement on annual income, for a total improvement of $210,100 over 20 years. Also, in this state, the policy's cash value was entirely protected from creditors as an exempt (+5) asset. Finally, this physician strongly believed that his tax rate would increase in the future and he wanted to hedge against that possibility with at least one asset class in his portfolio. For these reasons, Doctor 1 chose to move forward.

Doctor 2: 47-year old woman

This physician planned to contribute $50,000 annually to the plan and was a balanced investor. She told us that if she didn't go forward with the plan, she would allocate the funds to a balanced portfolio where she expected to generate a 7% annual return. She paid her investment advisor 1%, the underlying investments themselves had a 50-bps cost, and the portfolio generated about a 1% tax drag. She was in the middle of the group in terms of productivity and her income tax rate was around 35% when both federal and state taxes were considered.

Given her investment outlook, Doctor 2 opted for an equity-indexed universal life (EIUL) policy. As you can read more about in Chapter 4.2, EIUL is a very interesting and popular permanent life insurance policy structure because it grows with an equity index such as the S&P 500 stock index but has a floor (below which it cannot go, in terms of annual return) and a cap (which it cannot exceed). For Doctor 2's specific EIUL policy, the floor was 1% and the cap was 10.25%. For Doctor 2, this type of policy was attractive due to its stock market participation and downside protection.

Assuming that she contributed $50,000 each year for ten years into either her portfolio or this policy through the Non-Q plan, and assuming the portfolio's 7% return and a 6% annual return in the EIUL policy, we then compared what income each option would generate for retirement, specifically from ages 65 to 84.

While the doctor's portfolio would spin off $54,980 of annual after-tax income, the EIUL policy within the Non-Q plan would generate $85,103 annually – even with a lower assumed annual return in the EIUL policy. This equated to a 54% improvement on annual income, for a total improvement of $602,460 over 20 years. Also, per above, in this state, the policy's cash value was entirely protected from creditors as an exempt (+5) asset. For these reasons, Doctor 2 was excited to move forward.

Doctor 3: 35-year old man

This young physician planned to contribute $25,000 annually to the plan and was an aggressive investor. He told us that if he didn't go forward with the plan, he would allocate the funds to a stock-based portfolio where he expected to generate an 8% annual return. He paid his investment advisor 1%, the underlying investments themselves had a 50-bps cost, and the portfolio generated about a 1% tax drag. As the youngest physician in the group, his income was on the low end and his income tax rate was around 30% when both federal and state taxes were considered.

Given his investment outlook, Doctor 3 opted for the same EIUL policy as Doctor 2. For Doctor 3, this type of policy was attractive due to its stock market participation, but he also appreciated downside protection, which his other investments did not enjoy.

Assuming that he contributed $25,000 each year for ten years either into his portfolio or this policy through the Non-Q plan, and assuming the portfolio's 8% return and a 6% annual return in the EIUL policy, we then compared what income each option would generate for retirement, specifically from ages 65 to 84. With an assumed annual 8% return, Doctor 3's stock-based portfolio would spin off $76,938 of annual after-tax income, while the EIUL policy within the Non-Q plan would generate $121,316 annually, assuming only a 6% annual return. This equated to a 58% improvement on annual income, for a total improvement of $887,560 over 20 years. In this state, per above, the policy's cash value was totally protected from creditors as an exempt (+5) asset. For these reasons, Doctor 3 was also excited to move forward.

DOCTOR 1	DOCTOR 2	DOCTOR 3
MALE	FEMALE	MALE
53 YEARS OLD	47 YEARS OLD	35 YEARS OLD
GOOD HEALTH	GREAT HEALTH	GREAT HEALTH
$100,000 FOR 7 YEARS	$50,000 FOR 10 YEARS	$25,000 FOR 10 YEARS
40% COMBINED TAX RATE	35% COMBINED TAX RATE	30% COMBINED TAX RATE
CONSERVATIVE INVESTOR	MODERATE INVESTOR	AGGRESSIVE INVESTOR

HYPOTHETICAL ANNUAL NET DISTRIBUTIONS FROM AGES 65-84		
WHOLE LIFE: $68,096	INDEXED UL: $85,103	INDEXED UL: $121,316
BOND PORTFOLIO: $57,585	BALANCED PORTFOLIO: $54,980	AGGRESSIVE PORTFOLIO: $76,938
ANNUAL IMPROVEMENT: $10,511	ANNUAL IMPROVEMENT: $30,123	ANNUAL IMPROVEMENT: $44,378
TOTAL IMPROVEMENT: $210,100	**TOTAL IMPROVEMENT: $602,460**	**TOTAL IMPROVEMENT: $887,560**

Figure 3.6.1

TAKEAWAY: Most private practice physicians use qualified retirement plans (QRPs) to get to their retirement goals, yet so many are completely unaware of another tool they could be using: non-qualified plans (Non-Q plans). Non-Q plans avoid many of the drawbacks of QRPs and can be a great long-term hedge against the "tax trade" of QRPs.

CHAPTER 3.7

Avoiding High Fees, Conflicts, and Potential Liability In Your Practice's Qualified Retirement Plan

For physicians in private practice, qualified retirement plans (QRPs) can be extremely valuable tools. As we have described earlier in this Lesson and in previous Lessons, QRPs can provide current and future tax benefits, the highest level of asset protection, a forced savings vehicle, and a tax diversification tactic. However, QRPs can also create liability for the practice and physician owners personally. Moreover, because of the various parties involved in QRP management, many practices overpay fees and are harmed by conflicts among their advisors, all without the physicians realizing anything is wrong.

In this chapter, we will look at the potential pitfalls of QRPs and give tips on how they can be avoided.

A Time of Expanding Liability for Employers

During the last five years before the publication of this book in 2020, many medical practices became aware of the issue of potential liability related to their retirement plans. Perhaps this is because many well-known companies and even universities, such as those in the following examples, were hit with significant lawsuits for their alleged failings in this area. Here are some leading examples:

- General Electric 401(k) participants sued over poorly performing GE Asset Management funds. The lawsuit alleges that five funds managed by GE Asset Management during the period January 1, 2011, through June 30, 2016, caused harm to plan participants due to underperformance.

- A Novitex 401(k) plan participant sued over alleged fiduciary breaches, among other claims. The suit accuses Novitex of failing to fully disclose the expenses and risks of the plan's investment options to participants, resulting in "unreasonable expenses" being charged to participants for plan administration.
- A participant in the Gucci America, Inc. Retirement and Savings Plan accused the plan sponsor and its benefits committee of breaching fiduciary duties, including charging excessive administrative and investment fees to plan participants and "selecting and retaining opaque, high-cost, and poor-performing investments instead of other available and more prudent alternative investments."
- The University of Chicago agreed to pay $6.5 million to settle a class action lawsuit alleging that it failed to comply with its fiduciary duty to employees in ways that forced them to pay excessive fees to their retirement plan.

Note that in all these examples the employer was named in the lawsuit or paid the settlement. This is fundamental to understand because, as the employer, the company/university/medical practice has an inherent fiduciary duty to its employees. It must put employees' best interests first when managing their QRPs, including in how it chooses the firm to run the plan and how it periodically reviews those services.

A medical practice is exposed to this risk (among many others). Often, risks can be offset through the development of best practices and use of tools such as insurance. A retirement plan is no different. Ensuring that you have a detailed process is an important step in limiting the potential liability to which the practice owners, trustees, and underlying investment committee are exposed. It is important to know your role as a fiduciary to the employees of your practice.

Money damages for a breach of your fiduciary role in managing the plan can be substantial. According to Section 409 of the Employee Retirement Income Security Act (ERISA), "any person who is a fiduciary with respect to a plan who breaches any of the responsibilities, obligations or duties imposed upon fiduciaries by this title shall be personally liable to make good to such plan any losses to the plan resulting from each such breach, and to restore to such plan any profits of such fiduciary which have been made through use of assets of the plan by the fiduciary."

A civil action may be brought by a participant or beneficiary, or by another fiduciary. Even if a trustee delegates some of their fiduciary duties to others, the trustee is not relieved of fiduciary responsibilities because the trustee is obligated to monitor the performance of those to whom the duties have been delegated.

QRP Management 101

These are the key players involved in the ongoing management of a qualified plan:

Plan Sponsor/Trustee/Retirement Plan Committee

In a medical practice, the plan sponsor is typically the medical practice itself, the trustee(s) are one or more of the owners of the practice, and every practice will have a retirement committee, even if it is just one person. To identify these parties, one should refer to the retirement plan's plan document or summary plan document.

As fiduciaries under the plan, the primary responsibilities of these parties are the following:

1. Provide sufficient asset classes with different and distinct risk/return profiles so each participant can judiciously diversify their account
2. Prudently select investment options
3. Control and account for all investment, recordkeeping, and administrative expenses associated with the plan
4. Monitor and supervise all service vendors and investment options
5. Prepare and maintain an investment policy statement
6. Avoid prohibited transactions and conflicts of interest

Investment Consultant/Advisor

If it is following best practices, the retirement plan committee retains an objective, third-party consultant/advisor (the "advisor") to assist the committee in managing the overall investment process. The advisor will be responsible for guiding the committee through a disciplined and rigorous investment process to enable the committee to meet the fiduciary responsibilities outlined above. The specific duties and responsibilities of the advisor are the following:

1. Advise the committee about the selection of asset classes
2. Recommend investment managers for each asset class and monitor their performance
3. Provide the committee with quarterly reports
4. Communicate with the committee at least annually to review the investment policy statement objectives and evaluate the performance of plan investment options with respect to these objectives
5. Handle plan participant enrollment and education

Recordkeeper and Third-Party Administrator

The recordkeeper and third-party administrator is responsible for maintaining individual account balances, including these specific duties:

1. Maintain, update, and reconcile individual account balances
2. Process contributions, distributions, investment election changes, and transfers
3. Create and distribute quarterly plan and participant statements
4. Complete annual compliance testing and reporting
5. Provide an interface between the plan and the custodian

Custodian

Custodians are responsible for the safekeeping of the plan's assets. The specific duties and responsibilities of the custodian are the following:

1. Maintain separate accounts by legal registration
2. Value the holdings
3. Collect all income and dividends owed to the plan
4. Settle all transactions (buy–sell orders)
5. Provide periodic reports that detail transactions, cash flows, securities held and their current value, and change in value of each security and of the overall portfolio since the previous report

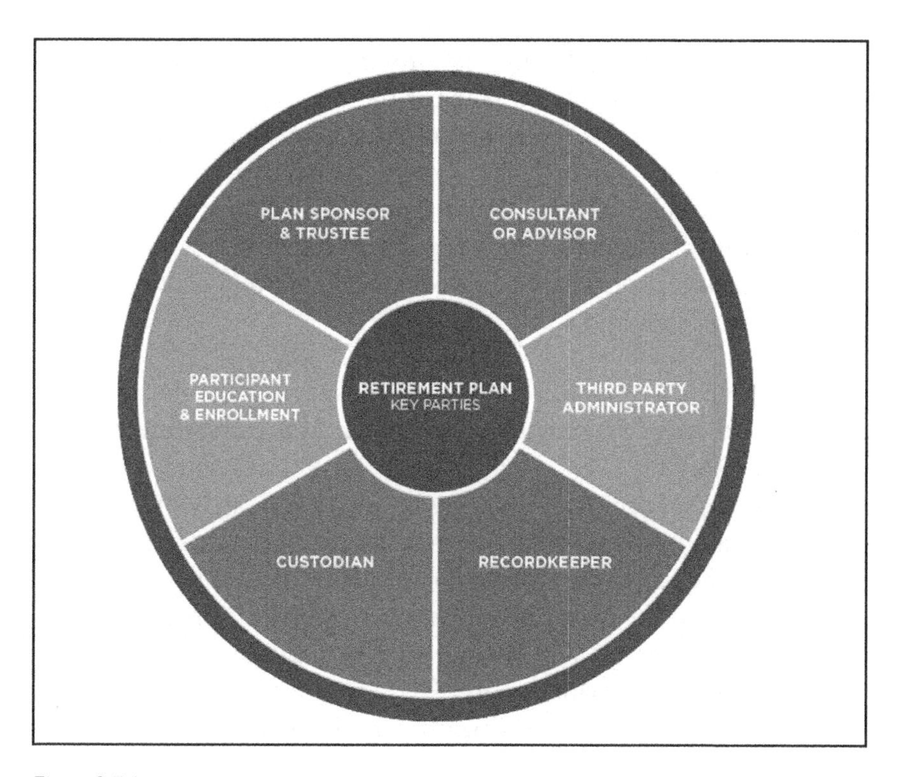

Figure 3.7.1

Common Pitfalls of Many Medical Practice QRPs

The practice pays too much in fees for recordkeeping, third-party administration, or investment advisory services.

Many QRPs are either paying far too much in fees or aren't getting much for the fees they are paying. Some fees are disguised in the underlying fund ratios from which the service providers are reimbursed. It is important that the trustees and practice managers overseeing these plans fully understand the plan design, the fees the plan is paying, and the role of each underlying party. A plan that fails to monitor any of these elements can expose the company to possible lawsuits.

One way to circumvent this potential service and fee issue is by having an independent company facilitate periodic benchmarking reviews. These reviews are compiled using third-party information to evaluate the services provided to a plan for the fees being charged and relate those services to other similar plans in a benchmark group. Not only will the benchmarking review help the plan meet its fiduciary responsibility, it can also save the company and participants money, identify substandard service providers, and improve the plan design and features.

There is a potential conflict of interest between the third-party administrator and the in-house investment advisor.

Despite recent technological advances and widespread access to low-cost index investing, many QRPs still include expensive mutual fund lineups or lack key elements of the major investment asset classes. A plan that has an average mutual fund expense ratio over 1 percent is probably paying too much.

These higher fees typically arise from an inherent conflict of interest when a plan chooses to bundle their third-party administrator, investment advisor, and recordkeeper. (The term "bundle" means that all three roles fall under one company relationship.) Such combined services can allow potential conflicts to flourish, as the investment advisor may have in-house or proprietary funds to use inside the plan. The real question becomes, "Is the advisor or firm paid more for having these funds inside the investment lineup?" (The answer is often yes, especially when a lineup is lacking significant low-cost options.)

Trustees and practice managers need to understand how each party is being paid, as that will often drive behavior. This information can easily be obtained through the annual 408(b)(2) disclosure required by ERISA. Transparency of fees is vital in today's regulatory environment.

The plan is lacking a robust investment fund lineup, or the fund lineup is too expensive.

There is a fine line between not having enough investment options in a retirement plan and having too many. For example, having ten large-cap value funds on the platform doesn't make a lot of sense considering the participants will have a difficult time choosing which one is right for them. On the other hand, offering only one fund is also a problem.

As an example of a middle ground, a low-cost passive fund could be offered along with a more expensive actively managed fund that aims to outperform the underlying index benchmark. This approach provides each participant with the flexibility to choose the option that fits their comfort level. We also recommend that a plan's fund lineup includes target-date retirement funds, which can serve as a one-stop investment option for participants.

There is no co-fiduciary to share potential liability for the plan and its management.

Medical practices, as employers, have a fiduciary duty to their employees to prudently manage the QRP. If they do not, they can face significant liability, as the University of

Chicago did. Without a financial firm acting as a co-fiduciary (as explained below), the practice and its physicians are "on their own" if any liability is found.

How to Lessen Your Practice's Liability

A medical practice should consider various means of limiting personal exposure for claimed breaches of fiduciary duty. Aside from establishing robust procedural prudence, here are other approaches to help mitigate fiduciary liability:

- Secure fiduciary liability insurance to cover losses from the acts or omissions of plan fiduciaries. (This doesn't cover fraudulent acts and doesn't satisfy ERISA bonding requirements.) This coverage is different than the required fidelity bond in that it protects only the retirement plan. Fidelity bonds permit recourse by the insurer against a trustee who engages in a breach of fiduciary duty.
- Delegate responsibility for investment decisions to an investment manager. This can be accomplished through a 3(21) co-fiduciary role or the 3(38) designation, which provides sole discretionary decision-making authority to a third-party investment manager.
    1. A 3(21) investment advisor works with the trustees of the plan to recommend the investment lineup for the plan but doesn't have discretion over plan investments. If you prefer to maintain control of your plan's investments, you will want to work with a 3(21) advisor.
    2. If your goal is to fully limit your fiduciary liability, choose a 3(38) investment advisor, who will have discretion and authority to manage the fund lineup.
- Allocate certain duties to others in accordance with plan procedures so that the scope of the trustees' duties is reduced. For example, a person who is not a trustee

may be designated as a fiduciary responsible for the participant loan program. (This is typically accomplished through an investment committee.)

- Allow participants to make their own investment decisions. If participant investment direction is implemented in accordance with Section 404(c) of ERISA, the trustees will be relieved of liability for the participant's investment decisions as to the participant's account. (Section 404(c) of ERISA requires the plan to give participants a choice of at least three investment alternatives that are diversified and have materially different risk and return characteristics.)
- Conduct regular trustees' meetings, keep meeting minutes, and document the basis for any changes made, particularly investment decisions and decisions concerning applications for participant loans.

Best Practice: Have Your QRP Reviewed

It is imperative that you periodically have a third-party firm review and identify potential issues in your QRP, as this analysis can identify material areas that are substandard. Establishing this process, in addition to the other actions recommended above, will help to reduce practice or personal liability for any potential breach of duty. Maintaining and reviewing key advisory relationships that help your practice navigate the complex qualified retirement plan world should provide some additional peace of mind. Most importantly, an audit of your plan through an independent benchmark study will allow you to better understand the fees you are paying and the services being offered to your employees.

TAKEAWAY: QRPs are important planning tools for all of the reasons explained in other chapters. However, as we described here, they can also create liability for the practice and its physicians and are rife with the potential for high fees and advisors' conflicts of interest. There are several important steps a practice can take to avoid these pitfalls, the most important of which is to have the plan independently audited periodically.

CHAPTER 3.8

Small Insurance Companies: What to Do Now

Physicians in private medical practices, as well as practice executives, are often looking for ways to protect the practice from potential claims, reduce risks, and reduce taxes. That is why small insurance companies (SMICs), often referred to as "captives" or "closely held insurance companies," have been popular planning tools for the last twenty years. In fact, those authorized under tax section 831(b) can trace their structure back to at least 1986.

However, in recent years, including the year of publication of this book (2020), we have seen several potential changes, both good and bad, in how these companies are being looked at by the federal government. This chapter provides an update on the changes affecting SMICs as of the time of publication.

What Is a Small Insurance Company?

The SMIC we will discuss here is a properly licensed, U.S.-based insurance company domiciled in one of the states that have special legislation for small insurance companies. While some advisors promote insurance arrangements in small international jurisdictions to take advantage of lower creation and maintenance costs, most domicile SMICs in the United States in one of the states that has special SMIC legislation. There are about twelve such states.

SMIC as a Risk Management Tool

A SMIC must always be established with a real insurance purpose, although it may also confer significant tax benefits. There are requirements for an insurance company to be a facility for transferring risk and protecting assets. Practitioners who specialize in this area have found ways to maximize long-term profit while reducing unnecessary risk under the insurance statutes. How risk is managed and how much risk can be insured in a captive will be answered based on your particular situation.

Specifically, clients can use a SMIC to supplement their existing insurance policies. A SMIC can insure deductibles, copayments, and excluded risks. Such "excess" protection gives the client the security of knowing that the company and its owners will not be wiped out by a legal judgment exceeding traditional coverage limits. You could think of a SMIC as a tax-efficient, asset-protected war chest to cover potential future losses.

Most doctors are acutely aware of the risk of a medical malpractice claim, but there are many other risks to doctors as employers and recipients of insurance (and Medicare). A SMIC can be used to protect the doctor and practice from employment liability claims, insurance audits, violation-of-HIPAA claims, and a variety of other risks that depend on your practice size, revenue, number of employees, and other factors. This protection can be of significant value and potentially very profitable to the SMIC if you manage risk well. In some instances, a SMIC may even allow the client to reduce existing insurance, as the SMIC policy will provide additional coverage.

Some doctors choose to use a SMIC to provide flexibility by using customized policies not easily found in the commercial space. For example, you may desire a liability policy that would pay your legal fees (and allow full choice of attorney) but not provide any benefit to creditors or claimants (what we call "shallow pockets" policies). This prevents the client from being a "deep pocket" (a prime lawsuit target).

Recent Changes Regarding the Taxation of SMICs

A number of important changes in the tax treatment of SMICs have occurred in the years leading up to the publication of this book. If your practice uses a SMIC, you should be well aware of these changes from your insurance manager and tax advisors. If you are considering using a SMIC, make sure you work with insurance managers and tax professionals to understand these issues.

2015 Statute Impacting SMICs

In December 2015, Congress passed and President Obama signed a so-called tax-extenders bill, H.R. 34, which included Section 262 entitled "Modifications to Alternative Tax for Certain Small Insurance Companies." This law, effective January 1, 2017, increased the potential annual exclusion for an 831(b) SMIC from $1.2 million to $2.2 million—the first such increase in thirty years. It was also indexed to inflation. This was seen in the captive industry as a great boon to SMICs.

While this law expanded the annual premium limit, it also codified a restrictive ruling as to who can own 831(b) SMICs. In the past, many SMICs were owned by estate planning vehicles for future generations, such as trusts and family-owned limited liability companies. The law limited the ability of a SMIC to have different types of owners than insured companies, virtually eliminating such estate planning options going forward. As a result, many clients with such estate planning tools in place had to remediate their structures or close them and potentially open new SMIC structures that were compliant with the law.

Notice Requirements Impacting SMICs

In November 2016, the IRS issued Notice 2016-66, which affected SMICs and their owners and advisors. This notice, while stating that 831(b) SMIC structures can be legitimate structures, deemed such tools "transactions of interest." This "transaction of interest" designation required clients and advisors involved with 831(b) SMIC arrangements that meet the criteria in the Notice to file Form 8886, "Reportable Transaction Disclosure Statement," or Form 8918, "Material Advisor Disclosure Statement." As one would imagine, the idea of having to file special notices to the IRS troubles many clients, even if their attorneys, CPAs, and captive managers feel that this is a positive development allowing the industry to weed out abusive players.

SMICs Listed on the IRS's "Dirty Dozen" List

Each year, the IRS publishes a list of "dirty dozen" transactions or tactics about which the IRS attempts to warn the public. SMICs taxed under code section 831(b) have been part of the list for a number of years. See the IRS's 2019 press release here: https://www.irs.gov/newsroom/abusive-tax-shelters-trusts-conservation-easements-make-irs-2019-dirty-dozen-list-of-tax-scams-to-avoid.

Taxpayers with SMICs Lose Three Court Cases

In the last two years, three different court cases have been decided in Tax Court involving 831(b) SMICs. While the cases may be appealed by the taxpayer, the IRS has won all three cases in Tax Court, with the court rendering judgments dictating that back taxes and interest be paid. Specifically, in 2017, the U.S. Tax Court disallowed the "wholly unreasonable" premium deductions the taxpayer had claimed under a section 831(b) arrangement, concluding that the arrangement was not "insurance" under long established law. (Avrahami v. Commissioner, 149 T.C. No. 7 (2017).) In 2018, the Tax Court concluded that the transactions in a SMIC structure were not "insurance." (Reserve Mechanical Corp. v. Commissioner, T.C. Memo. 2018-86.) Finally, in the Syzygy case (Syzygy Ins. Co. v. CIR, T.C. Memo. 2019-34 (April 10, 2019), the Tax Court determined the SMIC did not constitute insurance in the commonly accepted sense and its 831(b) election was invalid.

What To Do Now: You Don't Have a SMIC

As discussed above, 831(b) SMICs are still part of the tax code and the 2015 favorable statute is still the law of the land. On the other hand, the new reporting requirements and recent losses in Tax Court may prove to have a chilling effect on clients considering implementation of a new SMIC because many clients may not want to step into an environment where they will need to send a disclosure to the IRS about their "transaction of interest" while fellow SMIC owners are losing challenges in Tax Court.

For many medical practices, their tax advisors may recommend a wait-and-see approach focusing on monitoring future tax court cases. The hope is that, over the next few years, the taxpayer wins some cases and advisors can, from the various decisions, get a clearer pathway on what is allowed and what is not.

What To Do Now: You Already Have a SMIC

According to our discussions with captive insurance managers, many SMIC owners are now seriously considering closing their SMICs. Others are relying on their tax advisors and captive managers to keep their structure in place, confident that they are "doing it right."

If a physician or practice decides to shut down their SMIC, typically, there are two stages in this process:

1. **Revoking the SMIC's insurance license.** This is done with the local insurance department and may take months. Once the license is revoked and all outstanding requirements are fulfilled, the SMIC is no longer an insurance company. It then becomes a regular corporation under tax law. Typically, SMICs are set up as C corporations, so, once revoked, the entity is a regular C corporation.

2. **Determining what to do with the C corporation, including how to access funds.** Once the former SMIC is a "regular" C corporation, the owners have a variety of strategies to access the funds that have been accumulating. The strategies will depend on many factors including:

    - The need for liquidity for owners to spend for retirement or other lifestyle needs today, in the near future, and years out
    - The interest of owners in charitable planning and/or estate planning
    - The age and health of the owners
    - The interest of owners in tax-favored retirement income
    - Various others

The bottom line: there are several strategies that can be employed to leverage the funds built up in the former SMIC, and some are particularly tax-savvy. Like any sophisticated tax, charitable, or estate planning technique, such strategies are recommended to clients based on their particular facts, circumstances, and goals. Working with estate planning and tax advisors is fundamental to the process.

> **TAKEAWAY:** Because successful medical practices desire risk management and asset protection, consideration of the benefits of SMICs over the past two decades has been done with good reason. However, given the current state of tax issues surrounding SMICs, a wait-and-see approach may now be prudent for those considering the structure. Additionally, because of these tax issues, many physicians who have SMICs in place are looking at exit strategies.

LESSON 4

Using Insurance Effectively to Protect the Family and Build Wealth

In their prime practice years, most doctors will make many important decisions regarding insurances – especially disability, life and long-term care coverage. Unfortunately, many physicians make poor decisions when it comes to insurance because they do not understand the available product choices or are guided by less-than-ideal salespeople.

This Lesson explains the different options available for physicians when it comes to all three types of insurance, beginning with disability insurance. We then explain the various life insurance product choices and discuss why permanent life insurance may or may not make sense for a physician. We also offer case studies and success factors on how to make life insurance work best for a doctor and his or her family. We conclude with a chapter covering long-term care planning.

CHAPTER 4.1
Paying Bills Even if You Can't Work: Disability Insurance

We covered the topic of disability insurance in Chapter 1.2 for young physicians in training or the early years of practice, but we think it is an important enough topic to dedicate another short chapter to it. Many of you reading this now, in fact, may have skipped over Lesson 1 and we don't want you to miss this critical topic.

The probability of a disability over one's working life (ages 20–67) is 27.7%, according to the Social Security Administration.[1]

The reality is that inadequate disability income insurance coverage can be more costly to a physician's family than death, divorce, or a lawsuit. Responsible financial planning includes planning for the best possible future while protecting against the worst possible events. No one ever plans to become disabled, but half of 25-year-olds will have a disability of three months or longer at least once in their lives. This chapter explains not only why you need disability insurance but also what to look for in a disability policy.

The Need for Disability Insurance

The disability of the family breadwinner can be more financially devastating to a family than premature death, although both result in the breadwinner being unable to provide any income for the family. The difference is that a deceased earner is no longer an expense to the family, but if disabled, he or she needs to be fed, clothed, and cared for by medical professionals or family members. In many cases, the medical care alone can cost hundreds of

[1] https://www.ssa.gov/oact/NOTES/ran6/an2018-6.pdf

dollars per day. In short, with a disability, income drops or ends *and* expenses increase. This can be a devastating turn of events that can lead to creditor problems and even bankruptcy.

If you are older (near retirement) and have saved a large enough sum of money to immediately fund a comfortable retirement, then you probably don't need disability income protection. (Of course, you may have some long-term care concerns—that topic is covered in Chapter 4.5.) On the other hand, if you are under 50 years of age, or if you are older than 50 and have several pre-college-age children, significant debt (like a mortgage), or insufficient savings for retirement, you should consider *the right* disability insurance a necessity. The challenge is determining what type of disability income policy is right for you.

Employer-Provided Coverage is Often Inadequate

If you are an employee of a university, hospital, or other large corporation, your employer may provide long-term disability coverage. The premiums are probably discounted from what you would pay for a private policy. We advise you to take a good look at what the employer-offered policy covers and buy a private policy if you and the insurance professional on your advisory team decide you need it. For many people, this makes a lot of sense because employer-provided group policies are often inadequate. They may limit either the term of the coverage or the amount of benefits paid. For instance, benefits may last only a few years or benefit payments may represent only a small part of your annual compensation. Furthermore, since this is an employer-paid benefit, the money received during your disability will be taxable to you as income. For most of you, this would result in taking home less than half of your normal paycheck!

Give Yourself a Checkup

As just mentioned, most people with employer-provided disability insurance coverage will find the benefits inadequate. To determine where your existing coverage is lacking, we suggest that you give yourself an insurance checkup and answer the following questions:

- How long does the disability coverage last?
- How much is the benefit? (Some plans have a $5,000-per-month cap.)

- What percentage of your income is covered? (Generally, you cannot receive more than 60% of your pre-disability income and the benefit may be capped at $20,000, depending on your age). Though most group LTD plans are good for the purpose they serve, they are only a partial cure. Because of the cap, they have a built–in discrimination against higher-income employees—like you!
- Who pays the premiums? (Tip: If you pay the premiums from your personal funds rather than as a deductible expense through your business or practice, your benefits will be tax-free.) You may be seduced by the income tax deductibility of the premiums, but an extra tax burden today is much easier to swallow than a disability, with significantly reduced income and higher expenses, will be. When you and your family need the money the most, you will have more.
- Is the policy portable, or convertible, to an individual policy if you leave the group? If so, will you maintain your reduced group rate?
- If your business distributes all earnings from the corporation at year's end as bonuses to owners/partners (which C corporations typically do in order to avoid double taxation), you should find out whether these bonuses are covered by the group policy. If not, and if bonuses or commissions make up a substantial part of your income (which we have seen to be the case with many people), you'll probably need supplemental coverage.
- What is the definition of "disability" in the group policy? Own occupation, any occupation, or income replacement? (Please see the discussion of these three terms below.)
- Are your overhead expenses covered if you are disabled? If you can't perform your duties at work, will the business keep paying you? If you can't generate income for the business, that won't stop many of your expenses from piling up, will it? For professionals, a business overhead expense policy also covers hiring

an outside professional to replace the insured during disability for up to two years.

When you work with the insurance professional on your advisory team, keep these questions in mind. They will help you better compare coverage options from different companies so that you can find the best policy for your specific circumstances and goals.

Getting the Best Insurance Coverage for the Money

Now that you have given yourself a checkup and realize that you may need a new or supplemental disability insurance policy, you need to know what to look for in order to get the best coverage available at a reasonable rate. The following questions are important for you to ask when considering a disability policy.

What is the benefit amount? Most policies cap the benefit amount at 60% of income. Some states and insurance companies have monthly maximums as well. You must ask yourself how much money your family would need if you were to become disabled. Generally, you want to find companies that offer at least 60% of pre-disability after-tax income with maximums of at least $7,500 or $10,000 monthly. There are additional monthly benefits of $5,000 to $25,000 per month available through specialized channels for high earners who want more monthly income than is available with traditional policies.

What is the waiting period? This is the period of time that you must be disabled before the insurance company will pay you disability benefits. The longer the waiting period before benefits kick in, the less your premium will be. Essentially, the waiting period serves as a deductible relative to time—you cover your expenses during the waiting period and then the insurance company steps in from that point forward. This is not unlike the deductible you have on your car insurance except that auto insurance deductibles are in the form of amounts paid ($100, $250, $500, etc.) rather than being relative to time. If you have adequate sick leave, short-term disability, and an emergency fund, and you can support a longer waiting period, choose a policy with a longer waiting period to save money. Though waiting periods can last as long as 730 days, a 90-day waiting period may give you the best coverage for your money.

How long will coverage last? It's a good idea to get coverage that lasts until age 65, when Social Security payments will begin. Be aware that many policies cover you for only two to five years. Unless you are 62 to 65 years old, this would be insufficient because most people want coverage that pays them until age 65. Unless you are so young that you haven't yet worked long enough to qualify for Social Security, a policy that provides life-time benefits, at costly premiums, is generally not worth the added expense.

What is the definition of "disability" in your policy? Definitions vary from insurance company to insurance company and even from policy to policy within the same company. The definition of "disability" used in a particular policy is of the utmost importance. The main categories are own occupation, any occupation, and loss of income. Own-occupation policies, which pay a benefit if you can't continue your own occupation (even if you can and do work in another occupation after the disability), are the most comprehensive and, of course, the most expensive. Here are two important factors to consider in evaluating an own-occupation policy:

- Are you forced to go back to work in another occupation?
- Will you receive a partial benefit if you go back to work slowly after the disability and still make less than you did before the disability?

Does the policy offer partial benefits? If you are only able to work part-time instead of your previous full-time hours, will you receive benefits? Unless your policy states that you are entitled to partial benefits, you won't receive anything unless you are totally unable to work. Also, are extended partial benefits paid if you go back to work and suffer a reduction in income because you cannot keep up the same rigorous schedule you had before you became disabled? For example, this would be an important benefit for anesthesiologists, who often work extremely long hours in their younger years and most likely will work less if they become disabled.

Important note: Partial benefits may be added via a rider to some policies and should be seriously considered, since only 3% of all disabilities are total disabilities. Some policies even have a recovery benefit; that is, if a business lost patients or clients during the disability due to the insured not being able to serve them and the insured has lost income because of this, there may be a benefit payable. The insured does not have to still be disabled—loss of income due to disability-related attrition is enough.

Is business overhead expense covered? Whether you have $10,000 or $20,000 of monthly disability benefit, you likely don't have enough to cover your lost income *plus* the costs of running the medical practice. Though most companies have limited how much an individual can get in monthly benefits (often 60% of after-tax monthly income, capped at $10,000 per month), many carriers offer up to $25,000 or more per month to cover business overhead expense. Many practice owners who contact us have failed to take advantage of this important provision.

Is it non-cancelable or guaranteed renewable? The difference between these two terms—"non-cancelable" and "guaranteed renewable"—is very important. If a policy is non-cancelable, you will pay a fixed premium throughout the contract term. If it is guaranteed renewable, the policy cannot be cancelled but your premiums could go up. As long as "non-cancelable" is in the description of the policy, you are in good shape.

How financially stable is the insurance company? Before buying a policy, check the financial soundness of your insurer. If your insurer goes bankrupt, you may have to shop for a policy later in life, when premiums are more expensive. Standard & Poor's top rating for financial stability is AAA. A.M. Best Co. uses A++ as its top rating for financial strength. Duff and Phelps rates companies on their ability to pay claims and uses AAA as its highest rating. Moody's uses Aa1 as its designation for excellent companies. There are no guarantees in life but buying a policy from a highly rated company is the safest bet.

Other issues to consider when determining if you are getting the best disability insurance coverage for your money include the following:

- increased coverage
- cost-of-living increases
- waiver of premium
- return-of-premium waiver
- unisex pricing
- HIV rider
- multi-life pricing discounts
- protection of future pension contributions

The Importance of Reviewing Your Existing Policies

Most physicians reading this probably already have some type of disability income insurance in place. Although you have a policy (or two) in force, that does not mean you should "set it and forget it." In fact, there are many reasons why you should periodically review your disability policies, including the following:

- **Increases in income.** If your income increases, you should strongly consider bumping up your coverage to reflect the 60% target mentioned previously. With higher income, you will likely be able to qualify for more coverage through traditional or specialty carriers.

- **Increases in expenses/debt.** If you take on greater debt because of a larger home or mortgage or a second home, this may be enough to justify an increase in coverage. New children or other dependents or increased family expenses are also good reasons to have existing coverages reviewed.
- **New policies may provide additional coverages.** Because of changes in the marketplace, certain things excluded from coverage in older policies are now covered in new policies. For example, policies often used to limit coverage for mental or nervous conditions to two years, but now physicians can be fully covered to age 65. Furthermore, exclusions in older policies can sometimes now be removed.
- **New policies may provide longer coverage.** Older policies often limited the benefit period to age 65. Some policies today provide lifetime benefits.
- **New policies can be combined to reach higher levels of coverage.** With the use of major carriers and specialty carriers like Lloyd's of London, high-income physicians can access coverage of up to $50,000 per month—much higher than in past years.

TAKEAWAY: Physicians see patients every day who are hurt or ill and can't go back to work. Most doctors know this is a risk, but many fail to adequately address it in their own planning. Proper and adequate disability income insurance coverage is the best way to protect your future income.

CHAPTER 4.2

Permanent Life Insurance: What It Is

Perhaps no wealth planning tool discussed in this book is as strongly debated as permanent life insurance. On the one hand, permanent life insurance plays a major planning role for many individuals and businesses—from successful physicians, attorneys, and corporate executives to the country's wealthiest families, leading banks, and Fortune 1000 companies. On the other hand, innumerable commentators and advisors in the media deride permanent insurance as a poor investment.

In this chapter, we will explain what permanent insurance is and what it is not. In the next chapter, we will cover why many people use it, who should avoid it, and why it has a mixed reputation. In Chapter 4.4, we will examine key success factors and how they play out in a few case studies.

What Is Permanent Life Insurance?

Before we explain what permanent insurance is and is not, let's examine the alternative life insurance offering, term insurance.

Term insurance policies offer pure death benefit protection. They carry no cash value and provide protection for a limited period of time (referred to as a *term*). This limited time frame is usually ten to twenty years, though some companies offer a thirty-year term product. A term life insurance policy pays a specific lump sum to your designated beneficiary upon your death, so it can play an important role in providing temporary death protection for your family (or your practice or partners as part of a buy-sell arrangement).

Pros: Term insurance offers affordable coverage that pays only a death benefit. Term life insurance initially tends to cost less than other insurance policies because it has no cash value.

Cons: Term life insurance becomes more costly as we age because the risk of death increases as people get older. The premiums are generally fixed for the term of the policy, but if one needs a new policy when the original term policy expires, this increased cost can be a problem. It almost always is more expensive, and if the policyholder's health is poor it may be prohibitively expensive or unavailable. Even for the healthiest individuals, term insurance becomes unavailable at some point. For these reasons, term insurance is not a good tool for estate planning because the coverage cannot be continued at a reasonable price as you approach your life expectancy. For more on term insurance, please refer to Chapter 1.2.

The category of permanent life insurance comprises products that, unlike term, carry cash values along with death benefits and can last for the entirety of the insured's life—to age 100, 115, or beyond. (Of course, these products are "permanent" only as long as the required premiums are paid on time.)

Within the general category of permanent insurance there are a host of different products. Unfortunately, many physicians refer to all permanent products as "whole life," but whole life is only one category of permanent policies. Let's examine the leading permanent products.

Whole Life Insurance

Whole life insurance (WL) pays a death benefit to the beneficiary you name and offers you a cash value account with tax-deferred cash accumulation. Many physicians are "pitched" whole life by insurance agents for companies whose central product is WL, and that may be why many doctors think of the entire category of permanent insurance as WL.

Pros: WL has a savings element (cash value) that is tax deferred. The cash value grows based on the life insurance company paying a dividend. This dividend is determined by the life insurance company, is not guaranteed, and is likely to change annually. Because of the low-interest-rate environment over the last fifteen years, dividend rates on whole life policies have been decreasing.

You can borrow from this account free of income tax, or, if it is properly structured, you can cash in the policy during your lifetime. It has a fixed premium that can't increase during your lifetime (as long as you pay the planned amount), and your premium is invested for you long term. Because it has the cash accumulation component, whole life insurance can offer benefits such as tax reduction, wealth accumulation, asset protection, estate planning, and tax diversification of asset classes.

Cons: WL does not allow you to invest in separate accounts (e.g., money market, stock, and bond funds). Thus, your policy's returns will be tied to the life insurance company's dividend credit based on that insurance company's underlying investments. It also does not allow you to split your money among different accounts or to move your money between accounts, and it does not allow premium flexibility or face amount (the death benefit amount) flexibility.

Universal Life Insurance

Universal life insurance (UL) is similar to WL but has more flexible premiums and death benefits.

Pros: The cash value grows based on interest crediting to the policy as determined by the insurance company. It may be attractive to younger buyers who have fluctuations in their ability to pay premiums.

Cons: If the insurance company does poorly with its investments, the interest return on the cash portion of the policy could decrease. In this case, less money would be available to pay the cost of the death benefit portion of the policy and future premiums may be necessary in addition to the premiums originally illustrated. Additionally, the cash value will grow more slowly than originally illustrated and there will be less money to borrow during distribution years.

Variable Universal Life Insurance

Variable universal life insurance (VUL) pays your beneficiary a death benefit in an amount of dependent on the success of your investments. If the investments fail, there is a guaranteed minimum death benefit paid to your beneficiary upon your death. VUL gives you more control of the cash value account portion of your policy than any other insurance type. A form of UL, it has elements of both life insurance and a securities contract. Because the policy owner assumes investment risks, variable universal products are regulated as securities under federal securities laws and must be sold with a prospectus.

Pros: VUL enables you to make withdrawals or borrow from the policy during your lifetime, and it offers separate accounts in which to invest. Essentially, VUL combines universal life's flexibility with the ability to invest in mutual funds. It also affords you an opportunity to invest in the equities markets on a tax-deferred basis.

Cons: It requires the policyholder to devote time to managing the policy's accounts. The policy's success is dependent on the investments you make. Premiums must be high enough to cover your insurance and your accounts. There are also increased expenses due to the underlying costs of the investment options in the policy. This can be a drain on the cash value growth.

Private Placement Variable Universal Life Insurance

Private placement variable universal life insurance (PPVUL) has most of the characteristics of VUL discussed earlier. However, PPVUL differs from VUL in a few ways that make it more attractive to the ultra-wealthy. Essentially, these policies are treated as private placement securities and have great flexibility in their design and management while still enjoying the tax and asset protection benefits of life insurance. Some of the unique attributes of PPVUL make it very attractive for wealthy clients:

- PPVULs are available only to accredited investors.
- PPVULs do not generate materials that are available to the public. They must be requested by a *bona fide* accredited investor.
- PPVULs have higher minimum premium requirements (which differ by company; minimum premiums generally range from $500,000 to $5,000,000 of premium in the first five years).
- PPVULs have lower fees than traditional insurance products.

- PPVULs offer more investment flexibility. Policy owners typically choose among hedge funds or can suggest their own investment management firm to manage the funds within the PPVUL if premiums are large enough.

Pros: PPVULs allow the client to choose potentially more sophisticated investment options like hedge funds or private equity options. Internal fees tend to be much lower than for traditional insurance policies.

Cons: PPVULs have very high minimum premium requirements and are limited to accredited investors only. Because this is a private placement, there is very little written marketing material to review. Very few insurance companies do enough of this type of work to be considered efficient. The investment fees may be higher than with traditional permanent life insurance options.

A Hybrid: Equity-Indexed Universal Life Insurance

Equity-indexed universal life insurance (EIUL) is a universal policy that allows you to select from a list of stock market indices to grow your cash value. If the investments fail, there is a guaranteed minimum death benefit paid to your beneficiary upon your death.

EIUL gives you more upside than a traditional UL policy because the insurance company contractually agrees to credit the policy's cash value with the same return as the stock market index the policy holder chooses (typically, the S&P 500 Index, but it can be the Dow Jones, NASDAQ, EAFA, Euro Stoxx, or others) realized over the same period of time, subject to a cap and a floor. Thus, the policy owner has the upside of the indices (up to the cap) but the risk of the same indices (but only to the floor). Typical floors for an annual return begin at near 0% (no loss of principal), with caps around 10%.

Pros: EIUL enables you to get potentially more upside in the cash value accounts than WL but also gives you downside protection, something VUL and PPVUL cannot offer.

Cons: Products are relatively complex, with many choices of indices, participation rates, floors, and caps, and they vary significantly from insurance carrier to insurance carrier. Working with a professional who can help you make good decisions about policy placement and annual management is essential.

Is Permanent Life Insurance a "Good" Investment?

When thinking about permanent life insurance, many physicians want to understand whether it is a "good" or "bad" investment. However, with just what you have learned in the last two pages, you should be able to see the fallacy of the question. How can permanent life insurance be a "good" or "bad" investment when the choices within permanent products are so broad and deep? In other words, the structure of a permanent life insurance policy allows for an almost limitless number of underlying investments within the structure—and those investments will provide the policy's returns.

As we explained, WL offers a bond-based, dividends-type return. Is this good or bad? It depends on what the rest of the market does, doesn't it? In 2008–09, an asset with such a return would likely have been the best-performing asset class on a physician's balance sheet.

With VUL, the performance of the policy is based on the owner's choice of mutual funds: large cap, small cap, medium cap, international, emerging markets, REITs, bonds, hedge funds, and on and on. Is the policy a good investment? That depends completely on the owner's choice and management of the funds.

For EIUL, the answer is the same, but replace "mutual funds" with "indices" (such as the S&P 500); for PPVUL, the same is true again, but think "money manager."

The fact is, a permanent life policy can be a fantastic, great, good, fair, or poor investment because it isn't an investment itself; rather, it's a structure that houses investments, the choices of which are almost innumerable.

That's why when someone says, "life insurance is a good investment" or "life insurance is a bad investment," it is no different than when somebody says "real estate is a good investment" or "real estate is a bad investment." The accurate statement is "it depends." We will return to the idea that permanent life insurance is similar to real estate in the next chapter.

Certainly, it is true that there are costs within a permanent life policy that you won't incur if you invest the "difference" outside a policy. However, as you will see in the next two chapters, permanent life insurance policies have valuable tax attributes that you cannot get anywhere else—benefits that more than cover those "extra" costs for many doctors.

This does not mean that *every* physician should own permanent life insurance. In fact, in the next chapter, we will outline the types of people for whom permanent life policies are probably not a good fit. But that decision should be made based on your particular facts and circumstances, not because of a more-than-forty-year-old saying that doesn't apply to the products offered today.

"Buy Term and Invest the Difference": Does this Make Sense Anymore?

You may have heard the old saying "buy term and invest the difference" (BTID). We refer to it as "old" because it was coined in the 1970s as an objection to whole life insurance. As you learned earlier in this chapter, whole life products are tied to the insurance carrier's dividend rates, which closely correlate with interest rates and bond returns. This makes sense, as life insurance companies, being conservative entities that must weather the markets for centuries, need to invest most of their capital conservatively. In fact, state regulations require it. This is a good thing—we want insurance companies to be around decades in the future, when death benefits need to be paid.

As we will discuss briefly in Lesson 5, and as covered in depth in our book *Wealth Management Made Simple*, bonds carry less risk and provide less return over the long term when compared to stocks, as well as real estate and other possible investments. Hence, the BTID adage meant that instead of using whole life insurance bond-type returns to grow wealth, you would be better off buying term insurance to cover death benefit concerns and using the remaining funds (because term premiums are less than those for whole life) to invest in something else, such as equities or mutual funds, with greater long-term growth potential.

How does the BTID logic apply today, when so many investments within permanent insurance exist? Why would it make sense to buy term and invest the difference in mutual funds or REITs when you can invest in those same mutual funds within a life policy (VUL)? Why would it make sense to invest in an equity index like the S&P 500 when you can invest in that same index within a life policy (EIUL)? Or, if you are very wealthy, why would it make sense to invest those funds with your favorite money manager when you can do the same thing within a life policy (PPVUL)?

The marketplace simply did not offer all these investment choices within life insurance when BTID arose as a catchphrase.

The point here is clear: the old BTID adage does not apply to permanent life policies today, given the array of investment choices within policies.

TAKEAWAY: Permanent life insurance offers a wide variety of investment options and has significant tax benefits. Because of this, it is a useful asset class for many physicians.

CHAPTER 4.3

Permanent Life Insurance: Why It May Make Sense for You

In the last chapter, we explained what permanent insurance is and what it is not. Here, we will cover why many physicians use it, who should avoid it, and why it is has a mixed reputation. However, we will begin with a discussion of how permanent life insurance is similar to a commonly used asset class, real estate.

What Permanent Life Insurance and Real Estate Have in Common: Tremendous Tax Benefits

Real estate and life insurance both confer such significant benefits under our tax code—and have for a century—that one might consider them "tax-favored asset classes."

With real estate, you can write off depreciation on business real estate, deduct interest payments on home mortgages within limits, write off local property taxes against your federal taxes (this was limited by the most recent tax law), and enjoy up to a $500,000 capital gains exemption on the sale of the primary home (for a married couple filing jointly).

With permanent life insurance, you can enjoy tax-deferred growth of gains within the policy and, with proper management, access such value tax-free in retirement. In addition, policy death benefits generally are paid to beneficiaries free of income tax and—of interest to those focused on estate planning—you can even structure the death benefits to be paid estate-tax-free within certain types of trusts.

Further, both asset classes offer a powerful tax benefit that few others provide: the ability to move from one piece of real estate or life policy to another using a tax-free like-kind exchange. These exchanges are controlled by tax code sections 1031 and 1035, respectively.

Finally, for many clients, from an economic perspective, these asset classes share two important characteristics as well:

1. **Longer time frames.** While there are certainly professional real estate developers or fix-up flippers who do well in the short term, most physicians buying real estate should think longer term when buying a home, rental property, or other real property. Because of the real estate business cycle and the previously mentioned tax benefits, thinking longer-term is often savvier. The same is true for permanent life insurance, as we discuss in the next chapter.
2. **Borrowing against the equity.** With both asset classes, borrowing against the equity—through refinancing or HELOCs for real estate or tax-free withdrawals and policy loans for permanent life insurance—is a key part of short-term or long-term financial planning.

Why Sophisticated Clients Use Permanent Policies

Many strategies call for permanent insurance in wealthy families' planning. The three leading reasons to use permanent insurance that apply to many physicians, wealthy or not, are estate planning, asset protection, and wealth accumulation.

Wealth Accumulation

Because of the varied investment options within permanent life insurance, the tax-free growth of cash values, and the ability to access such values in retirement (or whenever you want) tax-free, permanent insurance can be a powerful part of your wealth accumulation/retirement plan. Further, when compared to qualified retirement plans, with their income taxation upon withdrawal, and most after-tax assets' creation of capital gains taxes upon liquidation, the tax-free access to cash values in a permanent life policy provides extremely valuable tax diversification in a long-term retirement plan. We discuss this in Chapter 3.1.

Asset Protection

As discussed in Lesson 2, asset protection planning is an important area of wealth management for many physicians. Also noted there, cash value (permanent) life insurance is a (+5) exempt asset in many states—that is, it provides the highest level of protection. Further, many states give unlimited protection to cash values and death benefits, making permanent insurance policies a significant part of many physicians' asset protection planning.

Estate Planning

The tactics that involve using permanent life insurance in estate planning are many and varied. We will discuss a few of them in Chapter 6.3. For our purposes here, it is important to understand that permanent life insurance plays a very important role in estate planning because it is permanent (as long as premiums are paid) and because of the liquidity it provides upon the death of the insured (a single person or the second to die of a married couple). Also of importance is that the proceeds generally are paid income-tax-free and, within a properly implemented trust, can pay out estate-tax-free as well.

Term insurance cannot play the same role because it is never guaranteed to last until death.

Who Uses Permanent Life Insurance?

High-Net-Worth Clients

Anecdotally, based on our firm's knowledge of the industry, we can say that tens of thousands of high-net-worth clients incorporate permanent life insurance into their planning for all of the reasons explained in this chapter. The estate planning, asset protection, and wealth accumulation benefits justify the inclusion of this asset class in their portfolios.

Major Corporations

Many of our nation's largest public companies invest in permanent life insurance through a strategy commonly known as corporate-owned life insurance (COLI). Every year, major U.S. companies invest in permanent life insurance, primarily to finance employee benefit plan expenses and increase net income. For example, companies with substantial liabilities for medical, group life, and other basic insurance as well as qualified and nonqualified benefit plan expenses can finance these costs with COLI. Other reasons for companies choosing to use COLI include the following:

- COLI can earn a competitive after-tax yield compared to other investments.
- COLI can match the long-term nature of benefit plan expenses.
- COLI can act as a hedge against benefit liabilities.
- COLI death benefits can be used to help the company recover plan costs over the long term.

Banks

Our country's largest banks are among its major corporations, including the Fortune 1000. Certainly, these entities are sophisticated when it comes to financial instruments. Many of the uninitiated or misinformed regarding permanent life insurance might find it surprising that many of these banks own permanent life insurance (called BOLI)—and even more surprising how much of it they own. The numbers are staggering. See Figure 4.3.1. Not included in the Figure is the fact that these banks own $163 billion of permanent life insurance cash surrender value.[1] Many physicians find it significant that permanent life insurance can make financial sense even to the most sophisticated financial institutions in the world.

---

[1] March 31, 2017 Bank Call Reports - Schedules RC & RC-F

ASSET SIZE	BANKS	BANKS WITH BOLI	PERCENTAGE OF BANKS WITH BOLI
GREATER THAN $50B	40	28	70%
$5B - $50B	169	137	81%
$1B - $5B	540	446	83%
$750M - $1B	246	190	77%
$500M - $750M	430	320	74%
$250M - $500M	1,122	836	75%
$100M - $250M	1,807	1,085	60%
LESS THAN $100M	1,501	621	41%
TOTAL:	5,855	3,663	63%

Source: March 31, 2017 Bank Call Reports - Schedules RC & RC-F

Figure 4.3.1

Not All Physicians Should Own Permanent Life Insurance

Despite all the benefits of permanent life insurance and its use by large financial institutions, it is not appropriate for all physicians. For many, simple term insurance products are all that is needed. In fact, if all of the following are true for you, term insurance may well be your best option:

- **Tax-free growth and access are not important.**
  You may not need permanent life insurance if you are at one of the lower income tax brackets or otherwise pay little or no income tax or capital gains tax on investments because of other deductions or losses that will be applied against income or gains for the foreseeable future.

- **Asset protection is not a planning goal.**
  If you are not concerned about potential liability or you live in a state that does not protect life insurance cash values, you may not get as much value from permanent life insurance.

- **Asset diversification is not a priority.**
  The cash value within a life insurance policy can grow

in a variety of ways: as part of a fixed-income portfolio managed by the insurance company, through a mutual fund-based approach, or as part of a market-based strategy with downside protection featuring a floor that the insurance company guarantees the rate of return will not go below. You may not need permanent life insurance if you are satisfied with the diversification of your investments and any use of guaranteed asset classes in your portfolio.

- **State or federal estate taxes are not seen as impacting your planning.**
  If your projected net worth is under both your state's and the federal estate tax exemption amount, or you have no children or grandchildren, you may not need permanent life insurance as an estate planning tool. Of course, tax laws change often, so it is difficult to say for certain that they will not affect your planning decades from today.

Why Permanent Insurance Has a Mixed Reputation

As you have seen, permanent life insurance is an asset class with over $160 billion invested in it just by our largest banks and much more invested in it by other corporations, families, and individuals. However, Google it and you will see a long list of financial experts warning you to steer clear of it. Why is this? Part of the reason stems from advice given 50 years ago that's summarized by an adage regarding the investment choices within the asset class—buy term and invest the difference—that applied to a narrow range of products from the 1970s. See Chapter 4.2 for more on this.

There is more to the story. In our view, there are three additional reasons this product gets a bad rap. This is important background information to understand if you are considering using permanent life insurance or already have it in your portfolio.

1. The Industry Itself

To some degree, the life insurance industry has only itself to blame when it comes to the mixed reputation of its products. Here are two of the primary reasons:

The low barrier to entry and training for life insurance agents.
By taking a short course and passing an exam, anyone can become a licensed insurance agent in most states. No formal education or on-the-job training is required. In fact, in many states, the requirements for obtaining a driver's license are more rigorous.

Given this, it should not be surprising that there is a tremendous range of education, experience, and acumen in the pool of life insurance agents. While there are certainly high-quality, well-educated life insurance agents all around the country, considering how many life insurance agents there are in the United States and the low barrier to entry, what would you expect the profile of the bottom 10%, 30%, or 50% of agents to be? It is troubling.

If the life insurance industry wanted to improve its reputation, one change to consider would be stiffening the requirements for new agents—to include a college degree, at least.

An industry-wide compensation formula that may encourage poor ongoing product management.
Generally, an agent who sells a customer a life insurance policy gets paid a commission by the insurance company. The customer does not pay a fee to the agent. Further, the most common commission arrangement involves a large portion of the commission being paid in the first year. Of course, this is not the case with all products (term and whole life often work differently) or all insurance companies (some allow commissions to be spread over the first few years of the policy). Nonetheless, the general rule applies: most life insurance agents make most of their commission in the first year of a new life insurance policy.

Contrast this front-loaded commission schedule with the servicing the agent should do on the policy, especially for permanent products where there may be significant cash value to manage and important decisions requiring a professional agent's direction. The commissions paid to the agent in the short term simply do not line up well with the long-term service the agent should be providing to the policyholder, and this can create problems over time.

2. The Potential Complexity of the Product

While the industry itself is certainly partly to blame for the ambivalence much of the public, including physicians, have about their products, the complexity of the product plays a big role.

When you buy a stock or bond, or even an ETF, what you are purchasing and how the security works are fairly straightforward. (If you need some education on securities, be sure to get our book *Wealth Management Made Simple*. We go through all the relevant investment definitions in Lesson 1.)

On the other hand, permanent life insurance products are sophisticated financial tools and they can be complex—much more so than stocks, bonds, or ETFs. Surrender charges, surrender values, indices and fund choices, participation rates, dividend reinvestment options, policy loan provisions, segment maturities, death benefit reduction options—all are terms that one needs to know to understand what is going on within a permanent life policy.

Further, each of these terms reflects a decision that the policy owner needs to make, sometimes once but often each year as the policy is managed. Expand these factors and decisions over a long-time horizon and it becomes clear how much an experienced, professional insurance agent is needed to guide the policyholder.

The bottom line: permanent life insurance policies have tremendous potential tax, investment, asset protection, and estate planning features and benefits. However, because of these features and benefits, the products are complex. If not implemented and managed properly, they will not perform as expected—and this gap between expectation and performance is what leads to some people's disillusionment with the products. Good surgical outcomes occur when a seasoned surgeon chooses the right procedure for the patient, performs the procedure properly, and implements the correct follow-up protocol and management. Using these types of insurance products involves a similar process.

3. The Long-Term Nature of the Product

Finally, along with industry issues and the complexity of the product, the long-term nature of the asset class is also a factor in why some "experts" on the internet give it a hard time. As we have stressed, a permanent life policy may be in place for decades, perhaps 50 years or more. For some, that long-term horizon raises some concerns about uncertainty.

Uncertainty about the future—what tax changes may come, how the investments inside the policy will perform against assumptions, what changes the insurance carrier will make—causes some advisors to look at these policies with a jaundiced eye. While it is always important to use reasonable assumptions and be cautious, another important success factor to layer into planning with any long-term product is flexibility. If one can structure the policy with the flexibility to make changes, this alone can protect it from many of the long-term what-if questions that critics often raise. We will discuss flexibility in more depth in the next chapter.

TAKEAWAY: Permanent life insurance is a much-misunderstood asset class. It offers a wide variety of investment options and significant tax benefits. These are among the reasons that many sophisticated investors, from ultra-wealthy families to Fortune 1000 corporations and banks, use it in their planning. Some of the reasons for the misunderstandings are the life insurance industry itself and the often complex and long-term nature of the product.

CHAPTER 4.4

Five Key Success Factors When Using Permanent Life Insurance and Case Studies

In the last chapter, you learned that permanent life insurance has tremendous tax, wealth accumulation, asset protection, and estate planning benefits. You also saw that today's products offer a wide range of investment options within them and that the country's largest corporations and banks and wealthiest families routinely use this asset class in their planning. Despite all this, some physicians are not good candidates for permanent life insurance, and there are issues with these products because of industry practices and their long-term and complex nature.

In this chapter, we will explain five success factors to implement when using permanent life insurance, based on our experience working with these products and physicians for more than twenty-five years. In addition, through a few case studies we will demonstrate the good things that can happen when these products are designed and maintained properly and the bad things that can happen when they are not.

Five Success Factors in Using Permanent Life Insurance

The insurance professionals in our firm have over one hundred years of combined experience working with permanent life insurance and even more working with physicians. We have identified five crucial success factors that should be part of any allocation to permanent life insurance.

1. Long-Term Time Horizon

Whether a permanent life policy is designed to accumulate significant cash values for the policyowner's retirement, for an executive's buyout, or for any other purpose, it is important that the purchaser have a relatively long (fifteen years or more) time horizon. Of course, if the policy is designed for estate planning, the time horizon may be thirty years or more, depending on the age of the insured.

The reason that a long time horizon is important relates to the discussion in the previous chapter about the frontloading of expenses, including agent commissions, in many permanent life policies. Compare an A share mutual fund, where the sales load is charged up front and there are no ongoing charges, with a B share, where there is no load upfront but there is an annual fee. Which is more cost effective depends entirely on how long the investor intends to hold the fund: one can calculate a break-even point before which the B share is best and after which the A share is best.

One can think of permanent life insurance as being generally like the A share mutual fund example. Rather than a sales load in a fund, many life policies have a "surrender charge" that is imposed if you surrender the policy in full (but, importantly, not if you access some of the cash value). The amount of this surrender charge covers many of the insurance company's upfront expenses (including the agent commission), and it goes down over time. The surrender charge in many policies hits zero between eight and fifteen years. If you keep the policy in force beyond the surrender period, you have effectively amortized the upfront costs over time and will not be penalized if you surrender the policy.

Taxes are another important reason to keep these policies in place for a long time. This is especially true for people using them for future retirement income because the tax benefits afforded by a policy (tax-free growth within the policy and tax-free access through basis withdrawals and policy loans) gain value as the policy growth compounds over time. As with a Roth IRA, simple math dictates that the longer one can enjoy tax-free growth and access, the better. We noted in the last chapter that this is a characteristic this asset class shares with real estate.

2. Proper Design of the Policy Up Front

The insurance agent should design the policy to meet the specific client's plans from the beginning.

To do so, the agent must understand exactly why the client is purchasing the policy. Is it for death benefit proceeds to protect the family or pay off a business debt? Is the policy part of a retirement income strategy? Once the agent understands the objective for the policy, he or she can design it properly from the beginning.

When designing for the death benefit, the agent will look to maximize the policy death benefits for any level of premium. The agent may use guarantees and rely on very conservative assumptions in the death benefit modeling.

When designing for cash value accumulation, on the other hand, the agent should minimize death benefits for any level of premium (within tax rules) because lower death benefits mean lower cost-of-insurance charges. Also, the policy can be planned to reduce death benefits over time (within tax rules) and should be designed to do from the outset. You can see this in the case studies later in the chapter.

3. A Design for Flexibility Up Front

As we mentioned in the last chapter, the long-term nature of permanent insurance subjects it to the criticism that things change—for the owner, for the investments within the policy, with tax laws, and with insurance carriers. Best practices for an insurance advisor, therefore, call for designing a flexible policy. Flexibility can be built into the policy in several ways, including permitting changing investments within the policy, paying more or less premium, changing premium frequency, adjusting the death benefit, and adding or removing a beneficiary. The more flexibility the policy is designed to allow, the more options the owner has to adjust how it works in their plan as circumstances change over time.

This built-in flexibility, along with the ability under the tax code to exchange policies free of tax (noted in the last chapter and discussed further later in this chapter with respect to 1035 exchanges), is a powerful remedy to concerns about the long-term nature of the asset class.

4. Regular Reviews and Maintenance

In one way, permanent life insurance is like any other asset class in which you might invest: regular performance reviews are mandatory. Just as you review your investment performance with your investment advisor quarterly or annually, so should you review your life policy with your insurance agent. It is in those reviews where you can make decisions on a myriad of options within the policy, taking advantage of the flexibility mentioned earlier. Whether it means changing investments within the policy, paying more or less premium, changing premium frequency, adjusting the death benefit, adding or removing a beneficiary, or even exchanging the policy for a different type (further discussed later in this chapter), regular reviews are when the agent and policyowner bring the issues to light and make decisions accordingly. Permanent life insurance is not a set-it-and-forget-it asset—few valuable assets are.

5. A Sophisticated and Ethical Insurance Agent

The most important of the five success factors may be working with an ethical insurance agent who understands the plethora of products in the market as well as the details of the specific policy you might use. If you work with such an agent, they will make sure that the other four factors are in place. If you do not, the absence of any of the success factors could undermine the policy's performance and how you evaluate the use of the asset class in your planning.

What should one look for in a life insurance agent? It is important, in our view, to work with an agent who is not operating under a captive or quasi-captive arrangement (see the previous chapter)—one who is truly independent, with no restrictions on the policies they can provide and no overhead payment incentives to prioritize one company's products over another. Beyond that, they should have significant experience in working with permanent life policies— a few decades—so they understand what could go awry and build in flexibility to avoid it. True expertise in the field is also important (perhaps they have lectured to other agents or written on the subject). Finally, it is always a good idea to work with professionals who are well regarded in the industry and have numerous references to provide.

Case Studies: The Good and Bad with Permanent Life Insurance

The following case studies will demonstrate the potential value of a permanent life policy to a physician's planning, as well what can go wrong. We show four physicians who are the same age and have the same cash value life policy funding and distribution plans. Two are guided by a good insurance agent who designs and helps them manage the policy. Two are not, and the results show it. We have created four case studies to show the impact on equity indexed universal life (EIUL) and whole life (WL) policies.

Case Studies

Case Study #1:
Doctor Sheila Invests Properly in an EIUL Product

Sheila is a 45-year-old female physician who will invest $30,000 per year for ten years in premiums for an EIUL product. She will then take tax-free income out of the policy for twenty years, starting at age 65. Guided by a quality life insurance agent, Sheila chooses a product from a top mutual company. The agent makes sure the policy is designed at the outset for maximum cash value accumulation and is made more efficient whenever possible. Sheila and her agent choose the index, participation, and accumulation time frames initially and also evaluate them each year.

Case Study #2:
Doctor Samantha Invests Properly in a WL Product

Samantha is a 45-year-old female physician who will invest $30,000 per year for ten years in premiums for a WL product. She will then take tax-free income out of the policy for twenty years, starting at age 65. Guided by a quality life insurance agent, Samantha chooses a product from a top-rated company. The agent also makes sure the policy is designed at the outset for maximum cash value accumulation and is made more efficient whenever possible over time. Samantha and her agent also track the policy performance each year in their annual reviews.

Case Study #3:
Doctor Mary Invests Improperly in an EIUL Product

Mary is also a 45-year-old female physician who will invest $30,000 per year for ten years in premiums for an EIUL product. She will take tax-free income out of the policy for twenty years, starting at age 65. She works with an insurance agent who is not knowledgeable about EIUL products design for retirement income, so the policy has too high a death benefit when it is initially purchased. Further, after the first few years, the agent fails to conduct annual reviews, so Mary is on her own in managing the policy. Mary neglects to make premium payments in years 6 and 10. With no long-term agent to advise her, Mary plans to take the same annual distribution amount as Sheila, who has the same product.

Case Study #4:
Doctor Melinda Invests Improperly in a WL Product

Finally, Melinda is a 45-year-old female physician who will invest $30,000 per year for ten years in premiums for a WL product. She will also take tax-free income out of the policy for twenty years, starting at age 65. Melinda is a do-it-yourselfer and did the research to find a high-quality whole life product from a top mutual insurance carrier. That is the good news. The bad news is that without regular annual reviews, she was not educated on the significance of missing a few premium payments. So, like Mary, she missed premium payments in years 6 and 10. With no long-term agent to advise her, Melinda plans to take the same annual distribution amount as Samantha, who has the same product.

PRODUCT	SHEILA'S EIUL POLICY	SAMANTHA'S WL POLICY	MARY'S EIUL POLICY	MELINDA'S WL POLICY
INITIAL DEATH BENEFIT	$913,133	$924,209	$1,449,125	$2,040,816
ASSUMED GROWTH RATE	6%	CURRENT DIVIDEND	6%	CURRENT DIVIDEND
PROJECTED DISRIBUTION	$58,231	$33,551	$58,231	$33,551
PROJECTED TOTAL DISTRIBUTION	$1,164,620	$671,020	$524,079	$277,711
MISSED PREMIUM	N/A	N/A	YEARS 6 & 10	YEARS 6 & 10
TAXABLE 1099 AMOUNT	N/A	N/A	$325,447	$37,711
AGE POLICY LAPSES	N/A	N/A	75	74

Figure 4.4.1

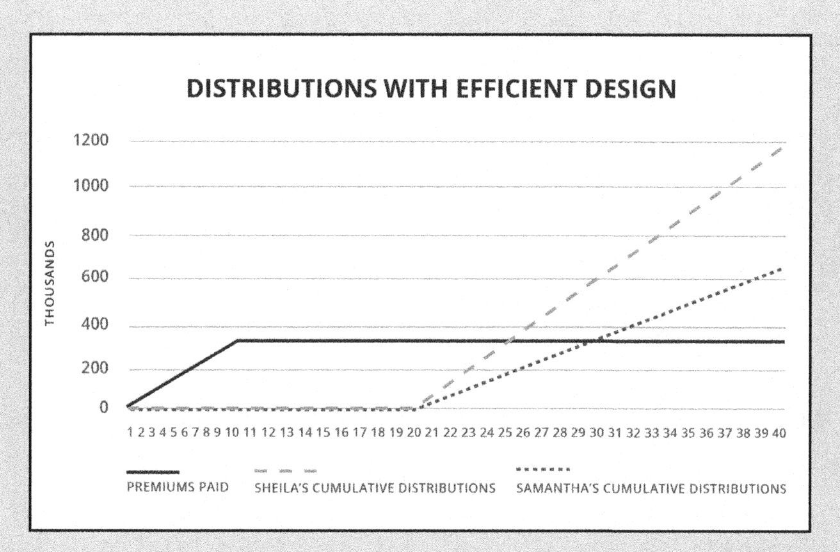

Figure 4.4.2

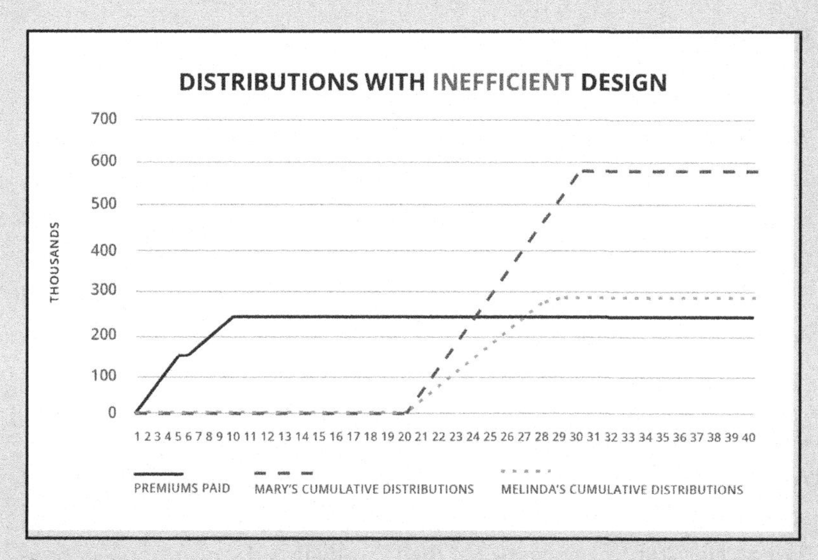

Figure 4.4.3

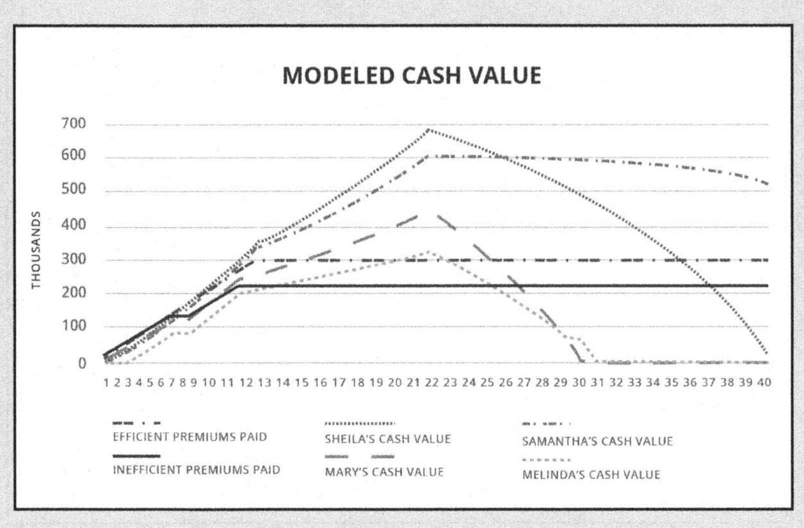

Figure 4.4.4

Results

Case Study #1: Doctor Sheila's EIUL

With proper initial policy design, premium discipline, and the guidance of an agent who advises her and adjusts the policy over time, Sheila's tactic of using EIUL for tax-advanced retirement income is a great success. With a 6% assumed return, Sheila is able to take out $58,231 in tax-free income for twenty years between ages 65 and 84. Even with the nearly $1.2 million of tax-free retirement income she enjoys, there is still a minimal policy death benefit until age 121.

Case Study #2 Doctor Samantha's WL

With proper initial policy design, premium discipline, and the guidance of an agent who advises her and adjusts the policy over time, Samantha's tactic of using WL for tax-advanced retirement income is a great success. With a return based on the insurance carrier's current dividend when the policy was purchased, Samantha is able to take out $33,551 in tax-free income for twenty years between ages 65 and 84. Even with the nearly $700,000 of tax-free retirement income she enjoys, there is still a minimal policy death benefit until age 121.

Case Study #3: Doctor Mary EIUL

With improper policy design, no professional guidance or adjustment over time, and the missing of two premium payments, Mary's EIUL policy lapses at age 75. With a 6% assumed return, Mary is able to take out $58,231 in tax-free income for nine years—$524,079—before the policy lapses. When the policy lapses at age 75, Mary must pay income tax on $325,447 of 1099 income. She has no death benefit since the policy has lapsed.

Case Study #4: Doctor Melinda's WL

With improper policy design, no professional guidance or adjustment over time, and the missing of two premium payments, Melinda's WL policy lapses at age 74. With a return based on the insurance carrier's current dividend when the policy was purchased, Melinda is able to take out $33,551 for a little more than eight years—$277,711—before the policy lapses. When the policy lapses at age 74, Melinda must pay income tax on $37,711 of 1099 income. She has no death benefit since the policy has lapsed.

As the case studies clearly demonstrate, the idea of using a permanent life insurance policy as an accumulation vehicle for retirement was a good one. Whether it worked as intended, however, was completely dependent on the execution of the concept — with proper direction by a competent insurance agent being the key success factor.

The Ultimate Flexibility Tool and Safety Valve for Permanent Life Policies

In the last chapter, we noted the similarities between permanent life insurance and real estate, including the ability to do tax-free exchanges. We will delve more deeply into this here, as it provides tremendous long-term flexibility for policyowners.

When interest rates fall, many of us consider refinancing our mortgages. We review the long-term savings versus the refinancing costs and make a decision. Physicians do this with their home mortgages, investment properties, and maybe even business loans. It is a common practice.

Simply put, this can also be done with permanent life insurance.

How To "Refi" Your Permanent Policy

Unlike with a mortgage, you do not actually refinance a cash value life insurance policy; you exchange it for a new one using the 1035 exchange provision mentioned in the last chapter. This is similar to exchanging one mortgage for another in a refi.

This is generally a simple process, but it usually requires new underwriting. This is important because just as you would not refinance your mortgage if the closing costs are higher than the expected interest savings, neither should you exchange a policy for a new one if your health has worsened since you first acquired the policy because the costs of the new policy will likely exceed the costs of your existing policy.

With the help of a knowledgeable advisor, you can assess these factors in advance and model the numbers so you have all the information before making the exchange. Note: if you have maintained a healthy lifestyle and remain in good health, there may be a financial incentive to exchange the policy.

Flexibility: Five Cost-Related Reasons to Exchange

Under the theme of flexibility for owners of permanent life policies, here are five potentially cost-lowering reasons for owners to exchange existing policies for new ones:

1. **Industry-wide cost-of-insurance reductions.** As a physician, you know that people are living longer today. As a result, the costs of insurance (COI) have been dropping across the industry. Lower COIs mean lower internal costs overall which mean better policy performance. If you purchased a policy more than ten years ago, exchanging into a new policy with updated COI could be reason enough to see better cash value growth and distributions in future years.
2. **You are still in great health.** Did you get a top rating when you purchased your cash value policy? Are you

still in good health? If you answered "yes" to both questions, you may have the most to gain financially from a 1035 exchange because of the way insurance carriers price their policies. The carrier had only a snapshot of your health when it issued your policy (perhaps a physician's statement and blood and urine samples). It has no knowledge of your current lifestyle or your health since the policy was issued.

With such little information and potentially millions of dollars on the line, it is not surprising that the carrier's internal cost accounting gradually diminishes the value of your "preferred" or "super-preferred" rating. After all, how does it know you haven't started smoking or gained significant weight? The bottom line: if you can still qualify for a top underwriting rating, you may have the most to gain by exchanging into a new policy to "revive" a lower COI structure. Your cash values and distributions could benefit significantly.

3. **Costs structures between companies.** Separate from the specific COI expense, insurance carriers vary in their overall product pricing structures, even within the top-tier companies. Because some carriers' products are known for being more expensive, additional long-term cost savings can be gained by exchanging from one carrier to another.
4. **Moving to policies with lower "access" costs.** What are "access" costs? The most important one by far is the "net loan rate" the insurance carrier will charge you for borrowing from your cash values. Beyond your basis (what you paid in premiums over the years), you will likely want to borrow additional cash value against your death benefits to *access* your cash value while you are alive—that's what makes your access to these amounts tax-free. Therefore, the loan rate your carrier charges is significant and, unfortunately, often hidden by unscrupulous agents selling high-loan-rate policies. If you own a cash value policy, it's likely you bought it partly because you can access those cash val-

ues, perhaps in retirement. If so, access costs are just as important as accumulation costs.

5. **Moving to mutual companies.** Some policyowners exchange their policies for new ones issued by mutual insurance companies—companies owned by the policyholders themselves. Their rationale is that they will be more likely to get the benefit of future COI reductions or avoid future loan rate hikes (and enjoy other cost efficiencies) as owners of the company than they would be if they own policies issued by stock insurance companies, where these savings may just mean more profits for shareholders. For a long-term asset like life insurance, eliminating the conflict between shareholders and policyowners may be a wise decision.

Flexibility: Two Reasons to Exchange Your Policies for Performance

Many life policy owners also consider exchanging their policies because of investment performance. Let's look at two reasons here:

1. **Taking advantage of new product features.** How much more can your cell phone do for you now than it could ten or fifteen years ago? While the differences in life policies may not be as visually dramatic as those in different generations of iPhones, they can be significant financially. Policy elements such as return multipliers, index participation rates, long-term care riders, and benefit distribution riders are new to the industry in the past few years and can be beneficial to the right person. If the underwriting rating has not changed, these factors alone may be attractive enough to justify a 1035 exchange.
2. **Moving from a bond-based whole life policy to one with some stock market exposure — or *vice versa.*** Anyone following investments knows that the last decade has not been kind to bonds and other investments that are based on interest rates. With the federal funds rate at 0% or close to it from 2009 to 2016, many bond-based or interest-rate–based asset classes have

underperformed expectations. A whole life insurance policy is such an asset class, as its growth is based on an insurance company's dividend. With insurance companies' portfolios heavily bond-based, it is not surprising that most of the top-rated life insurance companies have seen their dividend rates decline steadily for the past decade. Though rates have climbed a bit recently, it may be awhile before they rise enough to see whole life policies return to what they yielded pre-2009. Some whole life policyowners may want to move to a policy that has more upside potential.

On the other hand, we have seen some policyowners who have owned more market-based products, like variable or variable universal life, for the last decade. These owners have seen their cash values grow significantly as the market recovered from the crash of 2008. Now a dozen years older and a bit more conservative with regard to their portfolios, these owners consider moving their policy the opposite way, into whole life products, positioning them for less risk and more stable, if lower, returns.

Case Study: Doctor Dan Improves Performance with Policy Exchange

Dan purchased a whole life policy at age 40 from a large well-known carrier. He is now 52. While the carrier is solid, as is its whole life product, it is known in the industry to have relatively high expense charges. Dan was super-preferred when he initially purchased the policy and has maintained good health. Dan wanted to see how his whole life policy would compare with a different type of policy, perhaps one with more investments upside and lower cost structures, taking advantage of COIs and perhaps a different company's product.

We modeled several scenarios for Dan. We found that if he were to do a 1035 exchange of his whole life policy with a universal life policy issued by another top-rated company, he would enjoy significantly improved performance. While insurance carriers do not publish their COIs for whole life products, knowledgeable advisors can examine head-to-head performance numbers using identical ages, underwriting classifications, and assumed rates of return to see the difference in distributions from the policy, thereby comparing their underlying cost structures.

For Dan, a 52-year-old "preferred" risk, assuming a 5.85% rate of return for each policy, the results are dramatic. The distributions from his current whole life policy are projected to be $53,696 annually for twenty years beginning at age 65. With the same assumptions, the distributions from the new universal life policy would be $98,476 annually for twenty years beginning at age 65. This is nearly $45,000 of annual improvement and nearly $900,000 of increased distributions over twenty years.

This dramatic improvement is due to these factors: (1) probable lower COI moving from the whole life product to the universal product (we don't use exact numbers here because, as mentioned, COI for whole life products are not published) and (2) lower costs of accessing the cash values in the universal life policy versus the whole life policy.

TAKEAWAY: Permanent life insurance offers a variety of investment options within the structure and significant tax benefits. However, there are important success factors that must be present in order to use the asset class properly, as is obvious when one examines case studies. Finally, the ability to do a 1035 exchange (or "refi") provides significant long-term flexibility.

CHAPTER 4.5

Long-Term Care Planning: What You Need to Know About the Risk and the Role of Insurance

What comes to mind when you consider the phrase "long-term care"? You may think of the services provided by a nursing home, assisted living facility, or in-home care provider. In fact, long-term care can be any one or a combination of these services.

One might think that physicians anticipate the medical, family, and financial challenges of long-term care for themselves and their spouses, parents, and in-laws and make proper planning decisions before the need for care creates a tension-filled issue. Unfortunately, as a firm that has advised over a thousand physicians, we do not find this to be the case.

In this chapter, we will describe the background of long-term care planning and give an overview of some key issues all physicians should understand.

The Challenge

Physicians should be aware of the medical reasons people need long-term care services. Very simply, as we age, basic daily functions (called activities of daily living, or ADLs, in long-term care jargon) become difficult to perform without assistance. ADLs include eating, bathing, dressing, toileting, transferring, and continence.

Doctors should also be aware that assistance with such activities, whether in a nursing home, a skilled nursing facility, or even at home, can be very expensive—and the need for assistance may last for years. Thus, for both family and financial reasons, giving careful thought to these challenges in advance of a long-term care need is wise.

Looking at the macro statistics, just a few numbers tell the story:[1]

- 15 million: the number of Americans expected to have a high need for long-term care by 2050
- 52.3%: the expected percentage of people turning 65 who will have a long-term care need during their lifetimes
- $225 billion: long-term care expenditures in the U.S., 2015.
- $470 billion: the dollar value of long-term care provided by unpaid caregivers, 2013
- 129,000: the number of individual long-term care insurance policies sold, 2014
- 305,068: the number of hybrid life/long-term care policies sold to individuals, 2013

Bringing this home for a physician's family, ask yourself these questions:

- What would you do if you were suddenly faced with an additional yearly expense of $100,000 (much higher in New York, California, and other expensive states)? Also consider that this amount will double if a couple needs care simultaneously!
- How would this affect your retirement planning?
- How long could you afford these costs?
- How would this additional expense affect the estate you want to leave behind?
- How can you assure that you maintain your financial security and independence?
- How would you answer these questions with respect to your parents or in-laws?

---

[1] https://www.morningstar.com/articles/823957/75-mustknow-statistics-about-longterm-care.html

What the Government Provides

Generally, the government, through the Medicaid program, will pay for long-term care, but only after the individual meets certain state-specific income, asset, and physical minimums. Said differently, you must be poor by state standards before the government will assist you under the Medicaid program, and the assistance will likely be provided in a nursing home.

For most physicians and their spouses, meeting these minimums would mean losing most of the assets they have worked hard to earn over their careers—an unacceptable proposition. For some parents and in-laws, however, Medicaid qualification may be a suitable solution. With advance planning, the use of Medicaid trusts and other tools to qualify for benefits by moving assets to family members can be a viable option that should be explored.

Having Family Members Provide Care

While siblings, children, grandchildren, and other family members can play an important role in providing care, there are myriad issues to consider, including time management, geography, and funding. Think about how pressed for time most people are today as they balance the demands of their families and careers. Ponder also the challenges that could arise if some family members live near the person needing care and others do not. Will all geographically close relatives split duties equally? Will some be compensated for their time? At what rate? Can family members do a good job of providing care—or even an adequate one? Even in the best of circumstances, these are issues that can build resentment, anger, and stress and cause serious family repercussions.

Paying Out of Pocket

Certainly, many doctors can afford to pay out of pocket for months if not years for services for themselves and their spouses. But is this a wise choice from an overall financial planning perspective? It may not be, especially when insurance coverage is considered.

Even more problematic may be paying out of pocket for parents or in-laws, especially when siblings do not have the ability or desire to pay their fair share. Once again, anger, stress, and resentment are common in these situations.

Insurance Coverage

Purchasing insurance to cover long-term care needs can be a sound part of a financial plan. Long-term care insurance (LTCI) is an insurance product that pays for long-term care services in many settings: home, a nursing home, an assisted living facility, or an adult day care facility. Since there are many different LTCI plans and insurance carriers who offer them, it is important to make sure the plan you select will meet your foreseeable needs. Some plans cover facilities-only care, while others cover facilities care and home care. Some policies exist as stand-alone long-term care policies and others are hybrid life insurance/long-term care policies.

Types of LTCI Policies

Common types of policies include the following:

Traditional LTCI policies. Traditional LTCI policies feature benefits, options, and riders that vary in availability and scope among carriers. These traditional policies do not have cash value, nor do they have a death benefit. Once a person becomes eligible for LTCI benefits (by becoming unable to perform two of six activities of daily living and requiring substantial assistance), the traditional policy pays a daily or monthly reimbursement for approved expenses up to the maximum daily/monthly benefit chosen by the insured. Upper and lower limits vary among carriers but are in the $20–$300 per day range. Benefits can be received for a specified period of time, usually two to six years, as determined by a total insurance dollar value of the policy, often referred to as the "pool of benefits." "Facility-only" or "facility and in-home care" policies are also available. Elimination periods (deductibles) apply and can range from 0 days to 90 days.

Other features, options, and riders that vary among carriers are inflation protection, bed reservations, alternative plan of care, restoration of benefits, personal care advisor, respite care, joint policy discounts, premium waiver, rate classes, non-forfeiture benefits, indemnity benefits, and caregiver indemnity benefits.

A major reason for resistance to purchasing traditional LTCI is the possibility of paying premiums for a long time but never needing to use the policy's benefits. If this is the reason you do not have LTCI, you should seek a carrier that offers nonforfeiture or death benefit options. Nonforfeiture options allow for the policy to become "paid-up"—that is, not require any more premium payments—in exchange for reduced benefits. Often, the benefit pool is reduced to an amount equal to the premiums paid. Death benefit options allow the policy owner to name a beneficiary to whom a benefit will be paid when the policy owner dies, even if long-term care benefits have been received. The benefit amount varies but is usually either a return of premium or a multiplier of the LTC benefit amount. However, the policy must be in force at the time of death for the beneficiary to receive the paid premiums.

Universal life insurance policies. A different method of addressing long-term care needs is to purchase a universal life insurance policy with an attached rider that can accelerate all or a portion of the death benefit for payment of approved long-term care costs should the need arise. Benefits are received in much the same way as under a traditional long-term care policy. In most cases, an existing cash value policy can be exchanged for a universal life insurance policy with no tax consequence (consult your tax professional regarding your particular situation).

The monthly benefit amount is selected as a percentage of the death benefit, with the most common being 2% (but there are also options available that can go as high as 4%). As you use the benefit for LTC expenses, the death benefit will be reduced dollar for dollar and any cash value is typically reduced proportionally. This strategy can use many different product types, including lifetime guarantees on the death benefit and premium payments.

Case Study: Using UL for LTC Benefits

Sam, a 50-year-old man in good health, could purchase a universal life policy with a $500,000 death benefit and elect to be able to accelerate up to $250,000 if an LTC need should arise, at a maximum of $10,000 per month. If Sam has an LTC claim in the future and he takes the maximum $10,000-per-month benefit amount, the benefit pool will last for a little over two years and the policy will still leave a $250,000 death benefit for his beneficiaries.

The premium for this policy could be paid over any time period Sam chooses, beginning at age 50. For example, to be finished by age 65, Sam's annual premium would be $5,288. If he chooses to pay for life, the annual premium could be as low as $4,265. Alternatively, Sam could pay a single premium of $79,745.

Asset-based LTCI policies. Some companies offer LTCI policies that allow people with assets to invest those assets and secure leveraged LTC coverage (about 3:1). These policies are unique in that they pay regardless of outcome: if you need coverage, it is there; if you cancel your coverage, you get your assets back; if you never make a claim before you die, your children will inherit the assets you invested. When wealthier individuals have the funds to invest in this sort of policy, it can be a no-lose proposition. These products offer different premium payment options, ranging from single premiums to periodic payments until you reach age 100. Unlike the universal life options, most products in this category are fully guaranteed (LTC benefit, death benefit, cash value, and premium).

Overall, the most important feature of a good LTCI policy is a financially sound insurance carrier. Do not consider purchasing the cheapest LTCI policy that you can find. LTCI carriers must have the financial strength to sustain their ability to pay claims well into the future, when the millions of baby boomers will begin needing LTC benefits.

> **TAKEAWAY:** Many physicians will need expensive assistance when they are older, whether it be at-home or in-facility care. While paying out of pocket is an option, as is relying on family for care, using insurance to pay for such assistance may be the superior solution for many doctors. Long-term care policies and universal life policies with LTC benefits can play an important role.

LESSON 5

Out in Practice – Investing to Reach Your Goals

You could write a whole book on wealth management and investing—in fact, we have. It's called *Wealth Management Made Simple* (*WMMS*). We highly recommend this book for anyone looking to gain a better understanding of how investing fits within wealth management. Condensing our firm's 100+ years of advisor experience into one Lesson isn't a realistic task. Imagine being asked to explain everything you learned in medical school and residency to a room full of accountants, attorneys, and financial advisors. You may a be a great speaker, but you would not expect an attorney to diagnose a family member's medical problem after hearing your fifteen-minute lecture.

Recognizing this reality, in this Lesson, we focus on the areas we see as most pertinent for physicians as investors. We will refer you to WMMS in various sections of the Lesson. If you don't have a copy of WMMS you can visit *www.ojmbookstore.com* and order a free print copy or ebook download using the code **WPR2R**.

We will move forward with this Lesson under the assumption that you can read WMMS for more in-depth information.

In this Lesson, we will cover investing topics that we believe are of special interest to physicians, including:

- How physicians are dissimilar to typical U.S. investors and how they are similar
- A few of the scientific studies that show how our brains can physiologically hamstring us when investing
- The value of a professional advisor
- What physicians should look for in, and expect of, a professional investment advisor

CHAPTER 5.1

How Physicians Are Unlike, and Like, Most Retail Investors, and Why It Matters

One important success factor for physicians when it comes to investing is understanding how they are unlike most U.S. retail investors and how they are similar. Before we dig into these topics, a few comments about the financial media are in order, because all investors, including doctors, are influenced by what they read and hear about investing.

Advice From the Media

Let's focus on the two most prominent media: television and the internet. The goal of the media is to maximize ratings or clicks. Why? Media companies are compensated by selling advertising—more eyeballs equal more dollars. If the goal is to maximize viewers or readers, then what is the target audience? The answer is that there isn't a target demographic. As a physician, you need to be very careful about taking advice targeted to the masses.

Financial media need to keep you interested. If you hear that the economy is strong, the markets are stable, and your strategy is working, are you going to continue watching? No. Media companies understand this thought process. Because financial media need to keep viewers and readers interested, their slant will be negative. If the news you are regularly consuming is always negative, your way of thinking will be influenced by that. When was the last time you heard "stay the course, remain diversified, ask yourself if your goals have changed"? A bad quarter of earnings or a slowing GDP should not influence your retirement plan or your investment strategy.

How Physicians Are Different from Most Investors

As a physician, you are different from the average American retail investor in several ways. This is important to realize because most financial news, whether in print, online, or on television, is geared to the typical retail investor. Therefore, media messages on investing often will not apply well to your circumstances. We frequently speak with physicians who are operating under assumptions based on investment research that are ill-suited to their situation, and part of our job is to educate people on how and why this is so.

There are more, but we will discuss three important ways in which physicians generally differ significantly from the average retail investor: financial circumstances, amount of free time, and "highest and best use" of that time.

1. Financial Circumstances

Of these three factors separating physicians from the typical retail investor, this is perhaps most obvious. The reality is that most Americans are not as well off financially as physicians are. Let's examine income, as an example.

Americans on average earn nowhere near the income that physicians do. The median household income in the United States in 2019 was around $50,000,[1] while the average physician's income in 2019 was $313,000.[2] The average income of physicians in the top five medical specialties was $452,000.[3] This income difference is enormous and has implications in all disciplines of wealth management. Quite simply, many of the major concerns that physicians have as they go about their planning are not even minor considerations for the average investor. Nowhere is this truer than in tax planning.

The average retail investor cares little about tax planning because they don't have a significant tax problem. Did you know that approximately 44% of Americans paid zero federal income

---

[1] https://www.thestreet.com/personal-finance/average-income-in-us-14852178

[2] https://weatherbyhealthcare.com/blog/physician-salary-2019

[3] https://weatherbyhealthcare.com/blog/physician-salary-2019

tax in 2018?[4] Or that the average U.S. taxpayer has an effective federal income tax rate of 12.1%?

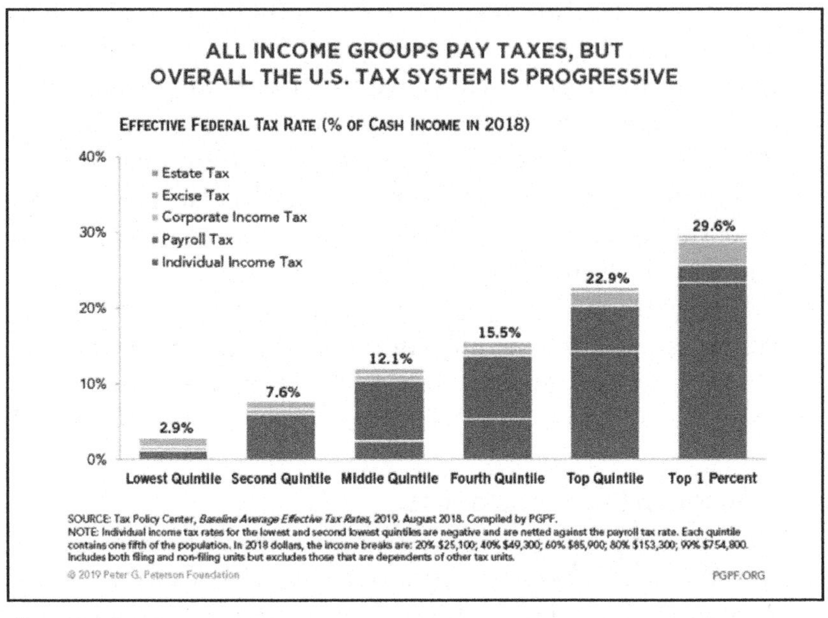

Figure 5.1.1

Compare an effective rate of 12.1% with the top marginal rate of a physician. The top federal rate is 37%. Add the 3.8% Medicare surtax on modified adjusted gross income over $250,000 (for married couples, or $200,000 for individuals) and state and local taxes, and it becomes clear that most physicians face a marginal tax rate of 40% to 50% or more, depending on their state of residence.

This difference in the tax situations of physicians and average retail investors has significant consequences for investing. This difference explains the following:

- Outside of the week before April 15, the financial media generally ignore the subject of taxes completely, yet it is top-of-mind for most physicians throughout the year.

[4] https://www.taxpolicycenter.org/taxvox/tcja-increasing-share-households-paying-no-federal-income-tax

- Almost all reporting on how an investment fund performed shows pre-tax returns rather than post-tax returns, when post-tax returns are all that really matters to a heavily taxed investor like a doctor.
- Mutual funds have, over decades, been able to avoid disclosing their internal holdings' built-in unrealized taxable gains, so new investors cannot understand the tax hit when they buy into the portfolio. Many physicians do not even realize this.
- Working with an investment advisor who uses a number of tax-reduction strategies (like asset location strategies and tactical tax gain/loss harvesting, among others) can be essential for physicians but almost irrelevant for most investors.
- Certain investment products can make sense for most retail investors but not for physicians. We will look at an example of this below.

Case Study: Separately Managed Accounts—Do They Make Sense for Doctor A?

A physician may assume that if an investment solution makes money, it is appropriate for everyone. You might be surprised to hear that investment solutions are often designed with scale and efficiency in mind, which benefits financial services firms but may not be a good fit for tax-sensitive investors like physicians. Let's examine separately managed accounts.

Separately managed accounts seem like a great concept to potential investors. The investor owns a pool of individual stocks professionally managed by a global asset manager who is, in theory, the best at their craft. Changes to the underlying holdings occur frequently, so the client feels as if the manager is earning their fee. However, this turnover creates an extremely high tax bill on the portfolio.

Doctor A was considering a separately managed account with a good portfolio return history given its risk profile and a portfolio of exchange traded funds (ETFs) with a similar risk/return-profile.

Portfolio A: Separately Managed Account
$500,000 earns 20% = $100,000 in appreciation. Half of the gains are short-term; the client has $50,000 in realized short-term gains. Because Doctor A lives in California, his marginal income tax rate is around 50% after accounting for state and federal taxes. Thus, the short-term gains results in a $25,000 tax bill. Portfolio A yields a net profit of $75,000.

Portfolio B: A Mix of Exchange-Traded Funds
$500,000 earns 18% = $90,000 in appreciation. The strategy is passive; therefore, the ETFs are not actively buying and selling underlying holdings. No gains are realized. Portfolio B yields a net profit of $90,000.

Imagine this scenario repeating for many years. Considering the compounding of gains upon gains, the result will be a sizeable difference in net worth. We acknowledge that equities aren't going to return 18% to 20% every year, which might lead one to say that this example is overstated. You should note, though, that portfolio B is statistically likely to outperform portfolio A at least 50% of the time. (A recent study by S&P Dow Jones Indices evaluating actively managed funds against their benchmarks suggests that the odds of portfolio A underperforming are much higher. The study found that 85% of large cap funds underperformed the S&P 500 over a ten-year period.[5])

Most mutual funds raise many of the same tax issues as separately managed accounts. If you would like to understand the tax

---

[5] https://www.cnbc.com/2019/03/15/active-fund-managers-trail-the-sp-500-for-the-ninth-year-in-a-row-in-triumph-for-indexing.html

efficiency of a mutual fund, find the fund's tax cost ratio. The tax cost ratio measures the percentage of the annualized return that is lost to tax as a result of the fund's distributions. A typical range for the tax cost ratio is 0% to 5%. The higher the tax cost ratio, the more of your returns are being lost to taxes. The tax cost ratio affects returns in the same manner as a mutual fund expense ratio. A 10% return by a fund with a 2% tax cost ratio results in a net return of 8%.

Why are so many investment solutions inefficient from a tax perspective? For most dollars invested in financial products, taxes are not applicable. The bottom line: many of these types of financial products are designed for investors who are subject to a lower amount of taxes than physicians are.

2. For Most Physicians: The Amount of Free Time

Ask almost any physician what their scarcest resource is and the answer is likely to be "time." The practice of medicine is nothing like the nine-to-five jobs that most Americans work. In fact, as we understand it, the practice of medicine has become more time-intensive as physicians' non-patient-care responsibilities have increased dramatically in recent years—think documentation and interacting with insurance companies and other payors.

What is a physician's typical day like? Beginning very early, see patients on hospital rounds and/or perform surgeries. Then conduct office hours. Then document patient care, return calls and interact with payors. Then stay up to date by reviewing medical literature. Get home at 6:00 or 7:00. Time to interact with young kids? Attend older kids' games or performances? Spend time with a spouse? Exercise? Eat a healthy meal? Unwind or enjoy a hobby? Get adequate rest? It is no surprise that physician burnout is so prevalent.

Add to that learning about all the various investment options, understanding the tax implications, and watching the markets, and there may literally be no time for sleep!

This is not to say that people who do other work don't have time stress. However, it may not be as pervasive as it is for physicians. A Bureau of Labor Statistics report published in October 2019 reveals that the average non-farm work week in the United States was 34.4 hours. For "private-sector production and nonsupervisory employees," it was 33.6 hours.[6] Conversely, in 2015 the AMA reported that fewer than 15% of physicians worked less than 40 hours per week.[7]

Because of this lack of time, focusing on the financial, tax, legal, risk, and insurance issues that must be understood in order to adequately manage a family's finances in general, and investments in particular, is a significant challenge if it is attempted without the assistance of a professional advisor. Add to this the consequences of managing a physician's higher-than-average income and net worth in less-than-ideal circumstances and the issue becomes even more important.

We are not saying that physicians cannot or should not take an active role in their wealth planning and investing. In fact, we delve more deeply into do-it-yourself (DIY) investing for physicians and the value of professional advisors in Chapter 5.3. However, compared to the average investor, physicians have much less time to do so and there is more at stake.

3. Highest and Best Use: For the Few Physicians with Spare Time

For the relatively few physicians who have the spare time to actively invest on a continuing basis, the question becomes, does it make economic sense to do so?

Certainly, most physicians are capable of researching investments if they have the time. A physician DIY investor can purchase sophisticated retirement software (or access very basic versions for free). They can, if they wish, take the time to keep up with evolving investment tax laws. Portfolio management software that will help them understand the correlation of their investments and the risk of the overall portfolio is available. They can access consumer-level trading platforms online as well. If they are extremely organized, they can create calendar reminders to ensure that they follow through and execute on every element of an investment process. Dedicating sufficient time, they can learn about estate planning, asset protection,

---

[6] https://www.bls.gov/news.release/empsit.nr0.htm

[7] https://www.ama-assn.org/practice-management/physician-health/how-many-hours-are-average-physician-workweek

business entity structure, buy-sell agreements, insurance products, and any other subcomponent of wealth planning.

Having the ability to perform a task, however, doesn't mean that you *should* perform the task. Investing the time to learn a skill, for one thing, does not equate to being good at the skill. One person cannot possibly be an expert in every discipline.

All in all, the most important question is not whether a physician *can* DIY invest. With enough time and commitment, they can. The important question is whether they *should*. In other words, would a physician be better off putting their time to its highest and best use—treating patients and being paid well to do so—to earn income and then spending a portion of that income to hire investment and wealth management expertise?

This highest-and-best-use analysis could just as easily be applied to other professionals, like attorneys, or compared with other services, like preparing tax returns, repairing a leaky sink, and mowing the lawn. Each professional has to balance his or her interest in doing these and a million other tasks with the economics of the opportunity cost of spending time on endeavors that they can pay other people to do for less than their own effective hourly earnings. Some physicians are natural DIYers and will gravitate to performing such tasks themselves rather than delegating, especially when the tasks are low-risk and failure or suboptimal outcomes can easily be seen and remedied (the sink doesn't stop leaking, the lawn isn't well-mowed). But consider jobs where it is more difficult to determine if it was done well: how can one know if the tax return one files or the portfolio one designs and attempts to rebalance or tax-manage is optimal?

For this reason alone, there is a much greater opportunity cost for higher-income investors like physicians who choose to spend their valuable time on tasks that they could pay someone else to do for them. This is so even if there is no skill differential (the doctor can mow the lawn just as well as the neighbor's son). And when the physician does *not* have the expertise to perform the task well (how well can most physicians prepare their own tax returns, compared to an experienced CPA?), it is not surprising that most physicians choose to outsource at least some of their investing and wealth management tasks. Basic economics dictate that they do so.

From an extremely high level, let's examine a few numbers. Most (though not all) of our physician clients work around 200 to 250 days a year and their income ranges from $250,000 to $1 million annually, so they earn $1,000 to $5,000 per day. If we estimate that the work involved in actively managing a portfolio, including researching public and private investments, assessing portfolio risk, trading and rebalancing, harvesting tax loss, locating tax-efficient assets, and implementing a spending strategy to manage sequence-of-withdrawal risk, would take one to three days per month, this equates to a time cost of between $12,000 and $180,000 annually. Obviously, this range is extremely large, with the highest-income physicians incurring the greatest opportunity cost because they are paid so well for the highest and best use of their time. Not surprisingly, though, even for the lowest-income physicians (who still are earning much more than the average U.S. household), their time cost almost always exceeds what they would pay a professional to handle these tasks — because they are likely to have smaller portfolios that generate lower professional fees, at least in an asset-based fee model.

This analysis is much like the one that dictates why physicians should not answer their own phones, book patient appointments, do the coding and billing themselves, or even perform medical tasks that a nurse or physician's assistant can do well. Doctors do not do these tasks at their practices because of the "highest and best use" concept.

To avoid the time cost of doing their own financial planning and investment management, most physicians elect to outsource it. If you make the decision to hire an advisor, though, that doesn't mean you can completely ignore your finances and become disengaged. Ask difficult questions, check for conflicts of interest, demand transparency, and expect regular communication. Once you perform these steps, you will be able to sleep well at night and you can make the highest and best use of your time—whether that is financial (seeing patients) or personal (spending time with friends and family, pursuing a hobby, etc.).

How Physicians Are the Same as Most Investors

Physicians are human beings and have brains like all human beings. Therefore, they face the same pitfalls as other investors. You may have heard of the impact of the basic human emotions of greed and fear on investing—getting overly optimistic when the market goes up, assuming it will continue to do so, and wanting to be in on the action (greed) and then becoming pessimistic during downturns and wanting out before losing everything (fear). Greed and fear can affect physicians like they do any other investor.

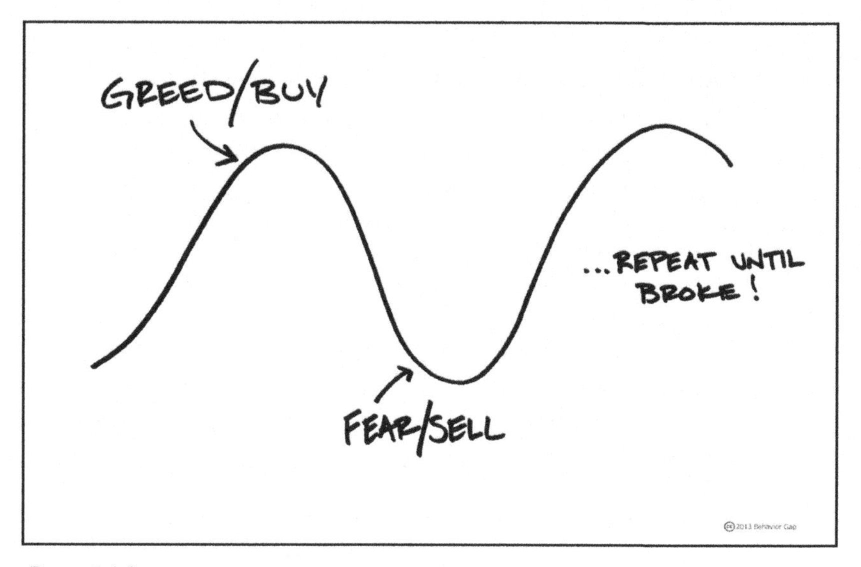

Figure 5.1.2

Here, we will discuss symptoms common to individual investors because of how our brains work when it comes to investing — physician or not. In the next chapter, we will discuss some of the scientific studies that explain how our brains react to investment decisions physiologically.

Individual Investor Mistakes

In a 2010 report that the Securities and Exchange Commission Office of Investor Education and Advocacy asked the United States Library of Congress Federal Research Division to prepare regarding the behavioral traits of U.S. retail investors, nine common investing mistakes that affect investment performance were identified:

Active trading is the practice of engaging in regular, ongoing buying and selling of investments while monitoring pricing in hopes of timing the activity to take advantage of market conditions.

The disposition effect is the tendency of retail investors to hold losing investments too long and subsequently sell winning investments too soon.

Paying more attention to the past returns of funds than to fees occurs when investors give too much credence to the past performance of funds and virtually ignore the funds' transactional costs, expense ratios, and fees.

Familiarity bias is the tendency of investors to gravitate to investment opportunities that are familiar to them.

Mania is the sudden increase in value of a "hot" investment because the masses rush to get in on the action. Panic is the inverse—investors try to abandon an investment that is performing poorly over the short-term.

Noise trading may occur when an investor decides to take action without engaging in fundamental analysis. When investors follow the daily headlines too closely and succumb to false signals and short-term volatility, their portfolios suffer.

Momentum investing is the practice of buying securities with recent high returns and selling securities with low recent returns, which assumes past trends and performance will continue.

Under-diversification occurs when the investor becomes too heavily concentrated in a specific type of investment.

Naïve diversification is diversifying between several investments in equal proportions rather than in strategic proportions.

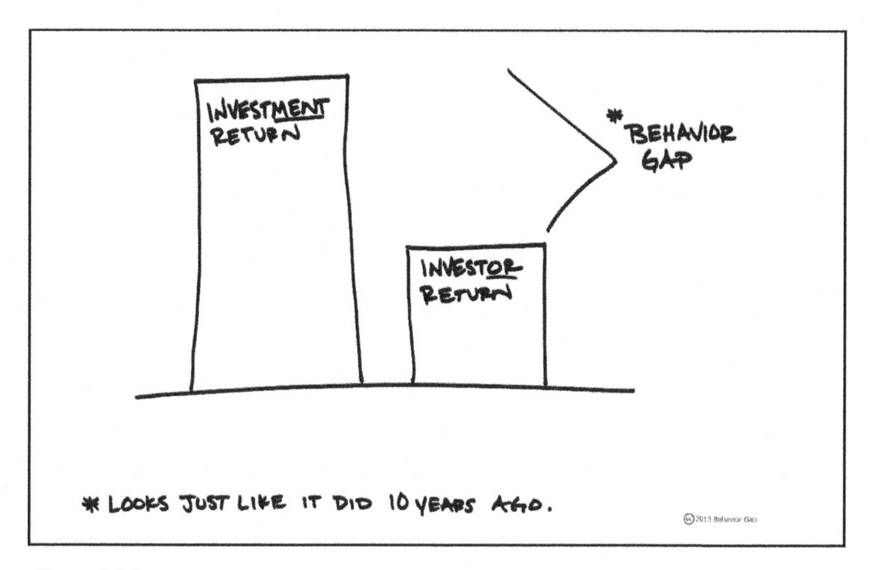

Figure 5.1.3

In *Wealth Management Made Simple*, we dedicate multiple chapters to the gap between how *investments* do and how *investors* do. Carl Richards drew this illustration over ten years ago to show this "behavior gap." Little has changed since he drew this modest picture. The point of this illustration is profound—the evidence is quite clear that most individual investors significantly underperform the investments within their portfolio because of the trends identified by the SEC. There is a gap between how the investments do in a vacuum and the investor's performance on those same investments because of the behavior of the investor.

TAKEAWAY: When it comes to wealth management in general and investing in particular, physicians are different than the average U.S. investor because of their income and net worth, the time they have available, and the highest and best use of that time. On the other hand, doctors are like all humans in that, in the area of investing, they can succumb to greed and fear and all the behaviors that these emotions cause.

CHAPTER 5.2
Why Our Brains Often Fail Us When We Are Investing: What the Science Shows

As physicians, you studied anatomy in medical school and probably in your pre-med courses as well. Some of you are neurologists or neurosurgeons—experts in the brain and its ailments. Nevertheless, few of you have studied how our brains work with respect to investment decisions and behavior.

In this chapter, we will briefly discuss the science of the study of our brains and investments—a field called "neuroeconomics." We will describe several studies that show how the human brain can lead investors down the wrong path.

If you are interested in more exhaustive coverage of the topic, we recommend *Your Money and Your Brain* by Jason Zweig. Many of the studies referred to in this chapter are described in more depth in Mr. Zweig's book.

Background

The human brain is a fascinating organ. It controls our thoughts and speech, the movement of our extremities, and the functioning of our autonomic nervous system. It has evolved to allow us to survive as a species for hundreds of thousands of years, but it is detrimental to successful investing.

You may be familiar with DALBAR's "Quantitative Analysis of Investor Behavior Study." This study has been assessing investor returns since 1994 and has found that investors repeatedly trail their benchmarks. In most years, investor performance lags by a substantial margin. You can review the details of DALBAR's study on its website. Most underperformance is tied directly to investor behavior, which, of course, is controlled by how investors think and feel as they make investment decisions.

The Reflexive Brain

The reflexive brain deals with the present. Like a physical reflex, it is triggered suddenly and powerfully. When short on time, the reflexive brain reacts and makes decisions based on experience. It is constantly searching for threats. The response of your reflexive brain is frequently complete before your conscious brain has recognized a need to respond, so your reflexive system gets the first shot at solving problems.

The amygdala is the part of your reflexive brain responsible for generating emotions, including fear and anger. It stores memories of events and functions as an alarm system. Our amygdala helps us focus our attention when a threat is present. A threat is not limited to potential physical harm; it could pertain to potential financial loss. In fact, the threat doesn't even have to be real—even anticipated threats can trigger the amygdala.

Why is This Problematic for Investing?

There is always a reason to be fearful in the world of investing. We would challenge you to find a time in history when anyone's environment has felt free of risk. Inflation, deflation, global tensions over natural resources or religion, political instability, corporate greed, wealth inequality, tax policy, and sovereign debt are a few examples of perpetual threats to financial markets.

The existence of risk is not a reason to talk yourself out of investing. It is exactly why you get rewarded with returns in excess of those of CDs or treasury bills. Unfortunately, accepting risk conflicts with what our brains are telling us to do. Accepting risk is particularly challenging when sudden large declines occur. Logically, we know we should buy low and sell high; however, our reflexive brain tells us to do the opposite. "There is an imminent threat to your survival—get out!" it screams. In other areas of life that involve risk, most of us are able to soothe the reflexive brain using the logical reflective brain described below. Consider plane rides. When we take our first flight, we may be extremely fearful of crashes. As we gain experience flying safely, though, we overcome our fears. Of course, some people cannot overcome a deep reflexive fear of flying no matter how much data they are given about how safe commercial flying is, even if they logically understand it with their reflective brain.

Investing presents a conundrum. We find that older, more experienced investors succumb less to the anxiety that market downturns can stimulate because they have been through it before and have seen their balances rebound over time. On the other hand, as investors age they typically have more to lose *and* have less time in their working years to make up significant losses with additional income. They literally have more to lose financially as they age and build larger portfolios. Because of this, we have seen even seasoned investors revert to fear-based decision making, if they are not properly advised, as their reflexive brains resurface.

The Reflective Brain

The reflective brain is, as the name suggests, responsible for critical thinking and problem solving. The reflective system is located in the prefrontal cortex. If we are assessing data or performing research, we are relying on our reflective brain. What are some examples of financial decisions that use our reflective brain? Determining your asset allocation and deciding which fund to invest in are two.

Why is This Problematic for Investing?

While more easily stated than practically applied, leveraging your reflective brain for investing is preferred. The problem occurs when there is too much information for the reflective brain—it will defer to the reflexive brain for the final decision. As we all know, there is a limitless amount of investment-related information and easily accessible data on the internet. Some investors are overwhelmed by it and allow their reflective brains to shut down. They just go with their gut and allow their reflexive brains to take over, making decisions that, in hindsight, do not seem to have any logical basis.

Scientific Studies

There are many interesting scientific studies from the field of neuroeconomics that teach us how our brains help or hurt us when it comes to investing. We will discuss three of them. The first shows how many of us use our reflexive brain instead of our reflective brain. The second demonstrates that even when we're using our reflective brain, too much information can hurt us. The third reveals that the brain reacts the same way to an anticipated jump in investments as a cocaine addict's brain does when it is anticipating another snort.

Case Study: Jellybean Syndrome

The first study demonstrates that even when making an extremely simple decision, when all information is easily known, most people act based on their reflexive brain's "gut" rather than their reflective brain's logic. People make decisions to follow a path knowing that the odds of it succeeding are worse than those of the alternative choice.

In this study, researchers at the University of Massachusetts Amherst conducted a simple jellybean experiment. Participants were asked to draw a jellybean out of one of two bowls, with the goal of grabbing a red one. They would win $1 if they did so.

The larger bowl contained 100 jellybeans: 7 red and 93 white. The smaller bowl contained 10 jellybeans: 1 red and 9 white. The participants were given these numbers.

Despite the probability of picking a red jellybean from the smaller bowl being higher, more people pulled their jellybean from the larger bowl. Their gut intuition (reflexive) overpowered basic math and logic (reflective).

When asked about their decisions, most participants explained that they preferred to pick from the larger bowl that they "knew" had lower odds of success because they "felt" it offered more ways to win.

Using logic and your reflective brain, the thought process should be very simple. A thorough analysis isn't required to determine that a 10% chance of success is superior to a 7% chance. Yet nearly two thirds of participants chose to draw from the larger bowl although they recognized the inferior odds for a favorable outcome. Participants "felt" the larger bowl offered more options to win—a classic demonstration of the reflexive brain beating out the reflective brain.

The mental disconnect in this experiment is called "denominator blindness." Subjects chose the larger bowl because it contained more red jellybeans (7, as compared to 1 in the smaller bowl) even though the percentage of red jellybeans was lower in that bowl than in the smaller bowl. They ignored the denominator—the total number of jellybeans in the bowl (100 as compared to 10).

An example of denominator blindness that is more directly relatable to investments is the way investors assess fluctuations in their account values. The most common approach is to look at the daily or weekly increases in their portfolio in raw dollar terms. While this seems logical, it is flawed because of the emphasis on the numerator.

Why? Although the numerator changes most, the denominator is more important. Assume that a portfolio valued at $500,000 experiences a $2,000 change in a day. A $2,000 decline is significant and can trigger negative emotions ("I lost $2,000 in a single day—maybe I should get out!"), while a $2,000 increase creates instant gratification and a sense of euphoria ("I made $2,000 today; I should go to Vegas!").

So far, we are comparing $2,000 to $0. But we should be focusing on the larger denominator.

A decline of $500,000 to $498,000 represents a 0.4%loss in the account value. If the portfolio increases from $500,000 to $502,000 the increase represents a positive return of 0.4%. The denominator represents your net worth and determines your ability to retire or achieve another investment goal. Rational thought would suggest we should not be concerned with a fluctuation of less than half of 1%of our assets.

Unfortunately, we are wired to focus on the smaller number, which fluctuates greatly on a relative basis. As one's assets increase, the absolute fluctuations in the numerator become larger.

A 0.5%change in a $1,000,000 portfolio is $5,000. The movement in the numerator triggers stronger emotions, and the need for risk management increases exponentially. An investor feels compelled to act, and the brain's defense mechanisms kick into high gear.

In fact, in a study of investment decisions, it was found that even investors who focus on stock price fluctuations alone are better off than those who review such fluctuations and are able to read the news about those stocks. Let's examine that study next.

Case Study: Information Overload

The proliferation of platforms from which we can consume financial news has created too much information for our brains to absorb. Twenty-four-hour financial channels, financial Twitter, podcasts, and a variety of other sources allow us to access breaking news in seconds. Distinguishing pertinent information from noise feels overwhelming to most investors. Research suggests, in fact, that you may improve performance by limiting your consumption of financial news.

Psychologist Paul Andreassan conducted an experiment with MIT business students in the late 1980s. The students were divided into two groups. The students in both groups purchased portfolios of stocks and were permitted to trade as they wished. The first group was allowed to see only the price change of their stocks. The second group was provided an ongoing stream of information, including all relevant news pertaining to their stocks, in addition to price changes. Interestingly, the group with less information substantially outperformed the better-informed group.

Andreassan's conclusion: the underperformance occurred due to the tendency of the students to overreact to news. Students receiving the news stream felt compelled to trade more frequently and did so with less success.

This research gives us insight into how the herd mentality can develop on Wall Street. It's a mindset that is particularly prevalent in times of fear. Ignoring consensus and standing alone as a contrarian is simple to understand yet very difficult to do. Groupthink leads to performance chasing, which is counter to buying low and selling high.

Speaking of "high," the next study that we will examine looked at the brain and how cocaine addiction compares with the high of making money on investments. The results are astounding.

Case Study: Cocaine and Making Money

Dopamine is a neurotransmitter produced by the brain that plays a role in reward and reinforcement in animals and humans. Improper amounts of dopamine, whether too much or too little, can lead to health problems. One could say that dopamine contributes to learning without awareness. If an event is rewarding, it gains our attention and helps us to focus.

While the release of dopamine plays a role in our desire to seek food and shelter, negative behaviors are also associated with the release of dopamine. Drugs such as alcohol, nicotine, and cocaine can trigger large releases of dopamine, contributing to addictive behavior. Cocaine use can trigger the brain to release dopamine at a rate fifteen times higher than normal brain activity does.

In a 2001 experiment led by Harvard Medical School's Hans Breiter, activations seen in four regions of the brain (the nucleus accumbens, sublenticular extended amygdala, ventral tegmental, and orbitofrontal cortex) in response to monetary prospects and outcomes overlapped with those observed in response to cocaine infusions in research subjects addicted to cocaine.[1]

Breiter and his colleagues recruited volunteers to participate in a game of chance. Subjects' brain activity was monitored through a neuroimaging process called high-field functional

[1] https://www.investopedia.com/news/study-investing-and-cocaine-look-same-brain/

magnetic resonance imaging (fMRI). The volunteers were given $50 and told that during the game, they might lose some or all of it, retain it, or increase it. Each subject was shown a sequence of spinners that were divided into three sectors, each with a different monetary value. There were good spinners ($10, $2.50, $0), intermediate spinners ($2.50, $0, -$1.50), and bad spinners ($0, -$1.50, -$6).

Subjects watched an arrow spin on each spinner for six seconds and then stop on one of the sectors to deliver a gain or loss. The scientists measured brain signals during the anticipation state (before the spinner stopped) and during the outcome phase (after the spinner stopped). The brain images recorded by fMRI displayed distinct patterns.[2]

Jason Zweig, in his book that we cited earlier in the chapter, describes the study and quotes Breiter: "Lay an MRI brain scan of a cocaine addict next to one of somebody who thinks he's about to make money, and the patterns of neurons firing in the two images are virtually right on top of each other." Breiter continued, "You can't get a better bull's-eye hit than those two. If there's an addictive process around chemicals and currency can be used to buy chemicals," he asked, "is it possible that the same process applies to money? It's a very, very good question that has not been answered, but there's a developing mass of anecdotal data that suggests that perhaps it is."[3]

What exactly does this study suggest? Several successful trades can trigger the same addictive behavior that's seen in someone using drugs or alcohol. The addiction in this instance is making money (or at least attempting to do so). Research has led us to the conclusion that over time, dopamine is no longer triggered by experiencing a specific event but rather by the cues we pick up in anticipation of the desired event. We are no longer stimulated by making money; rather, we receive stimulation from the cues we believe will lead to

---

[2] https://www.sciencedaily.com/releases/2001/05/010524062100.htm

[3] Jason Zweig, Your Money & Your Brain.

making money. The brain seeks patterns to identify the cues that it believes will result in successful trading strategies. Unfortunately, the human brain is not equipped to identify short-term investment trends. Our brains are not capable of competing with computer algorithms, which are able to process much larger quantities of data in a fraction of a second. The investor attempting to identify trends, therefore, is fighting a losing battle.

Overconfidence

Human beings tend to be convinced that they are above average and have a difficult time admitting they don't know something. We will share results from a few studies to support this statement in a moment. A healthy dose of confidence isn't a detriment in every aspect of our lives. If we lacked confidence, we would never take risks. Someone who is entirely risk averse would never start a business, invest in stocks, or try a new activity. Calculated risk taking may act as a catalyst to successful investing. Excessive risk taking derived from overconfidence, however, can be very troublesome.

Why is overconfidence problematic for investors? Overconfidence leads to excessive risk taking, eventually leading to larger losses. Lasting damage occurs when these losses are realized. How does this play out in the real world?

Imagine starting with an $800,000 portfolio. The economy is doing well, and the stock market is booming. You convince yourself that the gains in your account are attributable to the securities selections you made, and you elect to become more active. Rather than maintain a diversified investment strategy that you now find boring, you decide to invest your entire account in your winners, which have outperformed the market. Worry about losing money has dissipated and the result is a concentrated portfolio with 130% of the risk of the S&P 500. Riding the wave, the portfolio has increased to $1,000,000.

Suddenly the market pulls back. However, you are convinced that you have invested in great companies and you aren't fazed by a 10%correction. More unexpected bad economic news is released and now the S&P 500 is 25% off its high. Unfortunately, your $1,000,000 with 130% of the risk of the market is worth $675,000. Your reflexive brain kicks in after experiencing a $325,000 loss ("Get out! "You are in danger!") and you sell at the worst possible time.

While this may sound like an exaggeration, it is a scenario that we have witnessed time and time again. How does a rational, intelligent person make a series of mistakes that lead to such a disastrous outcome? Investors extend themselves into a level of risk beyond their comfort level, a mistake that would have not occurred without overconfidence.

Numerous studies and surveys cited in Jason Zweig's book refer to the tendency of humans to believe that their abilities are above average. The examples are not limited to investing. Here are two that we found especially interesting.

- Psychiatrists at the University of Washington published a study in which they asked drivers to rate their "skill, ability, and alertness" the last time they were behind the wheel. Nearly two-thirds of them rated their abilities as above average. All of them were in the hospital after a car accident that occurred while they were behind the wheel. Precisely 68%of them were directly responsible for their accident.[4]
- A survey asked three thousand entrepreneurs to rate the odds of success for a new business like the one they had recently started. Only 39%suggested that the odds of success were seven out of ten or greater. When asked to rate the odds that their own business would be successful, 81% suggested that they had a seven out of ten chance of being successful. An astounding 33%suggested that there was a 0% chance they would fail.[5]

The goal of this chapter is not to discourage you from investing. Rather, we want to help you understand the shortcomings of the human brain so you can avoid making the mistakes that so many investors make every day. In our view, understanding our limitations when it comes to investments is the first step to overcoming them.

---

[4] Zweig, Your Money & Your Brain, p. 85

[5] Zweig, Your Money & Your Brain, p. 86

TAKEAWAY: The field of neuroeconomics is dedicated to studying how human brains work when making investment decisions. Unfortunately, it is clear that our brains can hurt us as much as they help. Understanding our brains' limitations when it comes to investing is the first step to overcoming them.

CHAPTER 5.3

Investing With and Without an Advisor

In Chapter 5.1, we briefly discussed physicians investing without the help of an advisor. We talked about the time crunch most physicians are in and whether investing on their own is the highest and best use of their time. In this chapter, we will discuss do-it-yourself (DIY) investing further and delve into the value a professional investment advisor brings. Finally, we will discuss how technology has recently created a new alternative for investing: "robo advisors."

Investing on One's Own

Typically, investors who choose the DIY route do so for one or more of three reasons: reducing fees, enjoying the education associated with self-directing, and having not found someone they trust with their life savings.

Reducing fees is nothing to scoff at. Fee drag can make a difference to the overall performance of your investments. If you choose an advisor, it is imperative to understand how they are compensated and how your planning will be affected. And we have met physicians who love researching investments and creating their own plans—that is, managing their wealth.

It is possible to successfully manage your own wealth, but we find that typical DIYers are prone to bias, inconsistent attention, and other obstacles that hinder them from achieving long-term success.

Why not do it yourself? There are many reasons; we will focus on the most common.

- It takes time, so there is an opportunity cost. We covered this in Chapter 5.1.

- A professional advisor has access to the best technology and the benefit of scalability; a DIYer does not. This can impact trading performance and cost, eating into investment gains.
- DIYers are generally locked out of most private equity deals as well as alternative and private investment offerings that professional advisory firms can access.

Perhaps most importantly, money triggers emotions. Our last chapter mentioned just a few of the ways in which our brains are not wired to make rational decisions when emotions take over. Theoretically, no one has a greater interest than you in protecting and looking after your investments. However, that personal interest may be the single greatest factor working *against* your investment performance. Most investors are risk-averse, biased creatures prone to giving too much credence to noise, trends, and the herd mentality. In the legal field, there is an old saying (often attributed to Abraham Lincoln): "An attorney who represents himself has a fool for a client." Does this adage also apply to finance? In many cases, it does.

Despite these drawbacks, DIY investing can make sense for some clients for part of their portfolio. It can give you the opportunity to learn about your investments as you begin to build your portfolio and become an engaged investor. It will help you understand how markets work, begin to become aware of your tolerance for volatility and risk, and, most importantly, become familiar with the various investments and investment products available in the marketplace.

What Are the Quantifiable Benefits of Using an Advisor?

A recent Vanguard study[1] stated, "The value proposition for advisors has always been easier to describe than to define." Why is quantifying the value of advisory services so difficult? Because value

---

[1] "*Putting a Value On Your Value: Quantifying Vanguard Advisor's Alpha*; (September 2016) Vanguard Research; accessed on March 15, 2017 via url: https://www.vanguard.com/pdf/ISGQVAA.pdf.

is subjective and the perceived and actual value of wealth management advice will vary from person to person.

That said, we advisors spend significant time with our clients reviewing the components of wealth management that can be objectively quantified based on certain conditions. We can only estimate the value of each piece of wealth management because each piece will be implemented differently, for different reasons, for each individual and will react differently based on economic and market environments.

All advisors charge for their advice. It may be tempting to do a cost-benefit analysis to attempt to produce an annualized figure that clearly defines an advisor's value or the value of the tools they implement for you. But this, again, is very difficult because the value is likely to be sporadic, not consistent from year to year. Further, the value may be not in what is implemented but rather in what is *avoided* during mania and panic, when greed or fear tempt you to deviate from your course. On an individual basis, any cost-benefit analysis would be riddled with unprovable assumptions.

The Vanguard study did attempt, though, across the population and with big data, to quantify the value added by certain best practices in investing. They looked specifically at the following:

- Appropriate asset allocation/diversification
- Cost-effective implementation—i.e., taking into account all fees and costs concerning your investments
- Rebalancing
- Behavioral coaching
- Asset location/utilizing different accounts efficiently
- Spending strategy and withdrawal order
- Total return versus income investing[2]

As with most things, the value is in the whole rather than the sum of wealth management's parts. The value is difficult to discern

---

[2] Ultimately Vanguard determined that "value is deemed significant but too unique to each investor" to accurately quantify total returns versus income investing because each investor's spending, saving and portfolio composition is specific to them personally. *Id.*

at a granular level and rarely reveals itself in quarterly or annual statements. It is rare that advisors highlight the landmines that have been avoided, but the "value and impact on clients' wealth creation is very real."[3] Taking all parts into account, Vanguard estimated that advisors can potentially add 3% in net returns, calculated retroactively on an annual basis.

But that 3% claim comes with a heavy qualification—it will vary annually based on each person's unique circumstances and reveal itself only over the long term.

We are not claiming that every professional advisor *will* add value to your life. No one can make that claim. Rather, advisors *can* add value if they take the time and interest to consider *your* entire picture, and plan and manage according to your personal situation.

Paying for the advice and guidance of a trusted advisor can add meaningful value compared to the average investor experience. Therefore, it is helpful to know what options you have, what questions to ask, and how best to work with the advisor you choose. Let's examine these issues.

Morningstar Study

A Morningstar study[4] sought to "define the additional value achieved by an individual investor from making more intelligent financial planning decisions" with the aid of professional advice. It focused on retirees who received comprehensive wealth management advice, including assistance with strategies that consider customized withdrawal plans during retirement, tax efficiency, total wealth asset allocation, guaranteed income efficiency, and asset allocation predicated on future spending needs.

This Morningstar study is important because it demonstrated that a retiree could expect "an annual return increase of +1.59% [,] . . . a significant improvement in portfolio efficiency for a retiree."[5] The study states that the "results are strong enough to

---

[3] *Id.*

[4] *Alpha, Beta and Now…Gamma* (August 28, 2013); Morningstar Investment Management accessed on March 11, 2017 via url: http://corporate.morningstar.com/ib/documents/PublishedResearch/AlphaBetaandNowGamma.pdf.

[5] *Id.* At page 16 of 28.

highlight the difference that intelligent financial planning can make for investors."[6] The study is not an apples-to-apples comparison for all investment and wealth management planning. It focuses on income stability versus performance and reaching or exceeding specified goals.

Using an Algorithm: Robo Advisors

It should not be surprising that younger physicians are more comfortable with technology than their elders are. This increased comfort level finds its way into the field of investing. As in the general populace, younger doctors, generally with less to invest and often beginning their investment life, are more likely than more established physicians to use robo advisors. This investing option is relatively new, but because of its growth and potential popularity with younger physicians we will discuss it here. For further discussion, see our book *Wealth Management Made Simple*.

What Is a Robo Advisor?

A robo advisor is an automated service that an investor can use to invest assets. The cost is typically low. In fact, some robos will claim to be free. However, there is no free lunch. The robos electing to not charge an investment management fee for their service are making money from products inside the service. They may require a certain percentage in cash, or they share revenue from the funds or ETFs. The robo service is discretionary, so you do not have a say in how funds are allocated.

Why Have Robos Grown in Popularity?

Robo advisors provide a service at a very low cost. Working with a financial advisor can be cost-prohibitive for some people. Consider the following analogy. If you run your own practice, you are familiar with overhead. Not only do you need to pay rent and purchase medical equipment, you need staff to answer the phones, set appointments, greet patients, manage billing, and follow up on tests. Imagine that medical insurance did not exist and every patient had

---

[6] *Id.*

to pay out of pocket. You would need to set a minimum fee for your patients and many of them would not be able to afford your service.

Investors don't have the option of relying on insurance to cover the cost of advice, yet financial professionals also incur a minimum cost for performing a service. How do the largest financial institutions profitably serve clients who have very little to invest? They created high-cost, heavily front-loaded products (vehicles that were very common until a few years ago). Welcome to mutual fund A shares!

Funds charged a sales load of 5.75%, which they took right off the top. The broker would convince the investor that these costs could be made up over time. If you didn't want to take a big hit up front, you could elect for an investment that did not charge a load. Welcome to mutual fund B shares! Management fees for the alternative fund would be about 2.5% annually. If you decided to sell B shares before the end of seven years, you also experienced the pleasure of paying a penalty upon liquidation. Suddenly the broker had found a way to generate nearly $2,900 in commissions on a $50,000 investment.

This cost structure is absurd, yet very real. After reading the previous paragraph, you understand exactly why many people in our business have earned a poor reputation. Robos have filled a gap in the financial industry. Providing quality human service to an individual investor with $50,000 in assets is difficult under a traditional fee-based model. Robos have automated part of the process, using technology to rebalance portfolios. Investors complete a survey that reveals their risk tolerance and are placed into one of six to twelve strategies intended to match asset mix with risk tolerance. The approach of robos is reasonable for an investor who is beginning to build their retirement savings, does not have multiple accounts, or does not yet have complicated planning needs.

As a Physician, Why Shouldn't I Use a Robo Advisor?

We just highlighted several strengths of robos and pointed out flaws in the human advisor model (at least for emerging investors). Why wouldn't you simply hire a robo and call it a day?

You need to recognize that robo advisors were designed to serve the masses. Robos are designed to provide a reasonable service suitable for many people at a very low cost. A robo is similar to a fast food restaurant, a production home builder, or an online tax preparation service. For the appropriate customer, each is very good at what it does. McDonald's can quickly serve hundreds of customers at a reasonable price, a service your local downtown steak house can't match. Turbo Tax allows a taxpayer who is a W-2 employee with a mortgage, a 401(k), and a savings account to quickly complete a return for a price of less than $100. But a business owner with employees, property, rental expenses, a variety of tangible assets that may depreciate, and additional complex circumstances is unlikely to find an online tax preparation service suitable.

As a physician, you need to recognize that your needs are complex. A robo advisor is suitable for many investors, but automation does not provide the level of service a doctor requires. Let's consider a few reasons for that.

Taxes

As we discussed in Chapter 5.1, taxes are a very important aspect of investing and financial planning for you, though they are not as important for 99% of the U.S. population. A robo may provide year-end tax harvesting, which is a valuable service. Tax planning, though, extends beyond an occasional rebalancing trade. Is a robo going to run calculations to determine if you should be investing in corporate bonds or municipal bonds? Probably not. Is a robo going to evaluate the tax efficiency of your underlying investment and determine if that fund is appropriate for someone in a 37% federal tax bracket? Will your robo advisor suggest that you hold higher-yielding investments taxed as ordinary income in your IRA or 401(k)?

Also, although such platforms have boldly touted their tax-harvesting abilities in their marketing materials, third parties have challenged their numbers as inflated.[7] Moreover, Wealthfront, a leading robo platform, recently had embarrassing errors in their 1099 tax reporting that forced many customers to refile their 2017 tax returns after the deadline. A financial industry periodical stated, "As a result of having to refile updated tax information

[7] https://www.cnbc.com/2018/04/16/robo-advisers-may-be-overpromising-investors-on-tax-loss-harvesting.html

with the IRS after the 2017 deadline passed, Wealthfront clients may well face fines, an increased tax bill, and the roughly $400 cost of hiring a tax consultant."[8]

Behavioral Finance

As wealth accumulates, violent market swings become more difficult to accept. At the beginning of a physician's investing life, their entire account balance may be only $10,000. A 20% market correction results in a $2,000 loss. Years later, after saving aggressively and experiencing market appreciation, they may find themselves with $1 million in assets. The same 20% correction equates to a $200,000 loss. Greater wealth means larger losses; consequently, an emotional reaction at an inopportune time can have a devastating impact on your financial plan.

How does behavioral finance relate to robo advisors? Robos require investors to fill out a risk tolerance questionnaire. The questionnaire may even look very similar to the one a professional advisor would ask you to complete. Risk tolerance questionnaires are very similar to a fast food restaurant or online tax service. They are designed to quickly gather information and assign a portfolio closely matching the risk you indicated is acceptable. A questionnaire is not going to take a deeper dive into your personal circumstances. Typically, you will not be asked about real estate, other business ventures, potential risks to your current financial plan, insurance, debt, the likelihood of a sudden need for assets, taxes, or a range of other circumstances unique to you.

Ignoring these topics may be acceptable for the typical investor. However, physicians tend to have more complicated financial circumstances.

Relying exclusively on an online risk tolerance questionnaire can be a flawed approach for an entirely separate reason. Research suggests that many investors fill out questionnaires based on how they know they should behave in a volatile market environment. Actual behavior and rational behavior do not always align. Let's face it, we are human, which means we aren't perfect. Every one

---

[8] https://riabiz.com/a/2019/10/19/wealthfront-is-again-forced-to-disclose-a-bad-mistake-testing-how-far-the-move-fast-break-things-then-apologize-culture-can-go

of us recalls a moment we regret and wish we had handled differently. The odds are high that your patience has been tested by a coworker, one of your children, or even a sporting event. Sometimes we need someone who is rational to step in and serve as a voice of reason. Investing is exactly the same—a time will come when you need a professional to talk you out of a brief lapse in judgment. Your robo advisor is not going to have that conversation with you.

Robo advisory services have taken some media criticism for crashing during periods of high volatility. For example, customers were not able to make trade requests when the Brexit referendum occurred in the summer of 2016, and many were locked out when the Dow Jones tumbled 10% over a short few days in February 2018. Investors should recognize that robo advisors may not offer 24/7 access to trade their investments (a common misconception).

Existing Investments

Most robo services today allow only for cash transfers and deposits and are not capable of account transfers that include established positions. This will work for many small investors who are getting started, but long-term investors will be unable to participate because they hold quality investments and have large unrealized capital gains.

Limits on Types of Accounts

Many of the current robos have a multitude of limitations, including on the type of accounts that can be created, which may not allow for asset protection or estate planning (for example, the inability to create trust accounts or accounts for LLCs or FLPs). This makes a robo a non-starter for physicians concerned about asset protection, estate planning, or family wealth planning.

High Cash Positions Required

Most problematic for some investors are the large cash positions that robos require. These minimum cash positions can be a significant drag on performance, sometimes putting the client in a worse fee position than if they paid a reasonable management fee to a human advisor. Cash requirements provide an opportunity for robos to generate revenue from your assets that are not invested.

Even for smaller investors for whom the cost may not be as problematic, such required positions are a hidden expense that a non-astute investor may not recognize.

TAKEAWAY: Physicians may consider investing on their own, with a professional advisor, or through an online robo platform. Each has pros and cons that should be considered carefully.

CHAPTER 5.4

What to Look For In and Expect from an Investment Advisor

In the last chapter, we discussed the pros and cons of physicians investing on their own, with the services of a professional advisor, or through a robo advisor online platform. In this chapter, we will focus on working with a professional advisor, the most common way that doctors invest. We will briefly discuss the three most popular types of advisors (and the differences among them), key questions to ask an advisor, and what to expect in an advisory relationship.

Professional Investment Advisor Options

Here we will discuss only the three most popular human advisor choices for overall wealth and investment management, as we discussed robo platforms in the last chapter. For brevity, we will not cover less popular advisor options, like insurance agents, or limited-scope advisors, like hedge, private equity, or venture capital funds, which typically invest only a "sleeve" for wealthy clients. If you are interested in reading about these options, please turn to our book *Wealth Management Made Simple*.

The three most common investment advisor options for physicians are brokers/banks, fee-only advisors, and registered investment advisors.

Brokers and Banks

If you decide to work with a professional advisor, the first person you think of may be a broker dealer or bank-based advisor. Brokers and banks tend to be popular because they are the largest corporations who do the most marketing.

A broker-dealer is generally a person or firm in the business of buying and selling securities who operates as both a broker and a dealer, depending on the transaction. Here are some well-known examples:

- National or global broker dealers include Merrill Lynch, Morgan Stanley, and UBS.
- Regional brokers include firms like Raymond James and Edward Jones.
- Bank-based advisors are affiliated with large banks like Wells Fargo and Bank of America; they usually refer to themselves as "financial planners" or "financial consultants."
- Independent broker–dealers run their shops under their own names but are generally affiliated with larger corporations and sell products from outside sources.

We tend to lump these types of firms together because they share the following fundamental trait: *they are not fiduciaries and are required only to abide by the suitability standard* (more information about that later in the chapter).

Definition: A broker (also known as a registered representative) executes security trades for a commission or fee. Compensation is typically tied to the activity level in an account or embedded within the investment products used by the financial professional. The broker or bank representative is employed by the firm holding your assets (also referred to as a "custodian"). The term "broker-dealer," in U.S. securities regulation parlance, describes stock brokerages because most of them act as both agents and principals. A brokerage acts as a broker (or agent) when it executes orders on behalf of clients, whereas it acts as a dealer (or principal) when it trades for its own account.

Why would an investor use a broker? Many people are under the impression that value is tied to activity. In a traditional commission-based environment, clients are not paying a recurring annual or quarterly fee; they are being charged for activity. It is certainly possible for a broker's client to pay less for financial advice in certain circumstances, particularly if they own securities they intend to never sell. A traditional brokerage relationship is not discretionary, meaning that the investor will be able to direct investment decisions and receive suggestions on an ad hoc basis.

The benefits of working with some of the world's largest broker-dealers include tremendous research capabilities, unique investment offerings, and the convenience of branch offices throughout the world.

Why elect against using a bank representative or broker? The top reason, easily, is the conflict of interest present in a relationship where the compensation of the person making recommendations is based on the product they use for the investor. A lack of transparency in fee-based products also means it is very difficult for an investor using this type of advisor to understand what they are paying. Also, the broker's suitability standard is significantly weaker, from a client's perspective, than the fiduciary standard, discussed further below. Private banking advisors also lack independence and generally seem to only use their bank's products; bank trust departments administer trusts under similar conflicts.

How do you know if you are working with a broker? Simply ask the advisor how they are compensated. If you want to be more pointed with your question, ask the representative if they receive compensation from any financial products. Then follow up by asking if their employer receives compensation from financial products. An advisor should not be offended by these questions. In fact, they should welcome them. If the answer is not clear and concise, consider that to be a huge red flag.

It's important to note that most firms have realized that the title "broker" has negative connotations and have begun calling members of their sales force "financial advisors."

Another way to identify a broker is that they are employed by a firm where your assets are held. This can create many conflicts of interest that affect individual investors; there is a long history of proprietary products and incentives for the sales forces at these firms to push certain products on clients. Remaining objective and providing a transparent business model are the biggest challenges for broker-dealers.

In our opinion, for you (the client), the superior business model has a true fiduciary working on your behalf ("fiduciary" will be defined later), but the broker–dealer model today still uses the firm-favorable "suitability standard" in their relationships with clients.

Broker's Suitability Standard

As mentioned above, a broker is subject to the lower "suitability standard." *This means that the broker does not need to act in the best interests of the customer. Instead, their actions must only be "suitable" for the client.*

Broker-dealers are regulated by the Financial Industry Regulatory Authority under standards that require them to make "suitable" recommendations to their clients. The broker, instead of having to make their interests secondary to those of the client, merely has to reasonably believe that any recommendations are suitable for the client in light of the client's financial needs, objectives, and unique circumstances at the time of the interaction. *Loyalty is an important issue: a broker's duty is to the broker-dealer they work for, not necessarily to the client served.*

Most brokers even today have a very convoluted fee structure. In a time when clients are demanding transparency and lower-cost options, you will still see sales loads on mutual funds, trading commissions, and many account-servicing fees.

Fee-Only Financial Planners

Definition: A fee-only planner usually provides services for a set hourly fee ($200 to $500) or an annual retainer ($1,500 to $10,000).

Why would an investor use a fee-only planner? Fee-only planners are generally conflict-free fiduciaries. They also have a simple hourly or retainer fee structure. The cost and the fact that they will work in your best interests mean that you can certainly pick worse options.

Why elect against using a fee-only planner? Fee-only planners have their shortcomings. Most fee-only planners are in small shops with little in the way of resources. It's a positive that you will talk to the same person whenever you call, but this can be a problem in a long-term, business-continuity sense—would you be comfortable with your advisor retiring and sending you to a total stranger right before you retire?

Fee-only planners may be certified and have a professional designation, like certified financial planner (CFP®), but may not be licensed to buy and sell securities, in which case they can help you craft a plan but you have to implement it yourself. They generally have fewer technological resources and may also be shut out of more complex but potentially advantageous investments like real estate investment trusts (REITs) or other non-traded options often used by high-net-worth people to diversify their wealth.

Finally, if you are looking for comprehensive wealth management, many fee-only planners are also not insurance licensed, so they are not able to evaluate, review, or help clients make decisions on disability, life, or long-term care insurance options. As you have learned in Lesson 4, these products provide significant protection for physicians and their families.

Registered Investment Advisors

A registered investment advisor (RIA) is a person or firm engaged in the investment advisory business and registered either with the Securities and Exchange Commission (SEC) or state securities authorities. An RIA is defined by the Investment Advisors Act of 1940 as a "person or firm that, for compensation, is engaged in the act of providing advice, making recommendations, issuing reports or furnishing analyses on securities, either directly or through publications." *Investment advisors have a fiduciary duty to their clients, which means that they have a fundamental obligation to both provide suitable investment advice and always act in clients' best interests.*

Why would an investor use an RIA? An RIA must adhere to a *fiduciary standard* of care laid out in the Investment Advisors Act of 1940. This standard requires RIAs to act and serve a client's best interests with the intent to eliminate, or at least expose, all potential conflicts of interest that might incline an investment advisor, consciously or subconsciously, to render advice that is not in the best interests of their clients.

The following illustration is helpful. Note that for a fiduciary, the client is at the center of the relationship. All advice must be in the client's best interest. For an advisor who must satisfy only the suitability standard, the product is central. It does not matter whether the product fits, or its procurement is in, the client's best interests as long as the product is seemingly suitable at the time of the sale and/or advice.

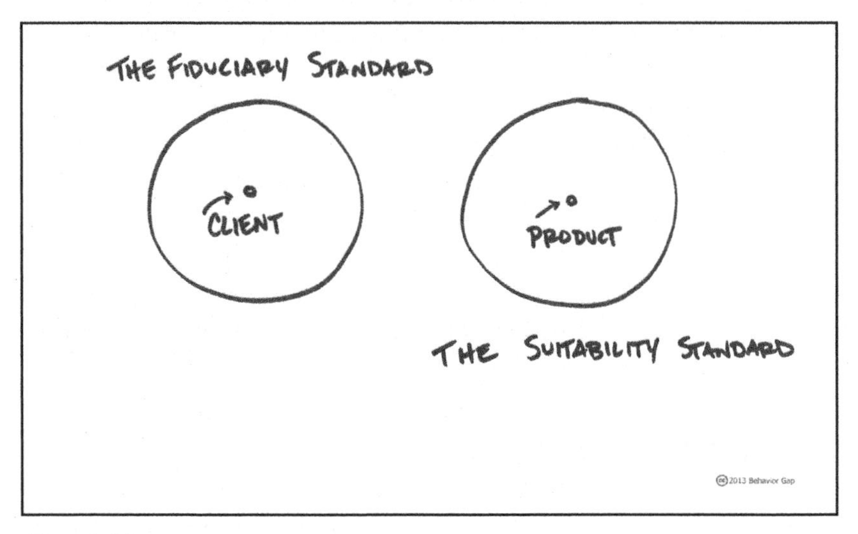

Figure 5.4.1

Key Benefits of Independence

RIAs are not tied to any particular family of funds or investment products. So, whether you need help with retirement planning, a tax situation, estate planning, or managing assets in multiple places, independent advisors have the freedom to choose from a wide range of investment options to tailor their advice to what's best for you.

High Level of Expertise

RIAs can help investors address the variety of complex investment needs that arise when they accumulate significant wealth. While specific services vary from firm to firm, RIAs are often described as financial quarterbacks with a holistic focus. A good RIA will speak to clients about their overall goals and objectives and review them with clients at regular intervals.

Independent Custodians

RIAs use independent custodians, such as Schwab, TD Ameritrade, and Fidelity, to hold clients' assets. Many investors feel that their money not being held by the same person who advises them about how to invest is a reassuring system of checks and balances.

A Simple Fee Structure (Transparency)

RIAs typically charge a fee that is a percentage of assets managed. This structure is simple, transparent, and easy to understand. It also gives your advisor an incentive to help grow your assets. When you succeed, your advisor succeeds.

Fees vary, but the average is around 1% to 1.5% Generally, the more assets a client has, the lower the fee they can negotiate. This serves to align the best interests of the client with those of the RIA, as the advisor cannot make more money on the account unless the client increases their asset base. All RIAs are required to include their fee schedules in their Form ADV filed annually with the SEC.

The most common definition of a high-net-worth investor is one with a net worth of $1 million or more. The reason for this is that most RIA firms will establish an account minimum for anyone wishing to become a client. Amounts below this tend to be more difficult to manage while making a profit.

Investment advisors might have a hybrid model, under which they sell products for commissions as well as charge fees for financial planning and investment advice. Others could be fee-based and not sell any products (which is different than the fee-only/retainer arrangement discussed above). These advisors might charge a flat fee or a percentage of assets for creating financial plans, making investment recommendations, or managing money.

Advisors don't exist strictly to pick the best stock, mutual fund, or ETF or simply forecast economic conditions and make tactical decisions in a portfolio. While those are important, an advisor should act as a buffer between you and your investments, taking some of the emotion out of decisions. An RIA can be ideally positioned, through their business model, to play this role.

Why would an investor not use an RIA? Some investors want to use a brand name, big bank, or broker-dealer. Some investors understand the value of, and seek out, holistic planning, but choose to handle their investments themselves.

Is Your Advisor Working for *You*? Five Questions to Ask to Find Out

Here are five questions you must ask your financial advisor in order to better understand how they make money advising you and how they work for, or potentially against, you. A higher level of transparency will increase your trust level, and trust is the most important component of the advisor-advisee relationship. These questions concern transparency and enhancing trust in the relationship.

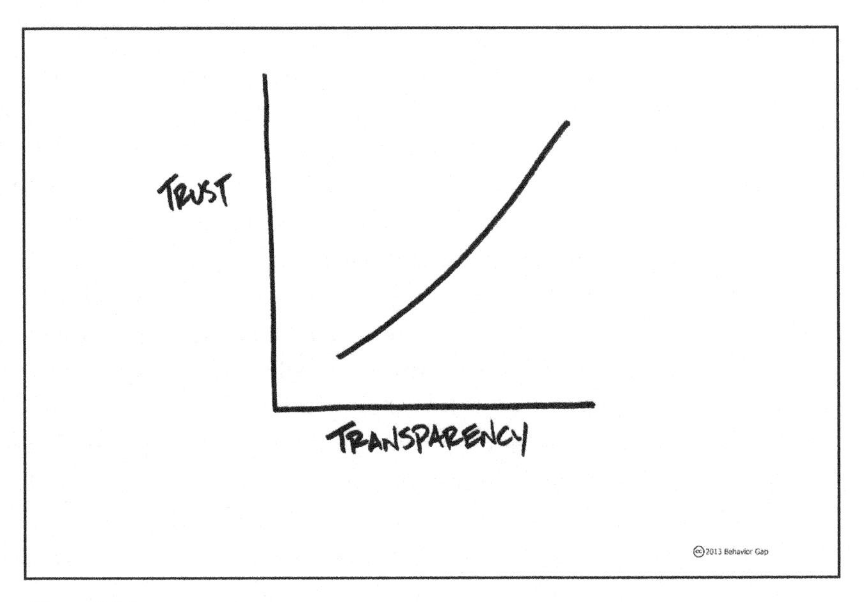

Figure 5.4.2

Question #1: Does your advisor owe you a fiduciary duty, or are they held only to a "suitability" standard?

Most investors are not aware that brokers and investment advisors are held to different standards in their dealings with clients. Registered investment advisors are held to a fiduciary standard. This means that they are required to make recommendations that are in the client's best interest. Contrast this with the "suitability" requirement that dictates that brokers are simply required to make recommendations that are suitable based on the facts at the time of the interaction. Recently, the Department of Labor has sought to even the playing field by forcing upon broker-dealers a fiduciary duty concerning retirement accounts, but the broker-dealer lobby has fought hard against this. As of this writing, only RIAs are held to the higher standard of always looking out for your best interests.

On the surface, this may seem like a subtle difference, but it can have a substantial impact on the client.

> *Example:* Physician A contacts his broker and expresses an interest in investing $50,000 in US growth stocks. The broker invests the client's assets in Fund XYZ, which charges a sales load of 5.75% and has operating expenses of 0.68% annually. The client will immediately pay a one-time fee of $2,875 on the trade on top of the recurring fund-management fee. In this case, the suitability standard has been met. Physician B contacts his RIA with the same request. The investment advisor purchases an ETF with a gross expense ratio of 0.18% and pays a commission of $8.95 on the trade. This client pays his RIA a management fee of 1% of the assets, which equates to $500 per year on $50,000. The advisor has met the fiduciary standard. In our very realistic example, the front-loaded fees paid by Physician A are significant enough that it would require a commitment of approximately nine years to this fund family before that commission is equal to the sum of advisory fees paid by Physician B.

Question #2: Can your advisor give a detailed explanation of how they are compensated?

Do your advisors receive commissions on any of the investments they will be recommending? Beyond commissions, compensation can come from sales charges on mutual funds or from a higher operating expense on a specific class of funds. An RIA typically has access to an institutional class of funds that will charge a lower expense amount than the retail shares commonly offered by brokers.

Private equities, structured notes, hedge funds, and non-traded REITs can offer various fee arrangements that may not be transparent. These investments may have a higher point of entry for an investor under the brokerage model in order to compensate the salesperson facilitating the transaction.

An RIA operating under the fiduciary standard may be able to offer the same investment at a lower cost simply because they are not taking a cut before your money goes to work for you.

> *Example:* Physician A is approached by his broker to invest in a non-publicly traded real estate investment trust. He sends a check for $100,000 and the security is priced at $10 per share, so he gets 10,000 shares. The broker receives a 7% commission from the REIT sponsor. Physician B is approached by her RIA to invest $100,000 in the same privately held REIT. The advisor charges a 1% management fee and does not accept compensation from the REIT sponsor. In this scenario, the commission is returned to Physician B in the form of a reduced purchase price for the shares. She receives a discounted price of $9.30 from the sponsor and is able to purchase 10,752 shares of the same REIT with her $100,000 investment. Physician A would have to hold the investment for approximately seven years before his 7% commission matches the sum of fees paid by Physician B to her advisor.

Question #3: Does your advisor's firm make money in other ways on your individual investments?

Request clarification of the ways that your advisor's firm may receive financial benefit from the securities you own in your portfolio. As an example, mutual funds commonly offer revenue-sharing arrangements with broker-dealer firms. In this scenario, your advisor at broker-dealer firm XYZ is receiving security analysis provided by its research department, which creates a buy list of securities. Unbeknownst to you, XYZ receives compensation from the fund company offering the recommended products. The result is a higher fee to you, the investor. You will not see these fees appear as a line item on your statement; they will be hidden within the underlying investments. This lack of transparency will not only prevent you from recognizing the true cost of the relationship, it may also create a bias in the research provided to the client's advisor. This scenario can apply to closed end funds, exchange traded notes, and other securities that will impact the bottom line of the firm, even if your investment representative does not receive additional compensation.

> *Example:* Discount brokerage firm XYZ offers to manage client assets at a reduced cost of 0.80% of assets under management for Doctor A. The rep at XYZ purchases $150,000 of retail shares of a bond fund with an operating expense of 0.75%. The rep does not receive compensation for choosing this fund; however, his firm (XYZ) receives revenue sharing directly from the fund company. An RIA for Doctor B charges 1% for his services and purchases institutional shares of the same fund with an operating expense of 0.46%. RIAs often have access to the lower-cost shares offered by certain mutual fund families. In this scenario, the discount brokerage relationship results in a slightly higher cost to Doctor A because of hidden revenue sharing, despite the brokerage charging a lower management fee for their service.

Question #4: Does your advisor use proprietary securities?
Proprietary products are not always easily recognizable, as they can be branded under a different name. In-house products are not necessarily poor investments at the moment the recommendation is made to a client. The problem arises when circumstances change and it is no longer in a client's best interest to continue to own the underlying security. Will the in-house research department recommend that their team of advisors liquidate the position in each of the firm's client accounts? Consider the impact of mass redemptions in a proprietary security. Who is going to be on the other side of that trade?

> *Example:* XYZ firm runs a highly rated international bond fund with heavy exposure to European bonds. A team of brokers is looking out for its clients and contacts its research team to express concern about the recent drop in price of the investment. The research team assures the brokers that they have adequately hedged the portfolio. A month later, concerned about potential liability for a poorly performing investment, XYZ firm removes the fund from the institutional portfolios it is managing. The large redemptions

create a significant drop in the price of the fund. A notification is then sent to the brokers explaining the firm's position after the price drop has occurred. The individual investor has suffered substantial losses while the firm has minimized the damage to its largest institutional clients.

Question #5: Does the advisor's firm engage in investment banking activities?

If the answer is yes, determine how your financial professional (and the firm) is compensated on your purchase of that investment. What is the incentive of the firm to see that the entire offering is filled?

Example: There are countless examples of initial public offerings where individual investors have been sold on tales of tremendous growth opportunities, only to experience disappointing returns and a substantial loss on their investment. The 2012 handling of the high-profile IPO of Facebook resulted in numerous lawsuits and continues to raise questions about conflicts inherent in the underwriting process.

This is not a complete list of questions to ask your current or prospective advisor, but it is a start. Our hope is that by asking these questions you will gain a greater understanding of the factors that may influence the recommendations of the advisor. If every action made on your behalf is not unequivocally for *your* benefit, it is time to reevaluate the relationship you have with your advisor.

In the next section, we discuss how your investment advisor and wealth management needs may eventually require ancillary coordination with other advisors like accountants, lawyers, and other specialists.

What Physicians Should Expect from Their Financial Advisors

"What does an investment advisor do for his or her fee?" This is a common question that investors, including physicians, often ask. We believe this question is fundamental because the decision of whom to trust to manage your wealth will be one of the most important financial decisions you will ever make.

We think physicians should receive the following seven benefits from their wealth advisor. They all make a quantifiable and qualitative impact on one's long term financial success.

Benefit #1: A Portfolio That Evolves with You

Does your advisor research funds to identify the best options in each asset category? Only with thorough data on a wide range of investment options can your advisor appropriately allocate funds for a custom-designed portfolio that evolves with you and your financial goals. Because asset values change, your advisor should regularly assess your portfolio to identify any drift from target allocations and take steps to rebalance as required.

Benefit #2: A Portfolio Designed to Match Your Risk Tolerance

Most physician investors initially give their advisors an idea of their tolerance for risk in their portfolios. With age and a shortening retirement horizon, changes to career and family can dramatically affect an investor's risk tolerance. Does your advisor periodically calculate the risk score of your current portfolio and compare it to your personal risk score? Nothing can take all the risk out of investing, but a thorough advisor will stress-test your portfolio in a variety of market scenarios and optimize asset allocation to match your risk tolerance, even if it has changed over time.

Benefit #3: Portfolio Management with an Eye on Taxes

Many investors focus primarily on portfolio performance while overlooking the impact of taxes on their investment returns. The impact of federal and state income and capital gains taxes on a portfolio depends on many factors, including the underlying investments, asset turnover, structure in which the investments are held, investor's other income, and investor's state of residence.

The ten-year recovery of the U.S. stock market has exacerbated this impact for investors in the top tax bracket. A tax-savvy advisor understands the effects of current tax law on the assets in your portfolio and works to maximize your net after-tax return.

Your advisor should implement tax harvesting strategies where applicable, coordinate the tax consequences of rebalancing, and allocate investments to optimize the tax diversification of your portfolio.

Benefit #4: Private Investment Opportunities

To offset the risk associated with market volatility, most advisors will recommend a portfolio that is diversified across a variety of asset classes. Traditional bonds are used as a risk mitigation strategy for many investors; however, physicians may turn to their advisors seeking investment alternatives with returns that do not correlate with stocks or bonds. An advisor who is well-versed in alternative investments can offer investors a broad menu of options, including REITs, commodities, managed futures, and private equity, and review the risk and fees associated with each option. Some advisors can also provide access to vetted private non-traded alternatives to help investors maximize returns while reducing overall portfolio risk.

Benefit #5: A Comprehensive Financial Plan

In addition to making investment recommendations, your advisor should work with you to develop a comprehensive financial plan that keeps *your* big picture in focus. A cash flow analysis, personal balance sheet, income projections, and goals for education and retirement are data that your advisor should gather to generate a dynamic plan that becomes your roadmap to guide the financial decisions you make for yourself and your family. As part of their wealth management services, your advisor should periodically review your financial plan and update it to incorporate any changes to your income, family situation, goals, and time horizon.

Benefit #6: A Clear Understanding of How You Are Doing

If reports from your investment advisor don't paint a clear picture of your portfolio's performance, this is a problem. Your reports should track net contributions and withdrawals, present a customized portfolio summary, and transparently show the performance of your portfolio, net of all fees.

Benefit #7: Total Wealth Management—Not Simply Investments

Does your advisor's firm work only with investments, or is your advisor backed by a solid wealth management team? A multidisciplinary wealth management firm includes specialists in areas of expertise affecting your overall financial well-being. For example, attorneys can analyze each asset and make recommendations to reduce the asset's level of exposure to lawsuits and other risks. CPAs can review tax returns and suggest ways to reduce or defer tax liability, and insurance experts can review existing policies and present options that could reduce premiums and/or improve coverage. An advisor who can offer these areas of expertise within his or her firm is well-equipped to become your financial quarterback, a resource to handle your questions concerning any financial matter.

The best advisors deliver significant benefits that can add both quantifiable and qualitative value to their clients' portfolios. This advisor advantage can help you achieve your long-term financial goals by aligning your portfolio with your personal risk tolerance, focusing on your net after-tax return, and developing a strategic wealth management plan that evolves with you and your family.

TAKEAWAY: Since most physicians will rely on a professional advisor's advice for at least some of their investments, it is crucial that they understand how advisors make money, along with their inherent conflicts and relative pros and cons. Asking the right questions and understanding what a top advisor brings to clients are also key success factors.

LESSON 6

Success Factors for Physicians Approaching and In Retirement

Achieving a retirement that meets their individual timeline and lifestyle goals is the number one financial goal for most doctors. As one approaches and then enters this phase, there are some crucial "dos" and "don'ts" from a financial perspective.

In this Lesson, we discuss three keys to success in long-term planning for retirement and four tactics to implement when approaching and then in retirement. We conclude with a discussion of estate planning, as this often becomes a renewed area of focus once a physician gets to this stage of life.

CHAPTER 6.1
Retirement Planning: Three Keys to Success

Getting to a comfortable retirement on their own timeline and with the lifestyle they want is, by far, the number one financial goal for most doctors. This is borne out by independent physician studies and our own experience of working with well over 1,000 physicians in our careers. In this chapter, we will discuss three important long-term strategies. In the next chapter, we will focus on shorter-term tactics to consider when retirement is closer.

Treat Your Retirement Like a Patient: Have a Plan and Monitor It

Certainly, your secure financial health is important enough to be treated with the care you would dedicate to a patient's physical health. A secure retirement requires a dynamic, flexible blueprint that outlines the steps you will take to reach your goals. Your plan should help you make sensible decisions about your money so you can achieve your goals in life. It should not be a set-it-and-forget-it static plan or be just about buying financial products.

Our vision of the best possible plan is one that provides you with evolving, well-coordinated wealth management that fits *your* needs. The plan should have an advocate/leader or *financial quarterback*—the person who will field your first call when you have a question concerning any financial matter.

Make Sure the Plan is Comprehensive

The elements of your plan may differ from those in someone else's plan. Your particular circumstances (age, income, goals, etc.) will often dictate which elements should be emphasized. A sound plan involves more than saving, investing, and rebalancing. If you want a plan that is truly comprehensive, you will need to consider additional sophisticated strategies as you begin to accumulate wealth.

Generally, a sound wealth management plan should include the following elements:

- investment planning
- asset protection planning
- tax planning
- insurance planning
- education planning
- financial modeling/retirement projections
- estate planning

We have incorporated all of these in this book in one Lesson or another. In working with a wealth manager, you should strive to include all of these elements in your plan. At certain times, obviously, one or two of them will be of much larger concern than others. That is the nature of life.

Wealth management planning will help you

- categorize your risk appetite;
- put a number to your goals (what is achievable and what looks difficult);
- map your current and future cash flows to your financial goals;
- map your existing assets to your financial goals;
- make a statement of your net worth;
- look at the adequacy of your insurance;
- shield your assets from potential lawsuits;
- reduce taxes where possible today, potentially increasing savings;
- employ tax diversification techniques;
- build a fund for your retirement; and
- guide your investment portfolio.

Build Flexibility Throughout Your Plan

So much of life doesn't work out exactly as we expect. Therefore, flexibility in your wealth management plan is fundamental. Many things that affect your ability to achieve your financial goals are beyond your control, so your planning should be flexible enough to roll with the punches.

Changes in income (or cash flow), changes in tax rates, market changes, potential changes in liability, and changes in your health can all hinder you from reaching your goals.

Changes in income and cash flow are important to consider in any wealth management plan. Most physicians cannot accurately predict their future income, so flexibility is essential.

You can incorporate income/cash flow flexibility into a plan by living below your means and prioritizing saving every month, quarter, and year. These two elements combined may position you to weather any temporary or even long-term hits to income or cash flow.

Another tactic could be implementation of a savings vehicle that allows for uneven funding/investments. An example in the qualified retirement plan arena is defined contribution plans that allow flexibility in contributions each year: profit-sharing plans or 401(k)s, as opposed to defined benefit plans, which can require a certain level of funding or cause underfunding penalties (cash balance plans or pensions). Even more relevant would be to use nonqualified plans that allow much higher contributions than defined contribution plans when income is high but allow contributions to be skipped entirely in years when income wanes.

Another example is in the asset class of permanent life insurance, discussed in Lesson 4. Funding flexibility would favor a universal life policy, for which funding is flexible year-to-year, over a whole life policy, which requires funding every year.

Changes in tax rates: In 2018, the tax code was overhauled for the first time in 30+ years. Of course, that doesn't mean that tax rates hadn't changed before—in fact, they changed during both previous administrations this century (Obama and Bush II). Moreover, all of the personal tax changes in the 2018 tax act are scheduled to sunset (revert to pre-act provisions) in 2025. At least, that is the law at the time we write this in 2020. The bottom line: the tax code is always changing, and even *permanent* tax changes are permanent only until a future Congress and president change them again. See the Figures 1.3.2 and 1.3.3 in Chapter 1.3 which show the highest marginal federal income tax rate over time and the federal capital gains tax rate over time.

From examining these graphs, it seems quite possible that we could see tax rates rise over the long term, regardless of any short-term changes in the next four to eight years. Even if they return to mean rates of the twentieth century, we will experience a sharp increase in tax rates. Thus, it makes sense to build in flexibility to account for this possibility.

As we discussed in Lesson 3, a tax diversification approach can help alleviate some potential problems. Essentially, this means building up wealth in three "buckets": those subject to ordinary income tax rates upon distribution in retirement, those subject to capital gains rates, and those not subject to tax upon distribution. While most plans focus only on asset class diversification in the context of investing, we believe it is crucial to also diversify your wealth vis-à-vis tax rate exposure. The graphic below may help you envision the value of having differently taxed "buckets" to draw on when you reach retirement. As the retirement/wealth distribution phase may last for many years, or even multiple decades, being diversified across such tax buckets puts you in a position of strength and gives you options for where to draw income from, depending on the tax rates then in effect.

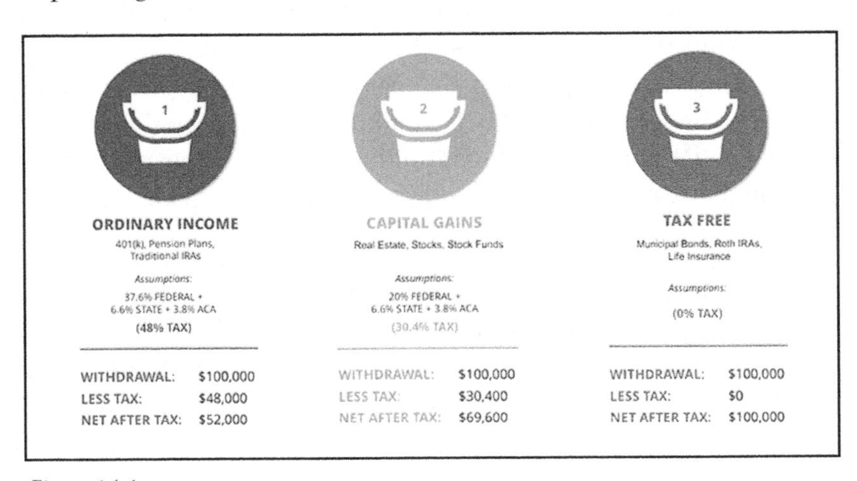

Figure 6.1.1

Changes in the "market": The reason we put the word *market* in quotation marks is that we mean more than a small sample of the stock market in the United States, such as the Dow 30 or even the S&P 500 indices. All securities, commodities, real estate, and other asset marketplaces in the United States and worldwide are volatile, and your portfolio and wealth management plan should acknowledge this.

A diversified portfolio has been shown to reduce overall risk and volatility, which creates flexibility to help you weather downturns in certain industries, asset classes, or even geographic regions. See the chart below showing returns from 2000 to 2019 as an example. You can see that the diversified portfolio came in third with an average annualized return of 6.2%. However, to achieve this return, this portfolio had significantly less volatility over the period (measured by its standard deviation), than the two asset classes that outperformed it. In fact, it was significantly less volatile than all asset classes, other than bonds and cash. Yet, the portfolio still had the third highest return.

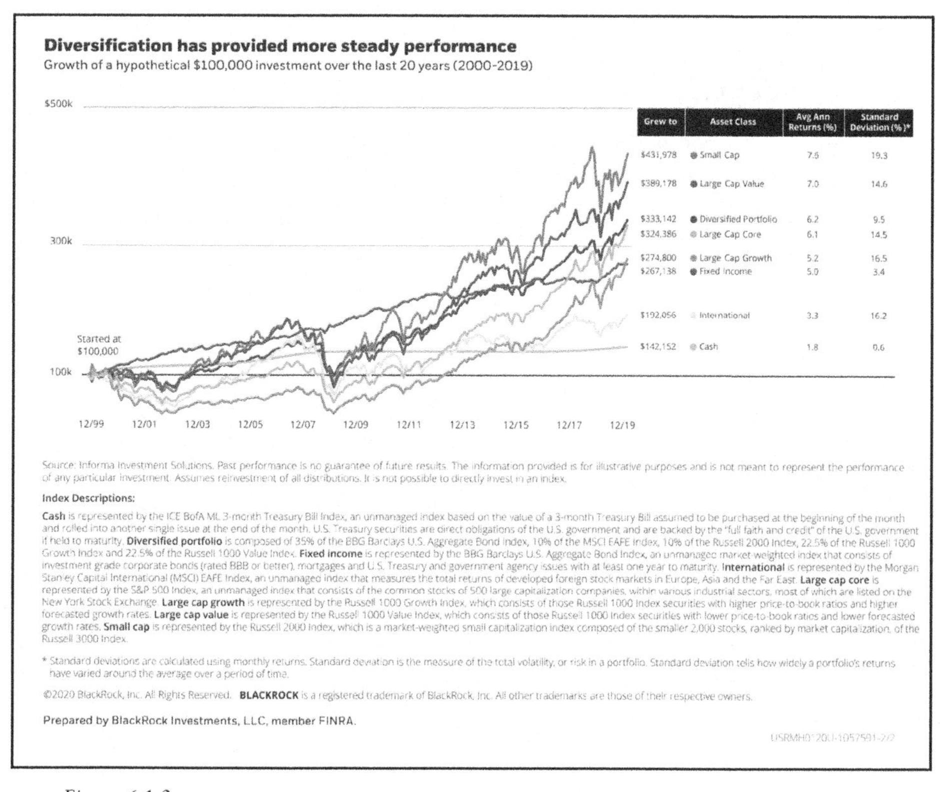

Grew to	Asset Class	Avg Ann Returns (%)	Standard Deviation (%)*
$431,978	Small Cap	7.6	19.3
$389,178	Large Cap Value	7.0	14.6
$333,142	Diversified Portfolio	6.2	9.5
$324,386	Large Cap Core	6.1	14.5
$274,800	Large Cap Growth	5.2	16.5
$267,138	Fixed Income	5.0	3.4
$192,056	International	3.3	16.2
$142,152	Cash	1.8	0.6

Figure 6.1.2

Changes in liability: As we discussed in Lesson 2, asset protection planning should be part of every physician's wealth management plan.

Changes in your health: Health is the most important element of all. At one extreme, being in good health is a blessing and allows you to continue to practice medicine and create more wealth, as well as to share it, enjoy it, and even give it away. At the other extreme, poor health can keep you from practicing and even lead to premature death, which can have a devastating economic impact on a family. For these reasons, it is fundamental for a conservative wealth plan to build flexibility around changes in health by securing the proper insurances to shield your ability to earn income (disability insurance and life insurance, as previously discussed in Lessons 1 and 4). Long-term care insurance (or riders that provide such coverage in life insurance policies) can also be an important part of your plan, even for parents or in-laws. See Chapter 4.5 for more on this.

> **TAKEAWAY:** Getting to a comfortable retirement on their own timeline and with their chosen lifestyle is, by far, the number one financial goal for most doctors. To achieve this goal, three long-term strategies are crucial: implement a wealth management plan and monitor it, make sure the plan is comprehensive, and build flexibility into the plan.

CHAPTER 6.2

Four Tactics to Use as You Approach Retirement

We will reiterate what we said in the last chapter: most doctors' number one financial goal is getting to a comfortable retirement on their own timeline and based on their chosen lifestyle. While our last chapter focused on long-term factors that affect meeting this goal, our focus here is more immediate.

In this chapter, we will discuss shorter-term tactics to implement when you are in what one insurance company calls the "retirement red zone" (football fans will understand this). At OJM Group, we begin to advise clients on these tactical approaches five to ten years out from retirement, whereas the last chapter discussed strategies that should be implemented decades out. Here, we will focus on four tactics: developing a budget, reviewing asset allocation, designing a withdrawal strategy, and, for those who own small practices, planning an exit strategy.

Developing a Budget for Retirement

This may seem like overly simplistic advice, but budgeting can either push a retirement plan to success or drive it to failure. While many believe a budget is just an awareness of spending, its actual purpose is to ensure that you live within your means and that every dollar earned is deployed strategically. To accomplish this, you must have a written and managed budget, not a mental tally of expenditures.

While budgeting is important for decades-long saving for retirement, it becomes even more crucial in your last working years. Now that you're closer to the day that retirement becomes a reality, your budget can be more specific and, ideally, much more accurate.

Consider: how accurate can a retirement budget be when you're thinking 20 years ahead, have kids still in school, and are living and practicing in a state that may not be where you will retire? It's a guesstimate. On the other hand, locking down an accurate spending range five years out, when you're an empty-nester and have a home in the state where you will retire, is doable.

Reviewing Asset Allocation

As physicians age, they need to reallocate their assets into increasingly conservative investments to limit their exposure to loss. Additionally, careful consideration must be given to properly limiting downside risk, potentially through fixed-income and alternative investments.

The idea of de-risking to more conservative assets can be troubling to those who are focused on maximizing returns because conservative investments tend to have limited upside potential. To understand why this move is often more beneficial than seeking higher returns in later life, a physician needs only to be familiar with *sequence of returns risk*.

Sequence of returns risk is the danger that liquidation and withdrawal from a retirement account will coincide with a downturn in the market. If it does, then the overall potential performance of the entire portfolio is effectively reduced because a greater number of shares will need to be liquidated to get the income expected, leaving fewer shares in the portfolio to grow.

Sequence of returns risk may not be important during the accumulation phase when time horizons are long, but during the withdrawal phase it is one of the most critical factors in the overall success of a retirement plan. This makes it a higher priority than chasing returns.

SEQUENCE OF RETURNS RISK *Hypothetical Example*				
	PORTFOLIO A		PORTFOLIO B	
YEAR	RETURN	BALANCE	RETURN	BALANCE
0	—	**$100,000**	—	**$100,000**
1	-15%	$80,750	22%	$115,900
2	-4%	$72,720	8%	$119,772
3	-10%	$60,948	30%	$149,204
4	8%	$60,424	7%	$154,298
5	12%	$62,075	18%	$176,171
6	10%	$62,782	9%	$186,577
7	-7%	$53,737	28%	$232,418
8	4%	$50,687	14%	$259,257
9	-12%	$40,204	-9%	$231,374
10	13%	$39,781	16%	$262,594
11	7%	$37,216	-6%	$242,138
12	-10%	$28,994	17%	$277,452
13	19%	$28,553	19%	$324,217
14	17%	$27,557	-10%	$287,296
15	-6%	$21,204	7%	$302,056
16	16%	$18,796	13%	$335,674
17	-9%	$12,555	-12%	$290,993
18	14%	$8,612	4%	$297,433
19	28%	$4,624	-7%	$271,962
20	9%	$0	10%	$293,658
21	18%	$0	12%	$323,297
22	7%	$0	8%	$343,761
23	30%	$0	-10%	$304,885
24	8%	$0	-4%	$287,890
25	22%	$0	-15%	$240,456
ARITHMETIC MEAN	6.8%		6.8%	
STANDARD DEVIATION	12.8%		12.8%	
COMPOUND GROWTH RATE	6%		6%	

Figure 6.2.1

NOTE: *Sequence of returns risk revolves around the timing or sequence of a series of adverse investment returns. In this example, two portfolios, A and B, each begin with $5,000 per year. Each experiences exactly the same returns over a 25-year period, but in inverse order, or "sequence." Portfolio A has the bad luck of having a sequence of negative returns in its early years and is completely depleted by year 20. Portfolio B, in stark contrast, scores a few positive returns in its early years and ends up two decades later with more than double the assets with which it began.*

Readers are likely to be shocked by this illustration. The hypothetical example demonstrates two investors taking 5% of the initial principal. Portfolios A and B have the exact same mean return over a 25-year period with identical risk (i.e., standard deviation). Portfolio A ran out of money. Portfolio B's value was 140% higher at the end of the 25-year period. Why? Because of the sequence of the returns.

Your initial feeling may be despair because you recognize that you have no ability to influence market returns in retirement. Neither physician investors nor advisors can control the timing of stock returns; however, they can control risk. By managing risk, you can manage the range of possible outcomes, ultimately increasing your odds of success.

Designing a Withdrawal Strategy

Selecting a Withdrawal Rate

A fundamental error in static retirement plans is setting a withdrawal rate that is fixed over a retirement period. Consider that, for many doctors, the retirement stage of life may last 20 years or more. In that time, investment yields may vary widely and both tax rates and personal spending habits could also change. Because of all these variables, it is essential that flexibility be built into retirement planning, both in initial models (high, middle, low) and when reviewing the plan each year (or more frequently). Only by having flexible planning models and periodically adjusting them based on real-time results can one expect to follow a model that can endure throughout retirement, no matter how many years, or decades, it may last.

Making Room for Taxes

No one knows what tax rates will be when they retire. This does not mean that doctors should ignore tax planning, but rather that they should model taxes as retirement expenses and design a strategy to minimize their effect. To do this, they must understand how taxes will impact withdrawals and liquidations. Having a plan that considers which withdrawals will trigger ordinary income taxes, which will incur capital gains, and which will realize no tax is essential. As discussed in Lesson 3, a long-term tax diversification "bucket" strategy will prove extremely valuable in the distribution phase of retirement.

If You Are in Private Practice, Begin Planning For the Exit

For the limited number of physicians who still own their practices and have few, if any, partners, the challenge of creating a lucrative exit should be addressed sooner rather than later. Too many doctors in this situation avoid the issue of a buyout or practice sale until a few years before their planned retirement, when it is often too late to plan properly. There are few, if any, sale opportunities, and even an internal transition to younger physicians is less lucrative than it could have been. To avoid this trap, consider implementing the following strategies at least five years, and in some cases much longer, before your planned exit.

Implement a systems-based practice.

Ask any business exit strategy consultant and they will tell you that it is crucial to systematize as many business operations as possible. When there are systems and written procedures for every element of the business, it is much more valuable to a potential buyer. It is no different with medical practices: every operation other than the physician's medical decisions and handiwork can be systematized. As a colleague and frequent speaker at plastic surgery meetings likes to say, one of his plastic surgery practices had a written 30-point procedure for cleaning the bathroom. It is that type of systemization that should be part of the DNA of the practice for years, if not decades, before any exit.

Recruit a younger physician.

Because the practice of medicine is tightly controlled by regulations, for many doctors it is not possible to sell their practices to non-physician investors (although that has changed in the last decade due to private equity firms' interest in buying medical practices in a variety of specialties).

As such, many medical practices are more likely to be "sold" internally to a younger doctor who starts as an associate and then becomes a partner and purchaser. If this is the plan for your practice, or even a likely possibility, recruiting that physician and seeing if he or she is the right fit cannot be delayed until close to your planned exit. It may take five, seven, or ten years, or longer, to find the right associate, train them properly, see that they can handle the patient load, and determine their financial ability to purchase the practice shares at a price you think is fair. In addition, getting them to buy in on the long-term plan is imperative, especially the formula on practice value and other possible ancillary issues, such as fair rent if you own the building and will continue to do so after the sale.

Design a compensation plan that fits the long-term plan.
When recruiting and hiring a younger associate, another tactic to consider is implementing a compensation package that ties in with the long-term plan. For example, a nonqualified plan could be designed so that the funding of the plan grows tax beneficially and is owned by the practice for years, even decades. If the associate hits their goals and stays for the duration, they vest into the plan. If they do not hit their goals, or leave the practice, the entire value stays with the practice (i.e., you). This may not only motivate and incentivize the associate to stay for years but also provide a significant part of their buyout fund if the timing of vesting coincides with your exit and sale of the practice.

TAKEAWAY: When a physician approaches retirement, there are several key planning tactics to consider, from developing an accurate retirement budget and de-risking their asset allocation to designing a withdrawal strategy. Physicians who own small private practices should also begin addressing their exit strategy.

CHAPTER 6.3

Planning for Estate Taxes

It is common sense that, as physicians enter retirement, they should review their estate planning and possibly revise their estate planning documents. A renewed focus on planning for estate taxes might be part of this process. In this chapter, we will describe a few planning strategies often implemented to efficiently pay or reduce estate taxes.

Overview of Estate Planning and Estate Taxes

In Chapter 1.5, we advised even young physicians to get their estate plans in order. In that chapter, we explained the basics of estate planning—what probate is and why to avoid it, the importance in many states of the revocable trust, and information about our estate and gift tax system. We recommend that you revisit that chapter to brush up on the basics.

At the end of that chapter, we noted that as of the date this book was published the estate tax exemption for a married couple was over $20 million, making federal estate tax planning moot for most physicians. We also explained that at the beginning of our careers the same exemption was less than $1.5 million and that it had changed many times over the last twenty-plus years. Therefore, we commented as follows:

Physicians—like all of our clients—do not know (1) when they (or their spouse) will die or (2) what UTC or federal estate tax rates will be in effect at that time. Also, many are not 100% sure what state they will be residing in when they die. For these reasons, and probability that most clients will live to their actuarial life expectancies, it becomes clear that estate tax planning must not only reflect what rules exist today but also allow flexibility for when things inevitably change in the near and not-so-near future. In sum, transfer tax management is a moving target. As such, it should be considered by physicians repeatedly over time as they accumulate assets.

We also noted that many states levy their own estate or inheritance tax. The families of physicians in such states may owe significant taxes to their state upon the physician's death even if the federal estate tax has no impact.

Given this reality, we think it is important to at least mention a few of the leading estate tax strategies used by wealthy families who are subject to the estate tax. They may become planning necessities for physicians at some point in the future.

Estate Tax Planning with Life Insurance Policies and Trusts

In Lesson 1, we explained that every physician with financial dependents should use life insurance to protect those dependents against a premature death. For many physicians, this means using term life insurance.

In Lesson 4, we described the various benefits of permanent life insurance related to its cash value (tax-free growth and access, investment options, and asset protection in many states) and why many physicians might consider using cash value insurance as part of their retirement planning.

Neither of those scenarios is what we are describing here. Rather, here we are focusing on the death-benefit proceeds of life insurance policies designed to pay estate taxes when the insured (an individual or a last-to-die spouse) passes away. We will call such policies "estate planning life policies" or "EPLPs."

Avoiding EPLP Pitfalls

EPLPs are life insurance policies that are purchased for the primary purpose of transferring wealth and creating liquidity for future generations. For estate tax planning purposes, it is important to remove the EPLP proceeds from your taxable estate. While you might consider having your spouse or children own the policy on your life to accomplish this, this tactic has pitfalls:

- You lose all control of the proceeds when you die. The assets will pass to the policy beneficiaries outright. If they spend them down, remarry, divorce, or are sued, your planning benefited someone other than your family members. As you'll see below, you can control the funds, even after you're dead, and keep them in the family for generations using a special life insurance trust that dictates exactly how the funds can be used.
- If the EPLP proceeds are paid to your children, your surviving spouse may run short of funds for living expenses. This can be a very big problem in second or third marriages, as children may not agree to support a stepparent.
- If the EPLP policy is a cash value policy (typical in estate planning situations because it is permanent insurance), your kids may be tempted to borrow against the policy, reducing the death benefit.
- If any of your children get divorced, the EPLP policy may be considered a marital or community property asset. Some of the cash value could end up going to a former son-in-law or former daughter-in-law.
- If your children are still minors, the policy would have to be owned by a custodian or a guardian.

To avoid these and other pitfalls, most well-advised physicians set up a particular type of trust to own EPLPs.

The Irrevocable Life Insurance Trust

Estate planning professionals know that they can remove a life insurance policy from a client's estate and avoid many of the pitfalls discussed above by creating an irrevocable life insurance trust (ILIT) to be the owner and beneficiary of an EPLP. Essentially, an ILIT is an irrevocable trust designed to purchase life insurance, own it, and distribute the proceeds when the insured(s) die.

ILITs offer many benefits. First, since the ILIT owns the policy, the policy is out of your taxable estate. Moreover, a properly structured ILIT can keep the proceeds from irresponsible children and their disgruntled spouses or creditors. The funds can then be used to pay estate taxes; provide an income stream; pay off debts, mortgages, or notes; and keep other valuable and needed assets intact for the family.

For people with significant assets, the ILIT may use the insurance proceeds to buy illiquid assets, such as shares of a closely held business, real estate, or other assets from the estate to keep them in the family. Alternatively, the trust can lend money to your estate, with the loan secured by the estate's assets. This is sometimes done to use the money to pay the estate taxes that are due on other assets. Because estate taxes are due nine months after the date of death, having liquid cash available is essential to avoid selling assets in a "fire sale," where the family may not get a reasonable price.

In either case, the estate will receive cash that can be used in a variety of ways. Later, the trustee can distribute the assets to the trust beneficiaries—the surviving spouse and children. This can be done in a lump sum or, if desired, the assets can be maintained in trust for the beneficiaries' later benefit and use. If kept in trust, these funds can be structured so that creditors of the surviving spouse, children, and even grandchildren will have no access to them, even in the event of lawsuits, bankruptcies, or divorces. In this way, the ILIT can be an asset-protecting tool for many generations.

The bottom line is that all the insurance proceeds will be available to help pay estate taxes and provide cash for whatever need might arise. Your family keeps control over the assets.

Charitable Estate Planning

Aristotle said that "To give away money is an easy matter and in any man's power, but to decide to whom to give it, and how large and when, and for what purpose and how, is neither in every man's power nor an easy matter."

Doctors spend their entire careers contributing to others. Many continue their altruistic ways later in life and want to give back to the world that gave them their success. What many physicians don't know is how to take this charitable intent and use it to create as much benefit for their family as possible while benefiting a charity at the same time. Here, we will briefly examine just one tool often used in charitable estate planning: the charitable remainder trust (CRT). Because charitable planning is a vast topic, we can only hope to give you a hint of the types of planning we implement for physicians.

Charitable Remainder Trust[1]

A CRT is a tax-exempt split-interest trust to which the donor transfers property, retaining an income stream. At the creation of the CRT, the charity's remainder interest must be at least 10% of the initial value of the CRT. The income stream retained by the donor may last for a term of years (not to exceed twenty years) or the lifetime of the donor or other specified beneficiaries. The CRT must make income payouts at least annually. At the termination of the CRT, the balance of the CRT assets is distributed to a qualified organization, such as a public charity, private foundation, or donor-advised fund, that was selected by the donor and identified in the CRT.

Because a CRT is a tax-exempt entity, it can sell a highly appreciated asset without incurring a current income tax liability. The donor will receive an immediate income tax deduction based on the estimated present value of the remainder interest that will ultimately be transferred to the charity. As an income beneficiary of the CRT, the donor benefits from the income-tax-free liquidation of the highly appreciated assets by receiving income from the sale of those assets. A portion of that income can be used to purchase a life insurance policy to replace the value of the assets transferred to the CRT.

By establishing and funding a CRT with low-basis, highly appreciated assets, such as stocks, bonds or real estate, the donor may be able to achieve charitable objectives, receive a charitable income tax deduction, reduce the size of their estate, and maximize wealth transferred to beneficiaries.

---

[1] This entire CRT discussion comes from "Wealth Transfer and Charitable Planning Strategies Handbook", NFP, 2017

Potential Benefits

- May increase current income, reduce the taxable estate, and provide a current charitable income tax deduction.
- Benefits donor's favorite charity.
- May provide tax-efficient asset repositioning.
- The life insurance death benefit can help to replace the value of assets transferred to the CRT and maximize wealth transfer to beneficiaries.
- The charitable beneficiary of the CRT may be a private foundation.

Planning Considerations

- Transfers to the CRT are irrevocable.
- When the CRT terminates, the CRT assets pass to charity, not to family members.
- Income tax deductions not used currently may be carried forward for five years.
- The current income tax deduction depends on the type of asset donated, the type of charity, and the benefits paid out to the income beneficiaries.
- The cost of creation and maintenance of the CRT.

How It Works

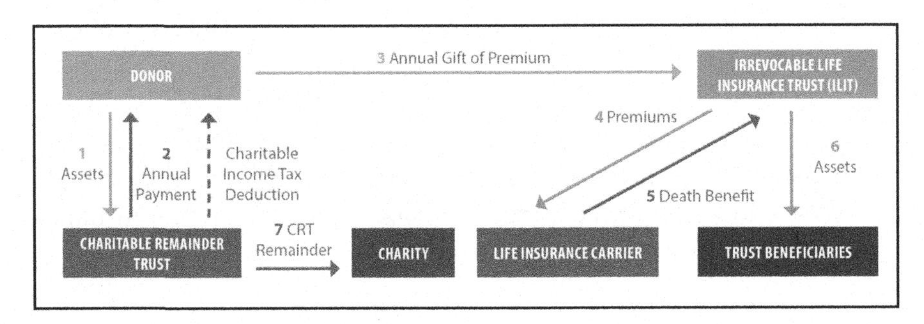

Figure 6.3.1

1. The donor irrevocably transfers property to the trustee of a CRT and receives a federal income tax deduction for the present value of the charity's remainder interest, subject to limitations.*
2. The trustee pays the donor either a fixed percentage of the initial value of the trust (annuity trust) or a specified percentage of the trust assets as revalued each year (unitrust). If the donor chooses to have the income assigned to a beneficiary other than a spouse, the donor is still responsible for income taxes. Payments to the beneficiary are subject to the federal gift tax but may qualify for the gift tax annual exclusion.
3. The donor creates an ILIT, the beneficiaries of which are typically the donor's family members.
4. The donor makes annual, scheduled, or lump-sum gifts of cash or other assets to the ILIT. Often, the amount of the gift made to the ILIT coincides with the amount of the life insurance premium.
5. The ILIT purchases a life insurance policy on the donor's life, retains ownership rights, and designates the ILIT as the beneficiary of the policy.
6. Upon the donor's death, the ILIT assets, including life insurance, pass to the ILIT beneficiaries free of income and transfer taxes.
7. When the CRT terminates, the CRT remainder is transferred to the charity.

* Trusts should be drafted by an attorney familiar with such matters in order to take into account income and transfer tax laws (including the generation-skipping transfer tax). If they are not, adverse tax treatment of trust proceeds could be the result.

TAKEAWAY: For physicians reviewing their estate planning in retirement, a renewed focus on estate tax planning may be relevant. Both federal and state transfer taxes should be considered. Because transfer tax rules have changed significantly and often over the last twenty years, doctors must plan not only based on the law as it exists today but also based on what may happen in the future. Two tax strategies that have stood the test of time are using life insurance within ILITs and charitable planning, including the use of CRTs.

Time is of the Essence

As we hope you have seen throughout this text, a physician's wealth planning is a process that will change over time. The important tactics and strategies to focus on in training and in the early years of practice will be different than those to implement in one's core practice years — and different again from those to consider when approaching or in retirement. In fact, what you take as most important from this book today may change if you come back to it in the future.

Time is influential on wealth planning not only because circumstances and priorities change over the years, but also because physicians generally are so pressed for time in their daily lives.

For most of you reading this, there will never seem to be enough hours in the day to do what you want to do, and there may always be other items at the top of your to-do list. For many of you, this means comprehensive wealth planning, where nothing is missed, is often put off for another day.

We encourage you to make such planning a priority and dedicate time to work on it or find an advisory team that can help you. If you are having a tough time getting started, need a little help bringing your planning to the next level, or want a second opinion on the planning you currently have in place, please contact OJM Group at **877-656-4362**, via our website **www.ojmgroup.com**, or by email at the addresses below.

We always enjoy hearing from our readers, and we would be honored to help you achieve your financial objectives, so you can achieve your ultimate goal of leading a more enjoyable life.

David B. Mandell, JD, MBA
mandell@ojmgroup.com

Jason M. O'Dell, MS, CWM
odell@ojmgroup.com

Carole C. Foos, CPA
carole@ojmgroup.com

Free Consultation

Schedule a complimentary consultation with OJM Group to learn how the topics discussed in our books, articles and presentations may benefit you and your medical practice.
OJM Group has helped over 1,500 physicians:

- Reduce their income taxes.
- Shield practice and personal assets from lawsuits.
- Implement a more tax-efficient corporate structure.
- Utilize superior qualified and non-qualified benefit plans.
- Protect their families and practices with life, disability and long-term care insurance
- Build investable wealth in a conservative, tax-savvy manner.
- Create and review dynamic retirement plans
- Coordinate all areas of planning.

Please visit www.ojmgroup.com or call (877) 656-4362 to schedule your free consultation.

Schedule A Seminar

OJM Group's education experts have presented seminars on asset protection, tax planning, benefit planning, investing, insurance and retirement planning for numerous medical societies, associations, hospitals and other physician groups nationwide. OJM Group can provide this content in various formats including lectures, podcasts, webcasts, and videos.

In addition, OJM Group can offer the opportunity to earn CME through its enduring material, the book *Risk Management for the Practicing Physician*. Now in its eighth edition since 1998, this monograph is nationally certified for 5.0 Category I CME credits.

Request Authors' Articles for Your Publication

OJM Group partners and team members have authored more than a dozen books for physicians and written articles for over 100 periodicals, newsletters and blogs. Article topics include asset protection, practice management, tax reduction, retirement planning, investing and estate planning.

OJM Group can provide this educational content to publications at no cost to the publisher and will offer readers a free print copy or ebook download of one of our books.

Please contact OJM Group at 877-656-4362 to schedule a seminar or request an article.

Visit www.ojmgroup.com to learn more about free educational materials and presentations for physicians.

Additional Resources for Physicians

These books for physicians are available in hard copy and ebook formats for Kindle and iPad. Please visit **www.ojmbookstore.com** and **use promotional code WPR2R** at checkout to request or download your free book(s).

Wealth Management Made Simple

OJM Group partners have authored this book as a resource that provides answers for the most common questions that we have heard during our work with over 1,500 physicians and other clients. Building wealth requires discipline, patience and education, and this book offers a time-tested approach that will help physicians and other investors reach their long-term financial goals and achieve a successful retirement on their terms.

Wealth Protection Planning for Orthopaedic Surgeons and Sports Medicine Specialists

Written by OJM partners and well-known orthopaedic surgeon Dr. Peter Millett of the Steadman Clinic in Vail, CO, this book features four concise lessons that may have a significant impact on your practice efficiency and long-term financial well-being. The book is structured in a Challenge-Solution format, including strategies for practice structure, tax and cost reduction, asset protection and building wealth.

Wealth Protection Planning for Dermatologists

Written by OJM principals and well-known dermatologist Dr. David Goldberg, this book features four concise lessons that may have a significant impact on a dermatologist's practice efficiency and long-term financial well-being. The book is structured in a Challenge-Solution format, including strategies for practice structure, tax and cost reduction, asset protection and building wealth.

Risk Management for the Practicing Physician

Now in its eighth edition since 1998, this monograph is nationally certified for 5.0 Category I CME credits. Co-authored by a practicing physician, an attorney, a CPA and a financial advisor, the book includes chapters on providing care in today's malpractice environment, effective patient communication skills, managing privacy risk and non-medical liability risks faced by practicing physicians.

Made in the USA
Monee, IL
14 November 2020